PROBLEMS OF THE MODERN ECONOMY

Agricultural Policy in an Affluent Society

PROBLEMS OF THE MODERN ECONOMY

General Editor: EDMUND S. PHELPS, *University of Pennsylvania*

Each volume in this series presents prominent positions in the debate of an important issue of economic policy

---

Agricultural Policy
in an Affluent Society

Edited with an introduction by

VERNON W. RUTTAN
ARLEY D. WALDO
JAMES P. HOUCK

UNIVERSITY OF MINNESOTA

NEW YORK

W·W·NORTON & COMPANY·INC·

"Agricultural Policy in an Affluent Society" by Vernon W. Ruttan: from the *Journal of Farm Economics*, Vol. 48, no. 5 (December 1966). Reprinted by permission.

"The Three Economies of Agriculture" by Harold F. Breimyer: from the *Journal of Farm Economics*, Vol. 44, no. 3 (August 1962). Reprinted by permission.

"The Crises in the Traditional Roles of Agricultural Institutions" by James T. Bonnen: in the *Proceedings* of the Great Plains Agricultural Council, Bozeman, Montana, July 28–29, 1966. Reprinted by permission of the author.

"The Implications of Changing Political Power on Agriculture" by Dale E. Hathaway: a paper presented at the National Agricultural Credit Conference, St. Louis, Mo., November 13, 1967. Reprinted by permission of the author.

"Parity Price": from *Agricultural Prices* by F. L. Thomsen and R. J. Foote. Copyright 1952, McGraw-Hill, Inc. Used by permission of McGraw-Hill Book Company.

"Commodity Programs for Agriculture" by Luther G. Tweeten: from *Agricultural Policy: A Review and Needs*. Technical Papers, Vol. 5, National Advisory Commission on Food and Fiber, August 1967. Reprinted by permission of the author.

"In Search of Principles of Farm Policy" by George E. Brandow: from the *Journal of Farm Economics*, Vol. 44, no. 5, (December 1962). Reprinted by permission.

"How Much Should Government Do?" by Kermit Gordon: from the *Saturday Review*, January 9, 1965, a special issue produced in cooperation with the Committee for Economic Development. Reprinted by permission of the publisher.

"The Food Commission: Its Product and Its Role" by George E. Brandow: from the *Journal of Farm Economics*, Vol. 48, no. 5 (December 1966). Reprinted by permission.

"Why the Growing Farm-Retail Price Spread?" by Jerome W. Hammond, Willis E. Anthony, and Martin K. Christiansen: from *Minnesota Farm Business Notes* (October 1967). Reprinted by permission of the University of Minnesota Agricultural Extension Service.

"Public Policy Toward Mergers in Food Retailing" by Willard F. Mueller: from *Agricultural Policy Review*, Vol. 7, no. 2 (April/May/June 1967). Reprinted by permission of the Agricultural Policy Institute, North Carolina State University, and the author.

"Agricultural Cooperatives and the Antitrust Laws" by Donald F. Turner: an address delivered to the National Conference of Fruit and Vegetable Bargaining Cooperatives on January 17, 1966. Reprinted by permission of the author.

"Proposed and Existing Organizational Efforts for Farmers" by Don Paarlberg: from *Agricultural Policy Review*, Vol. 7, no. 2 (April/May/June 1967). Reprinted by permission of the Agricultural Policy Institute, North Carolina State University, and the author.

"Bargaining in Agriculture and Industry: Comparisons and Contrasts" by Varden Fuller: from the *Journal of Farm Economics*, Vol. 45, no. 5 (December 1963). Reprinted by permission.

"Rural Poverty" by W. Keith Bryant: from *Minnesota Farm Business Notes* (February 1968). Reprinted by permission of the University of Minnesota Agricultural Extension Service.

"Political Pressures and Income Distribution in Agriculture" by Varden Fuller: from the *Journal of Farm Economics*, Vol. 47, no. 5 (December 1965). Reprinted by permission.

"Agriculture and Foreign Economic Policy" by D. Gale Johnson: from the *Journal of Farm Economics*, Vol. 46, no. 5 (December 1964). Reprinted by permission.

"Malthus, Marx, and the North American Breadbasket" by Orville L. Freeman: reprinted by special permission from *Foreign Affairs* (July 1967). Copyright the Council on Foreign Relations, Inc., New York.

"What Ails World Agriculture?" by Theodore W. Schultz: from *Bulletin of the Atomic Scientists* (January 1968). Copyright 1968 by the Educational Foundation for Nuclear Science. Reprinted by permission.

"The Old Agricultural Lag" by Kenneth Boulding: from *No Easy Harvest* by Max F. Millikan and David Hapgood, by permission of Little, Brown and Co. Copyright © 1967, by Massachusetts Institute of Technology.

Contents

PART FOUR: Bargaining Power for Farmers and Farm Workers

PART FIVE: Overcoming Rural Poverty

PART SIX: Agricultural Trade, Aid, and Development Policy

Introduction

FROM THE EARLY DAYS of the Plymouth and Jamestown settlements until 1900, America's three-hundred-year encounter with the frontier was the dominant theme in the nation's agricultural development. This long encounter forged an agriculture based on abundant land and scarce labor. Consequently, the agricultural technology that evolved was designed to obtain gains in labor productivity rather than gains in land productivity.

Since the closing of the frontier, agriculture's encounter with an increasingly dominant urban-industrialist sector emerged as the major theme in American agricultural development. In 1880, nonagricultural employment first exceeded agricultural employment, and by 1929 manufacturing employment alone exceeded agricultural employment. In 1970, it seems likely that agricultural employment will be only a little greater than total *unemployment* in the United States.

This fundamental restructuring of the relationship between the farm and nonfarm sectors of the American economy can be understood best by examining five sets of market linkages by which U. S. agriculture is joined to the rest of the national economy and to the world economy. These linkages include the *product markets* through which agricultural output is transmitted to the nonagricultural sector and through which agricultural incomes are generated in return; the *input and capital markets* through which manufactured capital equipment and other operating inputs move; the *labor market* through which manpower is allocated between the agricultural and nonagricultural sectors and among firms in each sector; the *land market* through which land is allocated among firms in the farm sector and between the agricultural and nonagricultural sectors, and finally, the *market for consumer goods* through which farm families achieve or are denied access to the patterns of consumption now identified with the American living standard.

During the past several decades these linkages have been modified by powerful forces of economic and political change. Students of agricultural policy previously have focused almost exclusively on *product market* linkages. The organization of this volume reflects the authors' convictions that a broader definition of agricultural policy is needed.

ECONOMIC DEVELOPMENT, POLITICAL POWER, AND AGRICULTURAL POLICY

The selections in Part One deal specifically with the economic and political changes that are reshaping the concept and role of agricultural policy. The paper by Vernon W. Ruttan reviews the impact of economic change, operating through the five markets, on the structure of agricultural policy. He stresses the implications of these changes for future policy development. He concludes that an unexpected by-product of agricultural change has emerged. It is the dual level of well-being among rural families. Even as commercial agriculture is being integrated effectively into our national economy, substantial poverty remains in much of rural America. Ruttan shows that the failure of these five markets to generate either effective resource allocation or equitable income distribution has stimulated federal policies which modify agricultural market behavior. These traditional policies are being supplemented in turn by new programs which directly influence the welfare of rural people and operate outside the five markets.

Harold F. Breimyer argues that the economic and technical forces described by Ruttan have shaped an agriculture composed of three separate and distinct economies. The first is the land-based *crop production* portion of agriculture which churns out raw materials. The second is the *livestock* economy. This sector is becoming increasingly industrialized and detached from the primary crop production economy of agriculture. The third, the *marketing and processing* sector, has become even more detached from crop and livestock production over a long time span. According to Breimyer, the marketing economy has grown in size and domination. It has almost completely isolated both the crop and the livestock sectors from the consumer. Although industrialization in the marketing sector is not new, the emerging industrialization of the livestock economy poses new questions about the ultimate economic structure of the primary crop production sector. One such disturbing question is, "who will control agricultural production in the decades ahead?"

One consequence of the basic changes in the structure of American agriculture is the erosion of the traditional political power base which has supported agriculture's role in the national political system. James T. Bonnen questions how well traditional agricultural institutions are responding to the vast technical, economic, and social change in modern agriculture. According to Bonnen, agriculture's major economic and political institutions (The United States Department of Agriculture and its many component agencies, the agriculture committees of the Congress, the farm organizations, the Land-Grant Colleges) once represented an effective, interdependent system for identifying and solving problems in both the agricultural economy and the rural society. But these dynamic changes, Bonnen observes, have brought rising levels of conflict, destructive tensions, and leadership failure in these organizations. He believes that, if this situation persists, the institutions serving agriculture will not survive as a meaningful system.

Dale E. Hathaway analyzes the implications of several major shifts in the political foundation of agricultural policy. He argues that Southern domination of agricultural affairs is eroding and that the political power of the Southwest and West is rising. As a result, the old corn and cotton political base on which the Farm Bloc once rested is no longer viable. A new political base built on Breimyer's "three economies" plus the agri-business sector supplying manufactured inputs for primary farm production is emerging. Hathaway believes that one consequence of this development will be a declining concern with the problems of the rural community. Thus, "it is possible that we may find increasingly prosperous and politically potent commercial farms in the midst of an increasingly disorganized rural society, where they (farmers) have power to influence their prices and markets but not their roads, schools, and social institutions."

PRICE AND INCOME POLICY
FOR COMMERCIAL AGRICULTURE

The agricultural depression of the 1920's and the economic crisis of the 1930's created a fertile environment for passage of policies designed to boost agricultural prices and thus obtain "economic justice" for farmers in the market place. For more than thirty years the controversy raging around the idea of "economic justice" for farmers has focused on the concept of "parity" prices—"fair" prices for the commodities farmers sell in relation to the prices of commodities they buy. The first three papers in Part Two focus on the drive to achieve parity prices for agriculture. In their paper W. D. Rasmussen and G. L. Baker review the legislative history of these developments.

In spite of its significance, a recent survey in Michigan showed that very few farmers have a reasonable understanding of the parity concept in agriculture. F. L. Thomsen and R. J. Foote describe how parity prices are calculated and what their economic significance is. Although most of the parity debate has focused on prices, the concept of parity or "fair" income for farmers always has remained an important consideration. In "Parity, New Concept Needed," the National Advisory Commission on Food and Fiber argues that "there is no longer any close relationship between the parity price index and parity of income to a growing proportion of farmers." The Commission recommends that parity prices be retained primarily as analytical tools; for policy purposes, parity should be defined primarily in terms of income rather than prices.

A careful review of economic studies on the impact of alternative agricultural policies and programs is presented by L. G. Tweeten. A major finding of these studies is that, in the absence of farm price programs, both the prices received by farmers and their net farm income would have been substantially lower than it actually was throughout the post World War II period.

The last three papers in Part Two attempt to set out the principles of farm policy for the agricultural programs of the future. In his presidential address to the American Farm Economic Association, George E. Brandow poses four criteria against which farm policy should be evaluated. These include: a) the productive use of farm resources, b) the equitable distribution of income among persons engaged in agriculture, c) consistency with other economic policy, and d) freedom of individual thought and action. Past farm programs received relatively good grades on objectives a) and d) while objectives b) and c) were not adequately served. Kermit Gordon, a former director of the Bureau of the Budget, is especially critical of the failure of agricultural programs to be consistent with general economic policy.

The final paper in Part Two summarizes the report of the National Advisory Commission on Food and Fiber. This summary presents both the majority position, supported by 16 of the 29 commissioners, and the minority position, supported by the remaining 13 commissioners. The report calls for a more market-oriented agriculture, continued market expansion, less government intervention, and freer international trade. The Commission also endorsed very progressive proposals for alleviating problems of low-income people in agriculture. Although the report shows substantial differences of opinion among commission members, it will point the direction for much agricultural policy discussion during the coming years.

FOOD MARKETING POLICY

Policy discussion in the agricultural marketing sector traditionally has focused very heavily on the farm-retail price spread—the farmer's share of the consumer's food dollar. Technical efficiency in the food marketing and processing sector itself has been largely overlooked. In 1964, Congress established the National Commission on Food Marketing. Although this commission was established in response to widening farm to retail price spreads it produced a comprehensive review of economic performance in the food marketing industry.

Jerome Hammond, Willis Anthony, and Martin Christiansen summarize and evaluate the technical findings of the Commission. George Brandow, who served as executive director for the Commission, emphasizes the findings and conclusions of the Commission. Willard Mueller, an economist with the Federal Trade Commission, evaluates the Food Commission's conclusions as they affect the Federal Trade Commission's role in preserving competition.

The main conclusion of the paper by Hammond, Anthony, and Christiansen is that the food marketing industry is performing well in terms of technical and economic efficiency. More stringent restrictions on structural change in the industry, argue the authors, would serve little economic purpose. This contrasts with the views expressed by both Brandow and Mueller. Indeed, the Federal Trade Commission's perspective seems to be that competition in the food industry already has been eroded seriously and any market-expanding mergers by retailers should be reviewed carefully by the FTC. The opposing views presented in these three papers indicate that the issue of competition in food markets will remain an unresolved policy issue for some time.

BARGAINING POWER FOR FARMERS AND FARM WORKERS

Farmer bargaining power has become a major policy issue. Bargaining power is not, however, new to agricultural policy discussions. Farmers have long organized to improve their political and economic bargaining power. For example, the Grange, oldest of American farm organizations, grew rapidly in response to the rural distress of the 1870's.

The most dramatic effort by farmers to grasp direct marketing power occurred during the 1920's. Special new legislation was passed to protect farmer cooperative associations from antitrust action. Then, under the leadership of California's Aaron Sapiro, national commodity cooperatives were formed for wheat, cotton, tobacco, peanuts, and many other crops. The organizational objective was to control a sufficient proportion of the entire crop so that prices and other terms of sale could be enhanced for farmers. Cooperative control was to be achieved by means of long-term contracts with producer members. The plan failed because widespread farmer participation was not achieved.

A major element in the bargaining power controversy has been the application of the "monopoly cooperative" and the "labor market" approaches. In the paper by Donald Turner, Assistant Attorney General and head of Antitrust Division of the Justice

Department, the history of legislation giving agriculture co-operatives advantages over other forms of enterprise in exerting monopoly power in the market is reviewed. According to Turner, "the very fact that farmers are allowed voluntarily to form a cooperative association suggests that they may lawfully obtain by the cooperative device a degree of market power which individual businessmen could not obtain by similar combination." It is clear that Turner views the potential market power of cooperatives as a threat to the competitive process.

Don Paarlberg and Varden Fuller focus attention on the outlook for increased bargaining power by farmers within the "labor market" framework. Paarlberg views current bargaining efforts as part of a long-term effort by farmers to gain control over aggregate production and marketing decisions. Fuller emphasizes the limitations for securing farmer bargaining power within this framework. At the same time he is optimistic about the prospects for bargaining if price objectives are relatively modest.

Bargaining power for *farm workers* is an issue that has been carefully avoided by most participants in the agricultural policy debate. The subject has been unpopular in Congress, in the U.S. Department of Agriculture, and among academic economists. The statement on "Hired Farm Labor" by the National Advisory Commission on Food and Fiber is a vigorous appeal for more political and economic bargaining power for farm workers. It points out that hired farm workers are the most disadvantaged class of workers in the nation. It recommends that rural workers be given the same rights as urban workers to bargain collectively for wages. The Commission argues that there seems to be no justification for treating farm labor any differently from the nation's other workers.

OVERCOMING RURAL POVERTY

Economic and technical change has driven a wedge between commercial and noncommercial agriculture. Farm policy has failed to deal adequately with the problems of the rural poor. Of the 34 million Americans classified as "poor" in 1965, approximately 14 million lived in rural areas. Contrary to the popular view, however, most of the rural poor do not live on farms. They live in villages, small towns, and the open country. Of the 14 million rural poor, 11 million are white and only 3 million are nonwhite. Poverty in rural areas, therefore, does not conform to conventional stereotypes. Many identify poverty only with life in the urban ghetto and, at the same time, picture the agrarian way of life with romance and nostalgia. The hard fact is that income is much less equitably distributed in rural areas than in cities.

In 1966 President Johnson appointed the National Advisory Commission on Rural Poverty. The report of this Commission, entitled *The People Left Behind,* was released in December 1967. W. Keith Bryant, a Commission staff member, summarizes the group's findings in the lead article of Part Four.

The second paper, "Six Reasons For Action on Rural Poverty Now," comes from the Commission report. It presents convincing evidence that rural poverty should be overcome. The third paper, by C. E. Bishop, Executive Director of the Commission, focuses particular attention on how and why American society has failed to mold effective policies and institutions to improve labor mobility. According to Bishop, the largest mass migration movement in history has taken place in the United States during the last half century. Furthermore, this vast movement of people has been unguided, unplanned, and almost unnoticed. But it has been the keystone in America's dynamic economic growth. Technical change, in permitting a massive drop in agricultural employment, has made this migration possible and has paid off handsomely in national economic growth. However, heavy penalties have been imposed on many of the families who participated in this population movement.

Varden Fuller sheds light on why the American political process has failed to devise effective programs for dealing with rural poverty. He suggests that our agricultural programs have contributed to the inequitable distribution of income among rural families. Moreover, he argues that the interests of land owners, as the chief beneficiaries of these programs, are being "served at the expense of the rural poor and of working farmers whose primary interest in agriculture is only occupational."

AGRICULTURAL TRADE, AID, AND DEVELOPMENT POLICY

Trade in agricultural products is a very large part of total world trade volume. The United States emerged from World War II as the world's leading exporter of agricultural commodities. These products have moved abroad under both commercial and noncommercial food-aid arrangements. During the past ten years commercial trade has increased sharply, and food-aid shipments have declined relatively. Today commercial exports of farm products account for approximately three-fourths of total agricultural trade. Food-aid shipments on concessional terms to less-developed friendly nations amount to less than one-fourth of United States agricultural exports. Total exports of agricultural commodities approach $7 billion annually. This is about one-fourth of the total value of all our merchandise exports, and is crucial to our international balance of payments.

The U.S. food-aid program has been controversial throughout its existence. There is no doubt that food aid prevented starvation in Europe after World War II. It has contributed to economic stability in many less-developed countries recently. However, many investigators insist that U.S. food aid has diverted the attention of policy makers in many recipient countries from the vital problems of agricultural development.

Our commercial trade policies do not always serve the national interest in a broad sense. We frequently sacrifice long-run national and international objectives in the short-run interest of politically strategic groups of agriculture producers or handlers.

In his 1964 presidential address to the American Farm Economic Association, D. Gale Johnson places recent agricultural trade policies of the United States and other developed countries in their long-run historical perspective. He argues that the protectionist policies of the developed countries may retard the growth of less developed countries. He observes, "an expansion in volume of food aid will not offset the adverse effects of the decline in export earnings. While it is comforting to the rich to believe that their bounty is being used to prevent malnutrition among the poor, and perhaps on occasion to prevent actual starvation, it is a delusion to assume such aid could be a major factor contributing to a rise in real per capita incomes in recipient countries."

Secretary of Agriculture Orville Freeman documents the crucial role which American agriculture's productive capacity has played in world growth and stability since World War II. Although Freeman's is a strongly positive outlook on American food aid, he shares Johnson's view that "if we are ever to solve the world food problem, we must now begin in earnest to increase food production in less developed nations".

In the final article, Theodore Schultz asks why U.S. technical assistance has not made a bigger impact on agricultural development in the postwar period. Schultz is highly critical of technical assistance efforts which assume that agricultural development merely involves the simple transfer of technology from the United States and other productive countries to the low income nations of the world. Schultz argues that poor countries must value farm products more highly in their development schemes, and they must reward their farmers more adequately for productive effort. He also stresses the importance of investment in research and development leading to the development of new high productive inputs. This section concludes with a wry bit of poetry by Kenneth Boulding. "The Old Agricultural Lag" skewers many current cliches about agricultural development used by professionals and amateurs alike.

Today's patchwork of farm commodity, resource and rural development, and commercial trade and food aid programs undoubtedly will be substantially changed during the 1970s. The programs cost too much. Their income effects are too regressive. The programs are biased in favor of plants, land, and animals and against people. Yet, the Food and Agricultural Act of 1965 is a real advance over previous legislation. It gives the Secretary of Agriculture a flexible instrument for adjusting production to utilization without accumulating burdensome surpluses. It permits agricultural commodities to move into world trade on a more competitive basis. It introduces the principle of direct income support. But the programs are costly—and likely to get more costly.

The experience of the last two decades shows that new agricultural programs closely resemble programs of the past. Progress is made by a process of incremental changes. Most improvements embodied in the Food and Agricultural Act of 1965 are likely to be retained in the 1970's. We can expect to see more effective programs dealing with the problems of hired farm workers. We can expect to see more effective programs for helping rural governments provide needed community services. We should be concerned about the new wave of trade protectionism that has been gaining momentum in Congress and elsewhere since the completion of the latest round of international trade negotiations. This movement toward "neo-isolationism" also threatens to snuff out our programs of technical assistance to agriculture in the less-developed countries. In the long run, such changes in our trade and foreign policy could disrupt economic progress throughout the world.

PROBLEMS OF THE MODERN ECONOMY

Agricultural Policy in an Affluent Society

PART ONE   Economic Development, Political Power, and Agricultural Policy

Agricultural Policy in an Affluent Society

VERNON W. RUTTAN

Vernon W. Ruttan is Professor of Agricultural Economics and Head of the Department of Agricultural Economics at the University of Minnesota. This paper was presented at the Annual Meeting of the American Farm Economic Association in August 1966. It was published in the Journal of Farm Economics *in December 1966.*

FROM THE TIME of the Plymouth and Jamestown settlements until the closing years of the nineteenth century, the encounter with the frontier represented a dominant theme in American agricultural development. This encounter created an opportunity for the evolution of an agriculture based on an abundance of land and a relative scarcity of labor. This in turn stimulated the development of an agricultural technology that was primarily directed toward achieving gains in labor productivity rather than gains in land productivity.

Since the closing of the frontier, in the last quarter of the nineteenth century, the encounter with an increasingly dominant urban-industrial sector has emerged as a major force in American agricultural development. By 1880, nonagricultural employment exceeded agricultural employment. By 1929, manufacturing employment alone exceeded agricultural employment. And by 1970, it seems likely that agricultural employment will be little greater than total unemployment in the United States, even

1

during periods of high-level economic activity (Table 1). This development alone opens up entirely new dimensions in the evolution of agricultural policy which could scarcely be considered when agriculture represented an important share of the nation's labor force.

The interactions between the farm and the nonfarm sectors that led to this fundamental restructuring of the American economy can best be visualized by looking in turn at each of five sets of market relationships: the *product market*, through which the output of the agricultural sector is transmitted to the nonfarm sector and through which incomes are generated in the farm sector; the *purchased input markets*, through which move the manufactured capital equipment and operating inputs used in agricultural production; the *labor market*, through which labor is allocated between the agricultural and nonagricultural sectors and among firms in each sector; the *land market*, through which the gains of productivity growth in the farm sector are transmuted into capital formation in the nonfarm sectors of the economy; and finally the *market for consumer goods*, through which

TABLE 1. *Employment by Sector in the U.S., 1880–1964, Projections to 1975 (in thousands of workers)*

	Agri- culture	Total nonagri- culture	Manu- facturing	Unem- ployment
1880	8,585	8,807	N.A.	N.A.
1929	10,450	37,180	10,534	1,550
1964	4,751	59,097	17,593	3,876
1975 (estimates)	3,808	78,871	21,111	3,745

SOURCES:

1880 and 1929: U.S. Bureau of the Census, *Historical Statistics of the United States, Colonial Times to 1957*, Washington, D.C., 1960.

1964: *Monthly Labor Review*, Vol. 88, No. 6, United States Department of Labor, Bureau of Labor Statistics, June, 1965.

1975 Projections: Howard Stumbler, "Man Power Needs by Industry to 1975," *Monthly Labor Review*, Vol. 88, No. 3, United States Department of Labor, Bureau of Labor Statistics, March, 1965. Projections assume a 25-percent increase in total nonagricultural employment, a 70-percent increase in employment in manufacturing, and a 20-percent decline in agricultural employment from 1964. Unemployment is estimated at 7 percent of the labor force.

N.A.—not available.

farm families achieve access to, or are excluded from, full participation in the patterns of consumption that are identified with the American standard of living.

The failure of these market relationships to generate either effective resource allocation or equity in income distribution has led to a set of policies designed to modify market behavior. These policies are in turn being supplemented by a new set of programs designed to affect directly the welfare of rural people outside of the structure of market relationship.

THE PRODUCT MARKET

Through most of American economic history, the product market—the market for things farmers sell—represented the primary link between the farm and the nonfarm sectors of the economy. It was the dominant channel through which shifts in the international terms of trade, national fluctuations in nonfarm income, and local variations in nonfarm demand have been channeled into the agricultural sector.[1]

In most low-income countries, where a substantial share of increases in per capita income is devoted to dietary improvement, the product market is still the main link between the peasant and the urban-industrial sector of the economy. As income per person rises, consumption of agricultural products expands less rapidly. At very high income levels there may be no additional farm-level food consumed as income continues to rise.

In the United States, the declining response in consumption of farm-level food and fiber to increases in nonfarm income has sharply reduced the commodity market effects of both fluctuations and growth in national economic activity in the nonfarm sector. Monetary and fiscal policy measures have tended to produce rather stable rates of growth in per capita income. Agricultural trade and commodity policies have tended to in-

1. The importance of interaction between the farm and nonfarm sectors of the economy represented the major thesis of T. W. Schultz's classic study of *Agriculture in an Unstable Economy*. Major attention was focused on product market interactions. A decade and a half later, D. E. Hathaway argued that there had been a major shift in this pattern of interaction, with the input markets having much greater significance.

sulate agricultural commodity prices, particularly crop prices, from normal trade and market fluctuations. Participation in the growth of foreign demand, except for a few products such as soybeans and some feed grain exports, has been heavily dependent on export subsidies or food aid throughout most of·the postwar period.

Changes in the product markets which link the agricultural to the urban-industrial sector have also modified the local market effects of urban-industrial development. The production of some products has become essentially industrialized. Broiler and turkey "factories" have almost entirely replaced farm production of poultry meat. Commercial production of fruits and vegetables is becoming highly concentrated. Regional specialization in production of fruit, vegetables, and animal products, resulting from technological and organizational changes in processing, transportation, and distribution, have reduced the impact of local urban-industrial development on the demand for locally produced farm products. Although there are a few minor exceptions, fluid milk, which is protected by a series of local market trade barriers, remains one of the few major farm products whose demand remains responsive to local urban-industrial growth.

The decline in the significance of the product market as a generator of either dynamic growth or instability in the agricultural sector is a consequence of both a) the economic development of the United States economy and b) the monetary, fiscal, and commodity policies that have been implemented since World War II. As a result, it is no longer reasonable to suggest that the farm problem is primarily a product of "business fluctuations and unbalanced expansion of the [national] economy."[2] There is, however, a very substantial possibility that commercial policy in western Europe and U.S. policy with respect to food aid for the developing countries may become an important source of instability in the product market during the next decade.

THE MARKET FOR PURCHASED INPUTS

The markets for manufactured capital equipment and current inputs have become increasingly important in transmitting the

2. T. W. Schultz, *Agriculture in an Unstable Economy* (New York: McGraw-Hill Book Company, 1945), p. 2.

effects of changes in the nonfarm economy to agriculture. Much of the new agricultural technology is embodied in the form of new capital equipment or more efficient fertilizer, insecticides, and other manufactured inputs. In 1870, the typical American farm was still in some respects a subsistence unit, with the value of intermediate products supplied by the nonfarm sector amounting to less than 9 percent of the value of gross farm product. By 1900, intermediate inputs still amounted to only about 13 percent of gross farm product. In recent years, nonfarm inputs have exceeded 60 percent of the value of farm output.

Growth in the use of purchased inputs has been closely related to developments in the labor market. The demand for labor, resulting from rapid urban-industrial development, reinforced the economic pressure for substitution of capital equipment for labor in American agriculture at precisely that period when the frontier was disappearing as a major factor in agricultural development.

The rapid growth of labor productivity in American agriculture was not, at first, accompanied by parallel changes in land productivity. Aggregate grain yield per acre in American agriculture remained essentially unchanged from the end of the Civil War until well into the twentieth century.

By the mid 1920's, however, a new biological and chemical technology was beginning to emerge. This combination of rapid advance in biological research and a high volume of relatively inexpensive agricultural chemicals created a new dimension in agricultural productivity in United States agriculture. Land productivity, which had experienced no real growth between 1900 and 1925, rose by 1.4 percent per year for the period 1925–1950 and by 2.5 percent per year between 1950 and 1964. This higher output per acre combined with continued mechanization to produce a rate of growth of labor productivity of 6.6 percent per year between 1950 and 1964 (Table 2).

The productivity gains in agriculture have been achieved, to a substantial degree, through advances in technology that are embodied in inputs produced by the farm-machinery, chemical, feed-processing and related industrial sectors. These industries have increased the quality of the technology embodied in their products and have achieved rapid productivity gains in the use of factor inputs. The results have been transmitted to agriculture through improvements in the physical productivity of factor in-

TABLE 2. *Annual Average Rates of Change
in Total Outputs, Inputs, and Productivity in
U.S. Agriculture, 1870–1964 (percent per year)*

Item	1870–1900	1900–1925	1925–1950	1950–1964
Farm output	2.9	0.9	1.5	2.0
Total inputs	1.9	1.1	0.3	0.3
Total productivity	1.0	—0.2	1.2	1.9
Labor inputs[1]	1.6	0.5	—1.8	—4.5
Labor productivity	1.3	0.4	3.3	6.6
Land inputs[2]	3.1	0.8	0.1	—0.9
Land productivity	—0.2	0.0	1.4	2.5

[1] Number of workers, 1870–1910; man-hour basis, 1910–1961.
[2] Cropland used for crops, including crop failure and cultivated summer fallow.

SOURCES: Computed from USDA, *Changes in Farm Production and Efficiency*, Stat. Bul. 223, rev., July 1965; and D. D. Durost and G. T. Barton, *Changing Sources of Farm Output*, USDA, Prod. Res. Rep. 36, Feb. 1960.

puts and reductions in factor-product price ratios.

As purchased inputs have risen relative to the value of farm output, however, the market for purchased inputs has become not only a source of productivity gains for the agricultural sector but a source of instability as well. Agriculture is no longer an industry with a vested interest in inflation. The monetary gains resulting from the higher product prices associated with rises in the general price level tend to be rapidly converted into net reductions in real purchasing power by inflation in the prices of purchased inputs.

THE LABOR MARKET

The labor market has become an increasingly important channel of interaction between the farm and nonfarm sectors. Technical and economic developments have made it increasingly profitable to substitute inputs purchased from the industrial sector for farm labor. The slow growth in domestic demand for farm products, the insulation of domestic markets from changes in demand in other countries, and the rapid growth in labor productivity have all combined to place on the labor market the major burden of balancing the rate of growth of agricultural output with the rate of growth in demand for agricultural products.

With the demand for agricultural output expanding at less than 2 percent per year and labor productivity rising by more than 6 percent per year, the burden of adjustment in the labor market has been extremely heavy. The rate at which labor leaves the agricultural sector, either through migration or through local off-farm or part-time employment, is highly responsive to the level of unemployment in the nonfarm labor force.

Labor-market adjustments have also been particularly difficult in the low-income agricultural regions where local nonfarm employment has not expanded at a sufficiently rapid rate to absorb both the excess agricultural labor force and the new entrants to the labor force from rural areas. The labor surplus has been so large, and the obstacles to migration for the older and less-well-educated members of rural communities have been so great, that migration has generally not been sufficient to induce convergence of wage and income levels between high- and low-income regions or to narrow income differentials between farm and nonfarm workers, except where there has been substantial growth in local nonfarm labor markets.

Even in areas where the intersector labor market has functioned effectively, it has also served as a channel for transferring capital from the farm to the nonfarm sector. The capital invested in the education of farm youth, while low relative to investment in education in the nonfarm sector, has been large relative to aggregate net farm income. Clearly, lower birth rates in rural areas could reduce the magnitude of the capital transfer associated with migration. And greater reliance on state and federal rather than local revenue sources to finance educational services could partially compensate rural areas for the capital drain through investment in education.

THE LAND MARKET

The land market has, throughout American agricultural history, played a major role in facilitating the redistribution of the ownership of both land and nonland assets between the farm and nonfarm sectors. Yet there is remarkably little quantitative evidence on the magnitude of intersector shifts in asset flows and ownership.

The success of land speculators in attempting to pre-empt the productivity gains from the opening up of new land in the West appears to have been greatly overemphasized in the Populist literature The extent to which economic rents resulting from national economic growth and local urban–industrial development have contributed to rising land prices is also a question that appears to generate more heat than light.

Nevertheless, it seems reasonable to hypothesize that the system of owner-operatorship of land which requires that farm property be refinanced each generation has served as an effective channel for the transfer of the ownership of capital accumulated in the farm sector to the nonfarm sector, at least since the beginning of the decline in farm population after 1910.

In recent years, the transfer of the ownership of capital accumulated in the agricultural sector to the nonfarm sector through the land market has been modified by a) rapid technological change, coupled with b) the institutional devices designed to maintain farm prices. In the absence of farm price support and production controls, the productivity gains in the agricultural sector would have been transferred directly to the nonfarm sector through the product market as a result of lower prices for farm commodities.

Price support and production controls have, except for short periods such as 1952–1955, effectively dampened such tendencies. During the last several decades, agriculture has been operating in an environment in which a) technological change has drastically increased both land productivity and the area that could be efficiently combined in one operating unit and b) price supports have been made effective by the willingness of the government to stockpile the major agricultural commodities. In addition, the government itself has entered the land market in an effort to bid land away from crop production.

In this environment, farmers have apparently utilized both the actual and the anticipated gains from higher productivity to bid against each other for the reduced acreage available to the agricultural sector for farm production. The effect has been to capitalize the benefit of technological change and commodity programs into land values. As farms have changed hands at higher and higher prices, a substantial share of the realized capital gains has been channeled into the nonfarm sector through inheritance by nonfarm family members. The result has been an increase in fixed costs and a reduction in net income to the new owner.

THE MARKET FOR CONSUMER GOODS

The market for consumer goods represents the channel through which farm families achieve access to, or are excluded from, full participation in the patterns of consumption that are identified with the American standard of living. In the past, it also represented an important source of demand for the products of an expanding urban-industrial sector. With the reduction in farm numbers and the decline in consumption expenditures relative to the value of farm output, the consumption expenditures of farm families no longer represent an independent dynamic factor in aggregate consumer demand.

Curiously enough, economists have devoted relatively little attention to the economic behavior of farmers as consumers. In an earlier era, it was assumed that farmers and other rural residents enjoyed a substantial advantage in real purchasing power as compared to urban families with similar money incomes. This was apparently confirmed by Koffsky's classic study of nearly twenty years ago. Although this work has not been repeated in comparable detail, there is evidence, from later estimates, that the purchasing-power advantage of rural residents, measured in terms of a market-basket concept, which included items consumed in both urban and rural areas, has declined sharply.

In contrast to these estimates, I would personally hypothesize, generalizing from the very inadequate data available on which to make such comparisons, that a valid analysis covering the broad range of commodity, social, and cultural components of consumption, with appropriate corrections for quality differences and transportation costs, would indicate substantially lower real purchasing power for rural than for urban families with similar money incomes.

Furthermore, I would hypothesize that purchasing-power advantages in rural areas that have been postulated in the past were based largely on the fact that the baskets of goods consumed in rural and urban areas were not really comparable. The rural basket was inferior in terms of both quality and the range of items included, not only in the areas of health, education, housing, and cultural amenities, but also in terms of the commodity components of food and clothing.

In the past, these disparities were disguised by what purported to be distinct rural and urban cultures—by a distinct rural economy and rural society—in which the rural and urban sectors presumably gave different weights to the elements entering into consumption patterns. This rural-urban cultural distinction is disappearing. There has emerged today a high-income commercial agricultural sector which does participate fully, both culturally and economically, in the consumer markets of a dynamic urban–industrial society. In most areas, the families who operate the nation's high-income commercial farms do their shopping at the same supermarkets and suburban shopping centers as the families of urban workers and professionals. They share the same cultural values and aspirations. But the real cost of full participation, I would argue, remains substantially greater for rural families than for the families that reside in or near the nation's standard metropolitan areas.

POVERTY IN AMERICAN AGRICULTURE

An unanticipated by-product of the effective economic and cultural integration of commercial agriculture into the national society is the emergence of a dual structure in the well-being of rural families. There is no sector of American agriculture that can be properly classed as a peasant sector. There is, however, substantial poverty in rural areas. Rural income is far less equitably distributed than urban income. The poverty problem has in the past been reflected primarily in terms of occupational, age, racial, and regional dimensions.

First, consider the occupational dimension. Incomes of hired farm workers are substantially lower than incomes of farm operators. The hired farm labor force is the most heterogeneous employee group in the American economy. Incomes of full-time hired workers on commercial farms have increased rapidly. Incomes of part-time and migrant farm workers, however, have not kept pace with the income of either full-time farm workers or farm operators. Mechanization of operations formerly performed by hand has actually reduced the number of days worked per year by some categories of hired farm workers.

The rapid growth in the size of commercial farms has also helped create an age dimension to the poverty problem. Many older farm operators have been caught in a situation where they have neither the financial resources to expand their farm operations nor the labor skills necessary to find remunerative off-farm employment.

There is also a racial dimension to the poverty problem. Roughly half of the farm families that fall in the poverty class are located in the South. Although the median income of white farm families in the South is only about half that of white urban families in the South, it is almost twice as high as the median income of nonwhite farm families (Table 3).

The regional dimension has, in the past, been closely interrelated with the racial dimension. Regionally, approximately half

TABLE 3. *Median Money Income of Farm and Nonfarm Families by Region and Color, 1964*

	United States	North-east	North Central	South White	South Non-white	West
1. *Median income*						
Nonfarm	$6,755	$7,277	$7,101	$6,136	$3,112	$7,378
Farm	3,558	4,804	4,160	3,168	1,721	5,248
Farm median income as a percent of non-farm	53%	66%	59%	52%	55%	71%
2. *Families with incomes of $5,000 or more*						
Nonfarm	68%	74%	72%	62%	24%	72%
Farm	36%	48%	42%	31%	4%	53%
3. *Families with incomes under $2,500*						
Nonfarm	12%	8%	10%	14%	40%	10%
Farm	35%	23%	30%	39%	77%	21%

SOURCES: U. S. Bureau of the Census, "Income in 1964 of Families and Persons in the United States," *Current Population Reports,* Series P-60, No. 47 and unpublished data.

of the nation's low-productivity and low-income farm families are located in the South. However, nonwhites have accounted for one-third of the total decline in farm population in recent years. This rapid decline in nonwhite farm operators since World War II means that the racial dimension is becoming less important in explaining poverty in rural areas in the South. There are also substantial pockets of poverty in certain peripheral areas such as the Ozark mountain area in Missouri and Oklahoma; parts of Southern Ohio, Indiana, and Illinois; certain cutover areas in the Northern Lake States of Michigan, Wisconsin, and Minnesota; and the areas of Spanish and Indian concentration in the Southwest and in other scattered areas throughout the nation.

It cannot be stressed too strongly that rapid growth in the nonfarm labor market is necessary for any successful effort to overcome the regional, occupational, age, and racial dimensions of poverty in American agriculture. However, neither off-farm migration nor local industrial development are capable by themselves of fully solving the poverty problem in American agriculture. Substantial numbers of the least mobile portion of the farm labor force remain stranded in rural underemployment—on small farms, in part-time employment, and in barely remunerative nonfarm employment.

Increasingly, this hard-core rural poverty must be analyzed in terms of the social structure of the low-income segment of society rather than in terms of the economic structure of rural areas. It is transmitted in part through the lack of cultural integration inherent in the dual structure of rural society interacting with the other poverty dimensions, particularly the occupational and racial dimension.

NEW DIMENSIONS IN AGRICULTURAL POLICY

American agricultural development policies have been uniquely successful in meeting national farm output and productivity objectives. These policies have clearly been less successful in meeting the income objectives of all of the families engaged in the production of agricultural commodities. One observer has pointed out that "behavior of rural people, their representatives and their institutions implies a materialistic bias in favor of plants, land, and animals and against people." While this is perhaps overdrawn, it is true that policies of the past were designed primarily to solve technological and commodity problems of rural people.

This was a valid choice at the time when these policies were established. It is important for United States economic development that the agricultural sector achieve a sufficiently high rate of output and productivity growth in order, simultaneously, to meet national food and fiber requirements and to release substantial numbers of farm workers for nonfarm employment. If technological change and farm output growth had continued at the 1900–1925 rate during 1925–1965, the United States would today a) be importing as much as one-third of its total food and fiber consumption, or b) be paying substantially higher prices for food. Instead, we are exporting approximately one-fifth of our total production and enjoying relatively low food prices.

There is no economic reason, however, for the continuation of a dual structure in American agriculture. And, in fact, a new set of agricultural policies, which are less commodity-oriented, is now emerging.

Employment Programs · Since the mid 1950's, the traditional commodity policies have been supplemented by a new set of employment-oriented rural development policies. Initiation of the Rural Development Program in 1956 represented belated recognition that the Employment Act of 1946 applied to rural as well as to urban areas. The Rural (later Area) Development Program was followed by a number of other efforts designed to expand farm and nonfarm employment opportunities in rural areas.[3]

A basic limitation of the rural employment programs is that they have not departed sufficiently from the production-oriented policies of the past. They continue to assume that the way to help rural people is to help them produce something of value to the rest of society—be it agricultural commodities, recreation

3. The literature on the Rural Development Program (RDP), the Rural Area Development (RAD), the Area Development Act (ADA), the Public Works and Area Development Act (EDA) and related employment-oriented programs such as the Appalachian Regional Development Act is too extensive to list in detail.

services, or automobile parts—without changing their geographic location. The employment-oriented programs are failing to make a significant aggregate impact on underemployment in rural areas simply because the resources in rural areas in which major effort is being concentrated (the Appalachians, the Ozarks, the Upper Midwest and others) are not underdeveloped—they are redundant. The employment programs may have a modest impact on location and investment decisions. They have no prospects of reversing the trend for greater centralization of industrial activity within standard metropolitan areas, and their contribution toward solution of the problem of rural poverty will be marginal at best.

Income Transfer Programs · The commodity policies have also been supplemented by a new set of policies designed to separate income-support payments from either commodity prices or direct participation in the production process. Extension of Social Security to farmers in 1955 was the first, and remains the most important, step in the separation of income-support payments from commodity prices. This action was by itself responsible for a sharp reduction in the disparity between the incomes of older farm and nonfarm workers.

Land retirement programs, which make rental payments to farmers for removing marginal land from intensive crop production, also operated as a mechanism to transfer income to farmers without directly affecting market prices. The Food and Agriculture Act of 1965 goes farther than earlier legislation in separating income-support payment from production-incentive and price-stabilization payment.

The use of effective income-protection programs, employing some criteria of a socially acceptable minimum standard of living and protection against the risks imposed on individuals through product, input, land, and labor market instability and trends is particularly important in the short run. Such payments permit the program participants to achieve a level of consumption more nearly in line with American standards. But they typically do not meet the additional objective of enabling the participant to contribute effectively to the further growth of the American economy.

Education, Training, Health Programs · To meet this latter objective, a stronger emphasis must be placed on investment in the human agent of production—in man. The current pattern of underinvestment in rural health, rural education and training, and other rural social services must be corrected.

New steps in this direction are now being taken. Government programs involving substantial investments in education, training, and health are being developed to assist low-income families to increase both their incomes and their contribution to national economic growth. In education, a) the Elementary and Secondary Education Act of 1965, b) the Adult Basic Education programs of the Economic Opportunity (Poverty) Act of 1964, and c) the Operation Head Start Program of the Office of Economic Opportunity are potentially of great significance. In the field of training, a) the post-high school vocational training possibilities opened up by the Vocational Education Act of 1963, b) the Work Experience Program under the Economic Opportunity Act of 1964, a) the Job Corps and Neighborhood Youth Corps programs under the same act, and d) the training and retraining provisions of the Manpower Development and Training Act of 1962 are all of potential significance. In the area of health, a) the Hill-Burton Act, which gives grants and loans for hospital and medical care facilities, and b) the 1965 Social Security Act amendments, which provide limited medical and substantial hospital-care benefits for the aged (Medicare) and low-income (Medicaid) families are of great significance.

Most of these new programs, except Medicare and Medicaid, must be classified at present as having potential rather than present significance for solution of the rural poverty problem. Many are just now getting under way. Among those that have been operating for some time, evidence is accumulating that they may be most effective for the lower middle class rather than for the very poorest families.

AGRICULTURAL POLICY FOR THE FUTURE

What kind of agriculture will emerge out of the technological and economic forces that currently impinge on the rural sector of the American economy? And what should be the orientation of the agricultural policies that can best serve a) the people who earn their living producing the nation's food and fiber, b) the rural society that emerges out of the changes that are under way, and c) the American economy in general? Let me attempt to respond to these questions, first with reference to commercial agriculture, and then with reference to the problem of poverty in rural areas.

Commercial Agriculture · In commercial agriculture, the decline in farm employment and farm numbers certainly will continue. Over the next decade, farm employment will decline to well below 4 million workers. This will be less than the number of unemployed workers, even in times of high-level economic activity. There are now about a million farms with sales of above $10,000 and less than half a million farms with sales of $20,000 or above (Table 4). This latter group alone produces over 60 percent of United States farm output. With family median incomes in metropolitan areas approaching $7500 per year, it is clearly only farms with sales of $20,000 or more that can come near providing family incomes sufficient to permit a level of participation in the market for consumer goods that is consistent with American standards.

If total production were to be concentrated on farms such as those with sales of $20,000 or more, the total United States farm output could be produced on 750,000 farms. If production were concentrated entirely on farms such as those with sales of $40,000 or more, the total United States farm output could be produced on less than 400,000 farms. It seems apparent that the technological capacity already exists that could permit production of 80–90 percent of the value of total United States farm output on between 50,000 and 100,000 production units.

The continued decline in farm employment and farm numbers will not be accompanied by a withering away of farm price and income programs. Even a highly concentrated food and fiber production industry would be subject to great price and output instability in the absence of public intervention. The rationale for public intervention in agricultural commodity markets is, and will continue to be, essentially similar to the rationale for setting

TABLE 4. *Estimated Number of Farms, Income, and Parity Income Position of Farms by Economic Class, 1965*

	Farms with (dollar) sales of						
	40,000 and over	*20,000 to 39,999*	*10,000 to 19,999*	*5,000 to 9,999*	*2,500 to 4,999*	*Less than 2,500*	*All farms*
Number of farms (thousands)	148	313	584	533	330	1,466	3,374
Percentage distribution (percent)	4.4	9.3	17.3	15.8	9.8	43.4	100.0
Cash receipts percentage distribution (percent)	38.5	22.2	21.7	10.3	3.2	4.1	100.0
Realized net farm income (million dollars)	2,351	3,326	3,909	2,117	809	1,597	14,109
Parity income gap, assuming a 5-percent return to farm operators' assets, and $2.61 per hour returns to operator and family labor (million dollars)	−294	−402	688	1,552	1,214	4,964	7,722
Indicated percentage change in realized net income required to achieve parity of returns.	−13	−12	+18	+73	+150	+311	+55

SOURCE: USDA (preliminary).

rates and regulating output in the transportation industry—that is, to lend stability to an industry which technological and economic forces would render chronically unstable in the absence of such intervention.

While the production and marketing of agricultural commodities will continue to be regulated through a combination of marketing allotments and quotas, multiple-price systems, marketing orders and agreements, and land-use contracts, it seems likely that these programs will be less oriented to achieving income goals in the agricultural sector than in the past. They will be directed to a greater extent toward the protection of urban consumers from price fluctuations and toward the achievement of international trade and development policy objectives.

It seems reasonable to expect that the programs designed to lend stability to product markets will increasingly be supplemented by efforts to dampen the new instability that is now channeled through the markets for labor and purchased inputs. Minimum-wage legislation covering a substantial share of the hired farm labor force can certainly be anticipated in the next several years. Efforts to organize agricultural labor are likely to receive more effective government support than in the past. There will be increased pressure for legislation regulating bargaining and other relationships among suppliers, growers, processors, and retailers, participating in vertically integrated systems. It also seems reasonable to anticipate that, in spite of intervention in product and factor markets, the land and labor markets will continue to function in such a manner that the value of an hour spent on the seat of a tractor by a farm operator will typically not exceed the hourly wage rate of a hired farm worker engaged in the same activity.

The situation which I have characterized opens up entirely new possibilities in the evolution of agricultural policy. With the level of farm employment less than unemployment in the rest of the economy even during periods of high-level economic activity, there is no longer any question of the capacity of the nonfarm sector to absorb displaced farm workers. The entire farm labor force could be absorbed into the nonfarm labor force in a relatively short time if it were deemed important for the national economy. It is now both technically and economically possible to develop policies designed to organize a food and fiber production industry capable of permitting that part of the population engaged in food and fiber production to participate fully in the level of material and cultural consumption that is available only in a modern urban-industrial society.

A food and fiber industry in which 80–90 percent of farm output could be produced by 50,000 to 100,000 production units is not only technically feasible but is in the process of evolving. This is resulting in a chain reaction by agricultural leaders that can best be described by the title of a recent Broadway musical: "Stop the World, I Want to Get Off." One manifestation of this tendency is the frantic efforts that are made every five years, after each new agricultural census, to prove that regardless of what else has changed we still have a "family" farm economy. Another is Secretary Freeman's recent promise to stop the outflow of population from rural areas.

Rural Poverty · A first step in a realistic effort to deal with rural poverty as it is now emerging is to recognize that it is no longer possible to make a significant aggregate impact on rural poverty by programs designed primarily a) to increase agricultural production or b) to increase nonfarm employment in rural areas. Production policy is an important element in the creation of a modern agriculture, but production expansion will not provide new jobs in rural areas. Employment policy oriented around regional development efforts can be important in achieving the efficient use of labor both nationally and regionally. However, the potential number of new jobs created by such activities in the remaining poverty pockets will at best be extremely limited relative to the size of the poverty problem.

Furthermore, with continued out-migration the absolute number of families in the poverty class living in the traditional depressed areas appears to be declining relative to the number of poor families in the areas that have traditionally been classified as commercial farming areas. Northeast Minnesota is classified as a depressed area, but the number of rural poor is greater in the commercial farming areas of Southwestern Minnesota. Iowa has more poor families in rural areas than some Southern states. This means that we must move beyond the charge that Schultz gave us to consider the regional and community dimensions of poverty in his classic "Reflections on Poverty Within Agriculture" to consider the psychological and cultural dimensions of poverty.

A second major element in the design of an effective attack on poverty in rural areas is recognition of the changing relationship between commercial agriculture and the rural community. The economic relationship that previously existed between commercial agriculture and the local community through the product market and the market for purchased inputs is rapidly disappearing. A prosperous agriculture no longer implies a prosperous rural community. The rural community and commercial agriculture are no longer joined in a mutuality of interest stemming from the possibility of a common solution to their economic problems.

A third major element in the design of an effective attack on poverty in rural areas is to reject the assumption that it is rural poverty in any significant respect except location. More positively, it is to recognize that the problems of both rural and urban poverty are essentially similar in their psychological, sociological, and economic dimensions and that the agencies that are most effective in dealing with these problems in urban areas will be the agencies best equipped to deal with them in rural areas.

The implication is that the problem of rural poverty is growing progressively less amenable to solution through use of the program instruments available to the USDA or to the colleges of agriculture. Indeed, to attempt to bend the program instruments available to these agencies into the direct service of antipoverty efforts would be to blunt their usefulness for agricultural production and employment policy.

The changing nature of rural poverty, with the emergence of the structural, cultural, and psychological dimensions as a dominant pattern, gives increasing importance to policies associated with direct income transfers, to assistance in the areas of health and education, and to greater reliance on small group or "case" approaches to the solution of individual poverty problems. Although the traditional agricultural agencies will not be heavily involved in administering such programs, the rural social sciences have an important role to play in policy analysis related to the poverty programs. The fact that they are not so directly involved in program administration may result in greater freedom of inquiry and greater impact than they have had in the commodity program areas.

The Policy Environment · The changing structure of power in rural America will, I anticipate, make it easier to face up to the policy issues both in commercial farm policy and in policy with respect to rural poverty than in the past. The redrafting of the legislative districts to achieve greater "parity" among individuals in voting rights will be a major factor in making state and federal legislatures more responsive to the needs of men rather than of land and commodities.

The policy actions of these more broadly based legislative bodies can be expected to reflect to a greater extent the concept that the rights of the individual depend upon an abstract conception of his dignity in relation to other individuals rather than upon a concept of freedom which relates man's freedom and independence to his concrete and tangible property rights. More particularly, they are likely to be more active in extending the full range of social and economic welfare legislation to farm families rather than in continuing to protect rural families from the mainstream of American social and economic development.

The Three Economies of Agriculture

Harold F. Breimyer is Professor of Agricultural Economics at the University of Missouri. His discussion of the relationship between the crop production, the livestock, and the marketing sectors of the agribusiness system was written while the author was serving as staff economist in the Consumer and Marketing Service of the U.S. Department of Agriculture. It was published in the Journal of Farm Economics *in August 1962.*

AMERICAN AGRICULTURE and its disciplinary companion of agricultural economics have long been troubled by uncertainties of self-definition. That agriculture begins with producing primary products of the soil is perhaps least disputed. Any challenge to this near-consensus is largely confined to the agribusiness school, which would push the baseline back to include the supplying of fuel and fertilizer and similar production items. As to terminal boundary there is less agreement. Nevertheless, evidence points to partiality for a wide compass. Certainly agricultural economists have addressed themselves freely both to the marketing sector and to the characteristics of final consumer demand for goods of farm origin. Market researchers have studied, in the presumed interest of farmers, the best design for food supermarkets and how to promote sale of lamb and apples. Secretary of Agriculture Orville Freeman laid claim to a considerable direct service to consumers as a proper function of his agency. Broad constructionists seem to be a working majority.

Clearly, a broadly interpreted agriculture departs far from a synonym with farming, and it casts the farm management origin of the discipline of agricultural economics into remote status. Yet there can be no rule of catholic definition. The right of scholarly choice is freely acknowledged. The scholar's obligation devolves into dealing consistently with whatever definition be selected.

The thesis of this paper is that modern agriculture as broadly defined to embrace the distributive destiny of its products is a composite, or sequence, of three separate and distinct economies. These are the production of primary products from soil, the conversion of feedstuffs into livestock products, and the marketing of products from farm to retail. As classification of itself is sterile, it will be pointed out further that the economic forces governing each of these three economies are distinctive, and that the differences are meaningful to analysis and to formulation of policy.

Of the three economies, the first constitutes what is probably the traditional or classic view of agriculture. The observations were essentially confined to crop production, with wheat ("corn") the commodity of common reference. Production of the herbaceous products of agriculture remains its peculiarly identified portion. It, and it alone, is an enterprise of producing primary products from that unique resource, the soil.

The second economy of agriculture is the production of livestock. Although commonly associated locationally with crop production, it is a secondary enterprise. It is a process of conversion of bulky raw materials into less bulky finished or semi-finished goods (largely the latter). It is no less a secondary enterprise than is the crushing of soybeans or the smelting of iron ore.

Habits of thought that conveniently have treated crop and livestock economics together arose from the association of the two enterprises on family farms. The association, in turn, is to be ascribed primarily to the economy of reducing bulkiness of feedstuffs close to their source. It is easier to ship cattle than corn, and cream than alfalfa hay. This saving of tonnage in shipment was an especially strong force when transport was slow and costly. Another factor in combining crops and livestock has been the advantage of sharing year-long use of family labor between complementary seasonal needs for the two enterprises. In addition, crop-livestock combination is implicit in the grazing of livestock on range and pasture—a kind of self-harvesting, a simple form of vertical integration. Despite their frequent physical association, crop and livestock production are of two separate economic categories, the former primary, the latter secondary.

The third economy of a broadly-defined agriculture is the long and complicated process of marketing. In it the products of crop and livestock agriculture are assembled, transformed, stored, conveyed and distributed. It is usually regarded as extending to retail sale. Formerly thought of as a non-productive junction between farm and consumer, a gap to be crossed, it is now recognized as a sector in which large economic values are created as well as the one in which the vital price-making function is carried out. The marketing economy, once partly farm-based, is now virtually entirely removed from the farm. It is the wholly nonfarm economy of agriculture.

TWO ECONOMIC MODELS

A reference point for review and interpretation of the three economies of agriculture is found in two basic economic models. Although the concepts are of long standing, they have recently been delineated with perception by Joan Robinson in two articles.[1] The first model is the earliest stage of development, in which land and men are the only existing factors of production and their native qualities are controlling. This is the primitive state, marked by the simplest economic pursuits. The second, and opposite, system is that of a fully developed economy. The latter is essentially capital-using. In its absolute version all factors of production are produced within the economy. Even labor and management are trained according to the needs of the market. As all are subject to change, "there are no persistent differences between factors of production."[2]

In their pure form these definitions describe in the one case an economy governed entirely by fixed, predetermined factors of production, and in the other a totally self-contained and self-sustained economy in which no factors are fixed, but all are variable. Neglecting for convenience both the obvious absence from the real world of either model in absolute state, and the influence of time on the fixity of any resource, the two definitions broadly distinguish between a primitive, fixed-resource economy and the ultimate form of an industrialized economy. They are polar categories for analysis, and therefore useful. For conve-

---

1. Joan Robinson, "Some Reflections on the Philosophy of Prices," *J. Manchester School of Economic and Social Studies*, May 1958; and "The Basic Theory of Normal Prices," *Quar. J. Econ.*, Feb. 1962.
2. "The Basic Theory of Normal Prices," *op. cit.*, p. 6.

nience they may be short-titled as primitive and industrial models.

The two models present two entirely different systems of value and income distribution. A primitive economy of immutable resources of heterogeneous endowment is a grim one indeed. All populations are in the iron grip of their particular resources. Demand schedules are practically non-existent, as most of the needs that can be met at all are vital ones. Production capabilities dominate valuation. The incapacity to offset natural deficiencies in productive resources (other than by territorial aggression, a not uncommon resort) gives occasion for tremendous unevenness in prices of products. The historical monopoly power of possession of salt is a familiar example. Scholars have often speculated on the elements of valuation in exchange in such a primitive economy, but it is doubtful that any system approaching a free market economy would be permitted. Its impact would be too oppressive. Much credence must be attached to the firm conclusion of Mrs. Robinson that a degree of conventional pricing usually existed historically and was warranted. Where there is natural monopoly of scarce resources and natural dispersion of plentiful ones, the "natural" consequences are product prices that are intolerably high to society in the former case and intolerably low to producers in the latter. Moreover, the inconstancy of crop harvests, due chiefly but not exclusively to variable rainfall, magnifies the problem. Some means to amelioration are probably universal in such an economy. The need for them is inherent.

The contrast between the rigorous primitive model and its opposite, the industrial model, forms a matrix for observing economic development. Economic development as a process is basically a progressive release from the shackles imposed by natural factors of production. It comes about through introduction of capital, both as production goods and as provision for training of labor.[3] This is what happened in the Western world during recent centuries and is happening worldwide today.

Unwitting prophet of the unfolding of an industrial economy was that inscrutable pamphleteer, David Ricardo. Nominally Ricardo was concerned with the price of corn and whether it made landlords exploiters. Yet, in the sort of contradiction in

3. In today's parlance the latter is cast as "investment in human resources."

which fate seems to delight, Ricardo anticipated the economic forces of the forthcoming industrial period with more clarity than did Adam Smith, who was vocal refuter to the agriculturally oriented Physiocrats and otherwise usually regarded as precursor to an industrial age.[4] Ricardo's genius was in seeing things in the large—he was an early macroeconomist. His principal, or at least most lasting, contribution was to bring an understanding of the economic role of land as a fixed natural resource. It will be remembered that Ricardo inveighed against regarding land as a slowly-consumable factor and thus akin to a capital good. In the passage that is assigned reading for every graduate student in economics, rent is a return ". . . for the original and indestructible powers of the soil."[5] In perceiving how the existence of a fixed stock of land of variable quality bore on rent as a distributive share, Ricardo gave great impetus to developing economic theory. The idea soon was extended into a general interpretation of rent or quasi-rent to any capital good that is scarce and not reproducible within the period under consideration.

Ricardo intuitively saw and dealt with, without explicitly recognizing it, the principle of diminishing marginal returns in production. That principle embraces combining one or more variable factors of production with a fixed factor. As such it relates to an economy that is at least one step removed from the primitive stage wherein all factors are fixed, yet that is short of a perfectly industrial economy of only variable factors.

In one notable respect the Ricardian vision was only a limited improvement over a primitive economy. This applies to his view of a mechanical and almost hopeless destiny for human labor, which he saw as usually striving for little more than minimum sustenance. Therein lies a moral. Theories of value and distribution based on a marginal return to a single factor that must do all adjusting have a sombre cast. They are doubly gloomy when labor is the variable. It was they which led to the "dismal science" tag for economics. Their import is the dominion of the least

4. Some Smithian scholars oppose calling him anti-Physiocratic. However, Smith himself declared he was. Cf. *The Wealth of Nations*, Cannan ed., pp. 627–52.

5. David Ricardo, *Principles of Political Economy and Taxation*, Gonner ed., p. 44.

common denominator: whatever return the most disadvantaged laborer or producer is willing, or forced, to accept shall set the standard of return for all. Unless the economy as a whole is thriving, that no-recourse marginal return can be low. (Hence the call for sustained economic growth.) Marginal-return valuation is the kind of principle to which many pay homage and few adhere. Organized labor has shown itself more than ready to avoid the income-autocracy of the marginal worker, even at the price of some unemployment. So has much of industry with respect to its marginal output—it has developed a wide repertory of protection devices. Likewise that part of present-day agriculture having the help of support prices. But this is an aside.

Back to Ricardo. Though he did not recognize diminishing returns well enough to call them by name, his successors did. For a generation or more they developed the theory of the diminishing returns that result as successive doses of a variable factor are brought to bear on an unchanging quantity of a fixed factor. Thus did the notion of a fixed land resource build the base for economic thought.

The system was brought to fruition as the counterpart in consumption, marginal utility, was introduced. When Léon Walras, among others, hooked diminishing returns in production with diminishing marginal utility in consumption an ingeniously symmetrical system was completed.

Three conditions are essential to the Walrasian system: a fixed-variable factor relationship in production; a matching marginal schedule in the psychology of consumption; and a close physical connection between the two. The third condition is easily overlooked, yet is indispensable. Unless the consumption and production functions are linked closely together, the nicely poised system breaks down. This condition requires both that the producer-to-consumer span be short and that products retain their essential identity throughout it. Significantly, at the time of Walras these three conditions were met fairly well.

An economic theory derived from agriculture, as was Ricardo's, could be applied well enough to nascent industry. As economic development progressed and industry took on more of its own distinctive character, it no longer sufficed. Emblem of change was the nature of marginal returns. Unlike an agricultural economy, epitomized in diminishing returns, a highly industrial economy is notable for a capacity for constant or increasing returns. Ricardo himself saw this, clairvoyantly. Marshall saw it also, in contemporary observation. He recognized it, however inadequately, in his theories. Joan Robinson has capsuled the transition in thought by naming Walras as still in allegiance to an extractive economy but Marshall, observer of the upsetting influence of economy of scale, as a scholar of a manufacturing economy.

The ultimate, purely refined form of an industrial economy, toward which economic life has trended and which, like rainbow's end, has visible meaning despite its unattainability, is in all respects the opposite of a primitive economy. In a pure version of an industrial economy all means of production are produced to order, including education and training of labor. In such an economy, if perfect divisibility of all factors be also assumed, there can be neither increasing nor decreasing returns to scale. There can be no rent or quasi-rent—no returns to a monopolizing factor.[6] The conclusions reached by Mrs. Robinson are pertinent and sound: "Where all means of production are produced within the economy and there are no economies or diseconomies attaching to the scale of production of particular commodities, the normal prices corresponding to any level of the money-wage rate and rate of profit are determined by the technical conditions of production; they are independent of the composition of output or the tastes of consumers. Demand has no effect whatever on relative prices. In Marshall's language, there is 'constant supply price' for each product . . . , so that their relative prices . . . cannot vary with their rates of output."

It is not that consumers' wishes are ineffectual or unmet. Quite the opposite is true. They are met perfectly, or at least to a universally equal degree of perfection. No shortcoming in a factor of production prevents attainment of that common level of satisfaction or gives rise thereby to a differential return to the factor.

The primitive is an economy of nature, the industrial an economy of man. The limitations as well as opportunities are natural in the former, man-made in the latter. Whether a primitive

6. Except when institutional devices create them—e.g., brand-name protection by patent and copyright.

economy turns out to be good or bad depends on the bounty or niggardliness of nature—including the native endowments of the aboriginal population. The achievements of an industrial economy are the outcome of the wisdom or baseness of civilized and educated man.

Until man improves his own character, it is interesting to speculate as to whether it be propitious if some forces remain outside his control. If scientists should learn to regulate rainfall, would mortal man be able to exercise that regulation equitably? What are his capabilities in joint self-management? The answer bears on farm policy, as will be noted below.

TWO MODELS IN THREE ECONOMIES OF AGRICULTURE

U.S. agriculture has moved progressively along the long trail from primitive to industrial sketched above. It did so first at a walk and then at a jog-trot. In recent years its motion has quickened to a dash. As such it has progressively taken on more of the characteristics of an industrial economy. This is the heart of the economic aspect of the technological revolution in agriculture.

This trend has encompassed each of the three economies of agriculture, changing the make-up of each. In so doing it has resulted in disproportionate growth of the more industrialized among the three. And it has detached each of the three economies of agriculture more sharply from the others. The impact is possibly most telling upon the first, primary-product, economy of agriculture, converting it to a natural resource-industrial composite and removing it farther from the other two economies and the consumer.

Use of Capital · Production on U.S. farms has been shifting at fast pace to an industrial, capital-using, character. Relevant data descriptive of this trend are computed and published by the Farm Economics Division of the Economic Research Service of USDA.[7] These are estimates of all inputs entering into farm production each year. Unfortunately, the published data do not

7. Data are from Ralph A. Loomis and Glen T. Barton, *Productivity of Agriculture, United States, 1870–1958*, U.S. Dept. Agr. Tech. Bul. No. 1238, 1961.

distinguish between the crop and livestock portions of farming. However, evidence is that trends are of roughly the same magnitude for each.

Total inputs for crop and livestock production scarcely changed at all between 1940 and 1960 (see chart).[8] Yet the composition of the total has been altered drastically. The proportion of "farm" inputs, land and farm-resident labor, decreased from 66 percent of the total in 1940 to 38 percent in 1960. Nonfarm inputs, which comprise machinery, fuel, fertilizer, pesticides, feed supplements and mixing, and many other goods and services including nonfarm hired labor, increased from 34 percent of total inputs in 1940 to 62 percent in 1960. Their relative proportion almost doubled within twenty years.

Inputs of U.S. Agriculture [1]

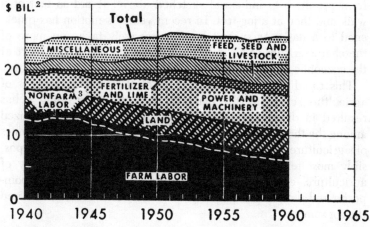

1. Annual inputs as computed from quantity–price aggregates.
2. Based on 1947–49 price weights.
3. Nonfarm residents hired for farm work.
SOURCE: Data taken from U.S.D.A. Technical Bulletin 1238.

The significant feature of the new, purchased, agents of farm production is that almost all of them are themselves the product

8. *Ibid.*, p. 61. As the authors point out, the statistical techniques employed influence somewhat the particulars of these comparisons but do not affect the overall picture.

of a production process. Their supply and use are subject to expansion and contraction. They are industrial goods and their use in primary agriculture makes it partially industrial. Thus does U.S. farming move away from the fixed-resource primitive model toward a capital-using economy of variable resources. It takes on ever more of the attributes of Mrs. Robinson's second model, wherein the quantity of inputs utilized and volume of output can be regulated according to the needs—or whims—of the market.

Since so much of the increase in use of purchased inputs in farming has taken place since 1940, those twenty years can justifiably be called an age of transformation. After countless centuries of history, production from farms is no longer so closely predestined by the mineral content of soils, the vagaries of rainfall, and the assiduousness of a labor force tied to the land. Now it is subject also to the governing influence of the resources fed into it. This is the fundamental significance of widely heralded "galloping technology": it is not that it necessarily expands farm output, but that it makes output expansible.[9]

And yet the primary, crop-producing economy of agriculture remains land-based. It is a hybrid, an amalgam. It is fish and fowl. It has some, and increasingly more, of the features of a flexible industrial economy. It also retains a solid core of the features of a fixed-resource primitive economy. From its composite character arise many of the conflicts and many of the knottiest problems in economic analysis and policy-making for primary agriculture.

The other two economies of agriculture, those of livestock production and of marketing, are highly capital-using. If livestock production be viewed as a secondary enterprise, its principal input is feedstuffs. Feeds are a capital good in all cases except possibly the grazing of native range. They are particularly to be viewed as a capital good now that an "ever-normal" reserve has made feed grains constantly available at fairly well stabilized prices. Urea and aureomycin are feed ingredients that never saw a farm. An outcome of the present system of feed supply is that annual livestock production is no longer tied closely to the size of each year's feed harvest. It can be expanded or contracted with

9. And contractible too, a derivation often lost sight of.

comparative ease.[10]

The marketing of farm products has become almost exclusively a nonfarm, capital-using undertaking. Any remaining tie to land is negligible.

Greater Growth of Livestock Production and of Marketing · The land-based, crop-production portion of agriculture is concerned with turning out raw materials ready for a long journey through processing, perhaps recombination, and ultimately final distribution for consumption. More value is created in that sequence of conversion and marketing than in the original production. Moreover, the difference in relative values has become steadily wider. Both the livestock production and the marketing economies have been expanding disproportionately to primary crop production. Their rapid growth, like the increased use of capital inputs in primary agriculture, reflects the extension of industrialization to all of agriculture.

For many years production of livestock has expanded more than crop production. A familiar outcome has been the increased portion of consumer's diets made up of livestock foods, in partial replacement of cereals. Evidence of production trends is gross output indexes which show, for crops, an advance from 71 in 1910–14 (1947–49 = 100) to 116 in 1957–61, but for livestock a more rapid rise from 62 in 1910–14 to 126 in 1957–61.[11] Moreover, as a source of cash receipts to farmers, all livestock and livestock products increased from 50 percent of total receipts in 1910–14 to 55 percent in 1956–60. If government payments be excluded as a source of receipts, the proportion of the total coming from livestock in 1956–60 was 56 percent.[12]

Marketing services for foods and other products originating on farms have proliferated in recent years. Standard source of data on relative values in production and marketing is the "food

10. It has at times been expanded too readily. Witness the broiler and turkey over-expansion debacles of 1961. Hog production has displayed some of the cyclicality formerly reserved to cattle.

11. *Changes in Farm Production and Efficiency*, U.S. Dept. Agr. Stat. Bul. No. 233, July, 1961, p. 11. Indexes are gross for both crops and livestock. Livestock indexes exclude workstock.

12. *Livestock and Meat Situation*, U.S. Dept. Agr., Econ. Res. Serv., July 1961, p. 25.

marketing bill" and "market basket" calculations of the Department of Agriculture. These data report the retail value embodied in original products as they leave the farm, and that arising between farm and retail. Over many years there was more cyclical variation than trend in the relationship between the two values. Since the end of World War II, however, the two have diverged persistently. From 1948 to 1960 the total value of all farm food products as they leave the farm increased only 7 percent, which is appreciably less than the growth in population. By contrast, the total food marketing bill increased 71 percent.

In 1948, the value of products at the farm was 51 percent of retail value. Marketing services thus received 49 cents—almost an even split. By 1961, the farmer's share was down to 38 percent, and the farm-to-retail margin up to 62 percent. The latter had become almost one-and-two-thirds times the farmer's share.

The published data on values at the farm include the value of livestock and livestock products marketed. These are secondary products. If data for the value of livestock products be replaced by the value of equivalent quantities of their primary constituent, feedstuffs, the farmer's share of the consumer's food dollar in 1961 is computed to be about 27 cents. Only 27 cents of each retail dollar spent for food in that year was returned to the farmer for his production of food and feed crops. Thus the approximate distribution of values for all food products of farming in 1961 was 27 cents to primary production, 11 cents to conversion of feedstuffs to livestock products, and 62 cents to marketing.

For nonfoods the value to primary production was even less. In 1961, only 14 percent of the consumer's dollar spent for 25 cotton products was returned to the original producer. Of the cigarette dollar for 1960, 15 percent reverted to the tobacco producer.[13]

The values created in primary agriculture are now a rather small fraction of values ultimately realized in sale of final goods at retail.

Mutual Detachment · Separation of the three economies of agriculture is old and now virtually complete for marketing, recent

13. *Marketing and Transportation Situation,* U.S. Dept. Agr., Econ. Res. Serv., Feb. 1962.

and still partial for livestock production.

Livestock enterprises have been undergoing progressive organizational detachment from feed production. Many cattle are concentrated for feeding in large commercial feedlots, especially in the West. These use little land and give a strong manufacturing flavor to the cattle feeding operation. Broiler production is not only semi-factory style but it seems to gravitate locationally to areas of the nation where costs are lowest or, it is sometimes reported, where contractees are most tractable. Egg production may be going the broiler route. Feeder pig production now rings the Corn Belt as a halo. And so it goes.[14]

Among factors that currently are wedging crop and livestock production apart are improved transport, notably barge shipping of corn; increased commercial preparation of mixed feeds; the need for, and premium on, specialized knowledge in livestock production; the mechanical, managerial, and manipulative forces underlying vertical integration in poultry; and the tremendous impact of the Commodity Credit Corporation's storage program for feed grains, which assures at all times a resting place for those feedstuffs between field and livestock and therefore facilitates separation of the two. The price support program makes clear distinctions between crops and livestock. It has been largely an aid to crop prices, as dairy products and wool are the only livestock products to be accorded continuous support. Price trends for livestock and feed have demonstrated more independence recently than in earlier years. Livestock prices, and livestock-feed price ratios, have been highly cyclical but have not trended downward since the late 1940's as have crop prices. Feeding margins for hogs and cattle, far from being narrowed by feed price supports, have if anything been wider during postwar years of feed support than before.

The marketing sector has been detached more and more from crop and livestock production. Only a few lingering ties to the farm remain. This observation needs only brief substantiation. Almost complete is farmers' withdrawal from turning out final

14. The separation between livestock and feed crops referred to here is managerial, not necessarily locational. Livestock production is independent to the extent it is managed as a separable entity, even though still located on combination farms. However, managerial independence is likely to lead to some locational change by livestock, and has in fact done so.

products such as home-churned butter. Vestige of direct market-ing from farm to consumer is just about confined to sale of fresh fruits and vegetables at roadside stands near large cities. Further-more, not only is the marketing sector now more completely separated, but the products it turns out depart more drastically from the original farm products. Food products at retail bear less and less resemblance to their basic raw material. For nonfoods the farm-retail contrasts are even more evident. If the test of parenthood be ability to recognize offspring, farmers must feel hard pressed to declare progenitorship for many foods and fabrics on retailers' shelves.

FURTHER IMPLICATIONS

An overriding implication of the presentation thus far is found in mere extrapolation of trends. There is as yet no sign of let-up in those under way. Primary production continues to become more capital-using. Livestock enterprises still threaten to leave their traditional home. Marketing gains ever more size and dominance. How fast and how far these trends will extend is a weighty ques-tion involving not only economic analysis but also prognosis as to policy. The economic and institutional character of agriculture has never in the nation's history been independent of influence by conscious act of government. It will not be independent in the future.

Analytically, the description of a tripartite agriculture presented herein can be useful. If the three parts of agriculture are signifi-cantly different, they should be dealt with differently. If "agricul-ture" is to be defined so broadly as to encompass all those parts, it cannot be equally broadly generalized for analysis and policy purposes. A degree of disaggregation is necessary.

Beyond that, as the three economies of agriculture take on ever more of the characteristics of Mrs. Robinson's second, industrial, model, countless other changes can be expected in addition to the broad ones enumerated in the previous section of this paper. A few selected ones will be described. They will be directed prin-cipally, but not exclusively, to primary agriculture.

Reduced Role of Land · As primary agriculture rests increasingly on inputs of nonfarm origin, the role of land as such becomes partly eclipsed. To be sure, the relative status of land and of variable nonfarm inputs depends on the conformation of production surfaces, as described by iso-cost and iso-product curves and the other paraphernalia of productivity analysis. Yet almost certainly the governing influence of inherent productivity of land is being compromised relatively if not absolutely. The land under a skyscraper seems astronomically valuable dollarwise, but is probably a smaller fraction of the value of the structure than is the land under an economist's suburban split-level home. Similarly, land values in agriculture are probably destined for gradual subordination relatively even though they may hold up well in dollars per acre.

Manifestations of this realinement are being obscured by various resistances and delaying actions. For instance, open-end price support to farm commodities has had such an effect. When support rates are at incentive level, open-end support encourages liberal use of nonfarm inputs in farming; but unless acreage allotments are very tight it also keeps land in productive use. Thus the Federal Government has subsidized both fertilizer manufacturers and landholders. Future changes in support policies, such as a shift to quantity marketing quotas, could change significantly both the amount and relative proportion of succor to each.

Ricardo saw land as single-purpose. Some farm programs have offered a competitive purpose; this too enters into land valuation. The Soil Bank was such a counter-offer. Land rental under the feed grain programs of 1961 and 1962 was another. The proposed Food and Agriculture Act of 1962 provided for a competitive recreational demand for land.

Changes in the relative status of the various factors of production reweight some of the vested interests in primary agriculture. At first glance, the interest of landholders might seem to fade. Yet bearing on this is the place seen for farm labor as a rival production factor. Is it to be viewed primarily as fixed or variable? To what extent do farmers and farm workers as seekers of employment look to a prosperous primary agriculture versus a vibrant, expanding nonfarm economy as augury for their future? For centuries farm labor was indeed almost fixed, chained to the land. It is held a mark of enlightenment that our industrialized modern society has tended to convert it to a variable—to make easier the departure of farm people from land. Recently a number of program proposals, such as the idea of homesteads-in-reverse, have sought to speed that exodus. Yet the process is not universally seen as unmixed blessing. Many farmers with modest acreages seek not the opportunity to be displaced from them, but to receive adequate income while remaining on them.

Similarly, the principle of management control has undergone some redefinition, and its resting place some change. Formerly, land ownership provided the major instrument of control. Now, control of variable nonfarm inputs, and notably the possession of technical know-how as to their use, are potent forces. They explain some of the transfer of management off the farm—more to date in livestock than in primary crop production but significantly in some fruit and vegetable crops, for instance.

Yet land remains essential to primary production, and the old conflicts between valuation of a fixed and a variable factor, while perhaps dampened, are not ended. Valuation of land as a fixed factor remains highly sensitive to any under- or over-valuation of variable factors. Relevant is Paarlberg's remark that "farmers subconsciously value their own labor and management at a low level," resulting in "well rewarded" land as "residual claimant."[15]

More Controllable Farm Output · A more industrialized primary agriculture, operating on more variable inputs than previously, should also be more capable of a managed variability of output. The new kind of farming ought to have a more responsive supply function. Nonfarm inputs are a spigot that can be turned on and off fairly readily; they provide an output-regulating device that was not so available in the days of simpler organization of agriculture. Of itself, this would seem to offer a welcome prospect for more stability in primary agriculture, and perhaps even for an ending of any need for farm control programs. In another sense, though, the new primary agriculture merely shifts the point of control. It posits it more on the forces and techniques by which the inflow of capital resources is managed.

15. Don Paarlberg, "Should We Have Supply Management to Improve Prices Paid to Producers?", paper presented at staff seminar, Dept. of Agr. Econ., Univ. of Illinois, March 21, 1962 (proc.), p. 3.

More Inelastic Demand for Primary Farm Products · Before the institutions of agricultural management are considered further it is necessary to consider the kind of market which primary agriculture faces. Perhaps unhappily, the industrializing of the three economies of agriculture which has made primary agriculture more flexible and adjustable has also made the farm-level demand for its products less flexible and harder to adjust to.

Demand for primary products has become less flexible, more inelastic, first because final demand by consumers has become more inelastic as their incomes have risen. But even more influential has been the widening of the marketing sector, which has pushed primary products into more distant, remote status. Due to that wider marketing gap, the pricing of products of primary agriculture is no longer a local facsimile of retail pricing. It is truly a pricing peculiar to primary commodities.

In a bigger and more complex marketing system, price signals are likely to be transmitted less efficiently. Prices at primary level will therefore lose sensitivity to small ups and downs in the consumer market. Contrariwise, prices at retail will be less influenced by small variations in prices at the farm; and this latter insensitivity will have the important result that the quantity utilized will not be very responsive to small price changes at the farm. Furthermore, the transformation so many goods undergo between farm and consumer can make the idea of price transmission less meaningful. Not only are many products now processed and blended but they often are sold under trade marking, brands, and other means of differentiation that affect their price and demand at retail but have little or no meaning for the original raw product. All these factors make the primary product market more independent and therefore usually more inelastic.

Yet even to the extent price signals are carried faithfully between the two market levels, the increase in size of the farm-to-retail price margin, reported above, results in greater inelasticity of farm-level demand. When farm-to-retail margins widen relatively and farm-level prices decline, as has happened in recent years, demand for primary commodities at the farm becomes more inelastic compared with consumer demand.[16]

16. The arithmetic is simple. A constant farm-to-retail margin conveys a given cents-per-pound price change at retail to an equal cents-per-pound

For a few commodities, demand for domestic utilization is so inelastic that the quantity so used is almost independent of their prices. This is true of wheat. Domestic food use will approximate a half billion bushels annually even though the price should vary over a sizeable range. An Iowa study, for example, projected domestic use of wheat to be the same quantity at either $1.15 or $1.50 per bushel.[17] The Department of Agriculture, in preparing its 1960 report to Senator Proxmire on the projected effect of certain farm programs, similarly held wheat use unchanged at alternative prices. Demand for cotton and soybeans is notably inelastic at the farm level.

A more inelastic demand at the farm puts a high penalty on instability of primary farm production. Or, from the opposite point of view, it establishes a premium on well-regulated production. Viewed according to the geometry of a demand curve, an inelastic demand also promises a dividend to farmers from designed underproduction, for the gross value or revenue curve derived from it peaks out well to the left of current supply levels. It was common practice a few years ago for economists to compute for various farm products the size of supply that would maximize total value. This exercise became less popular as the danger that too high a price would shrink a market was recognized. Moreover, that calculation was appropriate only to an older primary agriculture of more nearly fixed resources, that is to say, of fixed total cost. Where inputs, and costs, are variable, a maximum value calculation has little applicability.

A more inelastic demand and a more manageable supply constitute a change in demand and supply relationships in primary agriculture. In effect, the demand and supply curves have been rotated. A previously moderately inelastic demand curve and highly inelastic supply curve have turned clockwise into a more inelastic demand and less inelastic supply. Increasingly, the burden of achieving an acceptable degree of stability in primary

---

change at the primary product level. But that price change is a greater percentage of the lower farm-level price than of the retail price; that is, the demand elasticity is less elastic, or more inelastic, at the farm than at retail.

17. Arnold Paulsen *et al.,* "The Amount and Cost of Grain Land Retirement to Balance Production and Reduce Stocks Under Two Levels of Prices in the Mid-1960's," Center for Agr. and Econ. Adjustment, Iowa State Univ., Econ. Inf. 157, 1960 (proc.).

agriculture falls on the supply response.

The Institutional Organization of Farming · To recapitulate briefly, an earlier primary agriculture of more nearly fixed resources was notable for its uncontrolled and unpredictable output. That system forced most of the adjustment to a fluctuating production to be made in consumption. Fortunately for that era, the consumer market was close at hand and relatively elastic. A flexible and readily available consumer market can be a grand shock absorber to an erratic primary agriculture. It can take the blows, without intolerable recoil, of alternate surpluses and deficits in primary production. And analytically, a consumer demand so close at hand can permit consumer demand curves to be superimposed directly on a farm supply curve to describe a meaningful equilibrium, *a la* Walras.

Today's mixed primary agriculture combines the attributes of industrial and primitive economic models. Through use of non-farm inputs, its production is much more controllable than before. However, it also remains partly subject to the persistent if not perverse influence of that unique fixed factor, land. Demand signals that reach the farm can be partially but not wholly responded to. And those demand signals now originate from afar off and are more inelastic. Hence, pricing in primary agriculture will mix the rules of price-making under the industrial and primitive models. To the extent production can be adjusted to conform to changes in demand, no lasting differences in relative prices of commodities, other than those induced by technology, will result. To the extent production cannot adjust efficiently, but instead remains unresponsive, unstable and unpredictable, prices of commodities will be similarly quixotic and develop varying interrelationships.

Viewed differently, the larger role of variable inputs, partly unharnessing primary agriculture from the binding limitations of native resources, makes it more subject to the individual and collective controls of man. This conforms to the general characteristics of an industrial economy. It remains to be seen how, and how wisely, man uses his new power. The older agriculture, resistant to man's control, was protection against his errors. Its limited productivity, while not surfeiting consumers and often a harassment to farmers, yet served to prevent serious progressive declines of prices and values in farming. It was not so easy to over-produce then as it is now.

How, then, will the newer form of primary agriculture be employed? And of all farming, including livestock production? What institutional organization will farming take? These questions involve both the future for the traditional family farm organization, and the role of government.

The family farm structure is an anomaly. It is small-scale, decentralized organization existing in the midst of a nonfarm economy of large scale organization for mass production. Primary agriculture's historical reliance on a fixed, immovable, extensive resource, land, was a mighty force leading to the small family unit. Furthermore, the built-in limitation on total farm output helped to preserve land values and thereby protected against unsettling influences which would challenge that order.

Now some of the protections are weakening and the order is being challenged. It is being challenged because primary agriculture is loosened from its natural output-limitation bonds and, through use of nonfarm resources, is taking on a more industrial form. The question now faced is whether a system of small independent businesses in agriculture can meet the test of managerial techniques and competence to respond to market forces accurately enough to achieve an acceptable degree of stability. It is a question as to whether it can be adequately self-regulating. The long production interval that prevails in so many farm enterprises is a disadvantage. The increasing complexity of scientific knowledge in agriculture is another. These make the assignment doubly difficult. One school of thought and circle of farm organizations declares American farming can meet that test, as presently organized and without extensive government assistance; another asserts it cannot, and that if survival of the family farm system is desired the protection of government is necessary.

To complicate the matter further, some economies of mass production have begun to appear, as in broilers. In an atomized industry notable for the horizontal demand curve that each firm faces, constant or increasing returns to scale are frightfully disequilibrating. The family farm unit has always depended on its upsweeping marginal cost curve, the consequence of diminishing marginal physical returns, to achieve equilibrium. Without it, stable equilibrium for the individual firm is hard to come by.

Manufacturing industry has developed its own recourse for such a situation: it has arranged for a downsweeping demand curve. This has been done sometimes by means of monopoly or oligopoly, but far more often by that pervasive protective device of modern trade, product differentiation. But differentiation of product is unavailable to an atomistic farm economy. Its advantages could be obtained only by means of some form of horizontal or vertical combination. One of the ways to view vertical integration in poultry is to regard poultry production, lacking product differentiation of its own, as latching on to differentiation provided by nonfarm agents.

Emerging economy of scale relates more to production of livestock than to primary production of crops. As was observed above, livestock production has become more and more detached from production of feed crops; it is more disjoined managerially from land as a fixed resource. Grazing on native range is the only exception. Thus livestock production has much more of the character of the industrial model of an economy than does primary agriculture. It is therefore much more susceptible to taking on the institutional make-up of an industrial economy. Questions of evolving institutional organization of American farming have more immediate significance to the livestock portion of farming than to the crop portion.

The mechanics and powers of government have always been looked to for help in charting the course of U.S. farming. Yet the particular meaning of this analysis to programs of government is not easily discovered. As primary agriculture remains mixed, a certain ambiguity attends it. Stability in farm prices and incomes must increasingly be sought from the supply side of the supply-demand equation. The extent to which it can be attained without government programs is simply not known. Recent experience is of little help in pointing to an answer. The last quarter century of explosive technology in farming—of a rapid transition to a more industrial primary agriculture—has also been, unfortunately for researchers, a quarter century of Federal programs. It is a laboratory that yields few generalized and wholly conclusive findings.

Paradoxically, any need for government programs in farming could have two contrasting origins. One would result from the instability that remains in primary production due to use of land as a fixed natural factor of production. Government help in this respect is of the category of the conventional pricing Mrs. Robinson attached to a primitive economic model. Need for it arises not from technology, as so often asserted, but from its remaining partial absence. On the other hand, a second possible origin for government programs lies in uncertain capability of the present institutions of farming to accommodate a more industrialized agriculture. Nonfarm inputs are tools of supply control; can they, without government help, be utilized effectively enough by four million independent production units, under the handicap of the horizontal demand curve each faces, to attain a satisfactory degree of equilibrium?

This analysis neglects the problems of transition as such. It is important to distinguish between the throes of shifting from a primitive to an industrial primary agriculture, and the implications of the latter when achieved. And devices to ease the transition by freezing against the outcome can present some real dangers.

Farm Program Pointers · If national supply control is to be practiced, this analysis offers pointed lessons as to techniques. The importance nonfarm inputs have gained in governing farm output cannot be neglected in control design. If incomes to farmers were to be supported by means of attractively high commodity prices, it would probably be highly ineffectual to try to limit output by means of control of the single factor of land acreage. Incentive prices would induce use of too many nonfarm inputs. Some kind of quantity quota on marketings probably would be essential. If, however, incomes were to be sustained primarily by direct payments, in the form of compensatory payments on marketings or rental on land or reimbursement for practices performed, acreage allotments might well be reasonably effective. The lower prices would not be so great a lure to use of nonfarm inputs.

Differences by Commodities · This paper is necessarily general.

Let it be admitted that many distinctions are to be made by commodities. Economic and institutional issues in production of wheat bear little resemblance to those for winter pears. Those for producing beef calves are immensely different from those relating to commercial broilers.[18]

Revision of Concepts; e.g., "Cost of Production," "Surplus" · For decades various farm spokesmen have sought to build price support policies on a base of cost of production. Agricultural economists have usually opposed; some have scoffed. To the extent farm output now rests on variable nonfarm capital inputs, cost of production may at last achieve respectable status. At the least it is not as inapplicable as it once was.

Similarly, in the term "surplus" a notion of a predetermined normal volume of farm output is implicit. The excess beyond it is the surplus. As the idea of controllable variability in production is accepted, the surplus concept will tend to lapse.

Meaning to Marketing · Lastly, implications of the new organization of agriculture are to be found for the marketing economy. That economy has grown in size and dominance. It isolates primary agriculture, and secondary also, more completely from the consumer. Once regarded as a mere transmission agent, innocuous if not inert, it is now recognized as an active area indeed. It still conveys, however imperfectly, countless messages that originate with the consumer, and it adds a great many market influences of its own.

Various private and government services are directed toward improving the operations of the marketing system. Marketing research, expanded under the Research and Marketing Act of 1946, serves this end. Significantly, that research is undergoing redirection. It formerly stressed consumer behavior and physical

18. Beef cattle and potatoes offer a study in contrasts. A large industry still based on natural grass resources, runaway expansion in beef cattle is prevented by limitation on those resources, while a fairly elastic demand cushions the effect of supply fluctuations. Potato production is freely expansible as soil resources are not limiting and heavy fertilization is common, but demand is very inelastic, a combination guaranteed to bring instability.

Absence of natural limits to their production potential is doubtless a reason a number of fruit and vegetable producer groups have made use of marketing agreements.

efficiency. As products undergo more transformation between farm and consumer, consumer performance conveys a more blurred message to farm-level demand. The bread and pastries consumers buy are a long way removed from the farmer's wheat. Likewise salad oil and shortening from soybeans. It is highly doubtful that consumer preferences among various types of breakfast rolls or between white and yellow shortening can be translated with any precision into economic forces bearing on the price of wheat or of soybeans.

Similarly, it is by no means certain that improved physical efficiency in marketing universally or even generally redounds to the benefit of the farmer. A question may be raised as to whether the benefits of marketing research are more properly chargeable to society than to farming. Such a hypothesis is not new; it is often contended that all agricultural research should be viewed in such a light. And yet, even though not all improvements in marketing are automatically reflected at the farm level, the marketing system has great meaning to farmers. Both enhancement of its efficiency and understanding of its structure are needed. The system itself is called on to perform more services year by year. For instance, a more discriminating demand by consumers and processors has led to wide use of specification buying, always difficult to apply to the products of the farm. The grading and inspection services of Government are intended to facilitate specification trading, particularly in conventional open markets.

Furthermore, some of the trends within marketing have impeded its capacity to function well. An example is the waning of the influence of the open central market. Irrespective of whether that market was the best in all respects, it made prices more observable and reportable, and it thereby aided, as Collins has noted, the communication process in marketing.[19]

For all these reasons more critical attention is now being given to those aspects of the marketing system which extend beyond the physical getting-the-job-done and relate to performance in terms of the accuracy and equity under which prices are made. Received theory has been far from adequate for this purpose, for not only does much of it still hinge on the perfect-competition

19. Norman R. Collins, "Changing Role of Price in Agricultural Marketing," *J. Farm Econ.*, Aug. 1959, pp. 528–34.

model but it carries connotations of a Walrasian matching-up of a producers' supply schedule and consumers' demand schedule. In reality most prices are made through the agency of traders, whose supply schedule is a market rather than production schedule, and whose demand schedule is complicated by all the merchandising practices and gimmicks of modern retailing. Furthermore, the problem is made more formidable by arrangements such as vertical integration and contracting, themselves viewable as in some respects a reaction to, and means of circumventing, an over-extended marketing system.[20] Impressive and promising new market research is being directed to these subjects, usually employing the three concepts of market structure, conduct and performance. In addition, both the United States Department of Agriculture and various State Departments of Agriculture are stepping up market regulatory activities in an effort to protect against monopoly, collusion, and various other malpractices.

Lastly, the marketing system is looked to as the sector in which it may be desirable and possible to aid the management of production and marketing in a more industrialized primary as well as secondary agriculture—including the choosing of the kind of products wanted in the more discriminating markets of today. In so doing, not only the time-honored goal of "stability" might be pursued effectively but the institutional forms society desires for farming could be brought about or preserved. It may be necessary first to address attention to the institutions of marketing itself. Means to these idealistic ends run the gamut from informational services such as market news reporting and economic forecasting through market inspection and regulation to market controls by means of agreements and orders. Legal provisions for cooperative marketing are of the same nature. Typically these are partial devices, midway between *laissez faire* on the one hand, and strict regulation through the agency of government on the other. Most already exist in some form but could be modified, expanded, or extended to new commodities or areas. Their potential for the future is certain to come under increasing exploration. The marketing economy, the third and most industrialized of the three economies of agriculture, can be important

20. Collins, *ibid.*, p. 530.

to the first two economies in its own right, and also as a vehicle for determining the form those two will take as they progressively industrialize further.

The Crises in the Traditional Roles of Agricultural Institutions

JAMES T. BONNEN

James T. Bonnen is Professor of Agricultural Economics at Michigan State University. In 1968 he was appointed director of a study of the "Role of the University in Public Affairs" sponsored by the National Association of State Universities and Land Grant Colleges under a grant from the Carnegie Corporation. In this paper, presented to the Annual Meeting of the Great Plains Agricultural Council, he discusses the crises facing agricultural institutions in a post industrial society.

THIS NATION is midstream in a revolution in its social and political organization. We are today a society in search of new institutions and new political communities. Agriculture, whether it likes it or not, is involved. Agriculture itself has been experiencing a revolutionary rate of technological, economic and social change since World War II. And, increasingly the question is asked, "How well are we adapting the institutions of agriculture to this rapidly changing environment?"

The importance of this question to the institutions and people in agriculture cannot be exaggerated. . . In my opinion, four developments dominate any realistic description of the scene in agriculture today:

1. The general power structure of this society has been transformed. But the political leadership of agriculture has either not awakened to this fact or it is trapped by its own past policies and mythologies, unable—even unwilling—to adapt organization, policies, and tactics to be effective in the new political reality.

2. The commercial agricultural power structure has reached a state of extreme organizational fragmentation and its leadership—producers, suppliers, and marketers alike—is so engrossed in warfare amongst themselves that these fragmented elements of commercial agriculture are themselves contributing greatly to

48

a general erosion of the political power which together they exert.

3. The entire web of rural organizations had an original common goal of the economic development of American agriculture. Thus, no matter how diverse in origin they may have been, as a result of having a common general goal, they evolved into an *interdependent* set of organizations. Today this underlying web of *interdependent* commercial, governmental, political, and educational organizations in the service of agriculture is changing and no longer is as effective as once it was in identifying and solving the problems of rural life. The organizational system in agriculture is becoming socially disfunctional.

4. With few exceptions, in any direction you look, there are rising levels of conflict, destructive tension, and mounting evidence of what can only be described as a spectacular failure of leadership combined with "organizational dry rot." The generation of individuals who now man as well as lead these organizations do not understand their dependence one upon another; nor do they perceive the changing situation of their sister institutions well enough to be able to relate themselves in a manner that avoids unnecessary conflict. They are thus led into mutually self-destructive patterns of behavior.

If this situation persists the present interdependent web of institutions in agriculture will fail to survive as a meaningful system. In my judgment, no segment of this system can escape current indictment:

Not the United States Department of Agriculture (USDA) and its many component agencies,

Not the committees and members of Congress and our state legislatures,

Not the myriad of farmer organizations,

Not the Land Grant Colleges of Agriculture and Home Economics.

THE USDA AND LAND GRANT COLLEGES

Let me look most closely at two of these institutions: the land grant colleges and the USDA. Both were created as research and educational organizations for the purpose of generating and extending new technologies to farming and generally to aid rural people in attaining higher levels of living. Originally their organizations were strikingly similar. Today both have changed. The primary role of the USDA has been entirely transformed. Its research functions now account for less than 4 percent of its budget; about 85 percent of its budget is now devoted to gigantic programs of farm income support, conservation, and credit. As a consequence, it now is organized very differently and its decision-making structure is no longer dominated by researchers and academically oriented people. Thus, it no longer behaves (nor is it free to behave) as the university-like organization it was until the late 1930's—but many land grant universities complacently presume on their relationship with the USDA as if nothing had changed and as if the USDA were a large philanthropic foundation on the banks of the Potomac devoted to being kind to friendly and deserving colleges of agriculture. Needless to say, the USDA has failed to act in this image and the level of tension and misunderstanding between the colleges and USDA has risen greatly.

The land grant university has changed also. It was once exclusively devoted to the affairs of rural life and farming. Now, however, it is under the most intense pressure to become a full-scale, high-quality institution of higher learning. It is in the process of extending its research and public service functions not only to the rest of our society but into the international arena as well. . . . But the USDA, and farm people, and their representatives resent and do not understand the causes of these changes in the role, and therefore, the behavior of "their college."

Let me provide a few examples of specific attitudes and behavior that are destroying the fabric of the relationship between the USDA and the colleges of agriculture:

1. Many department heads and professors in the agricultural colleges willingly take any USDA money, if it supports their programs, but have such a negative attitude toward the USDA as a scientific environment that they would encourage their better students to seek employment almost any place rather than the Department. Yet without the high quality national research program of the USDA and its many services, these agricultural college professionals and their departments would have only a fraction of their present capacity.

2. Similarly many USDA research administrators frequently

express deep resentment that any of "their money" goes to the colleges, most of which they view as competitive and generally inadequate research organizations with high overhead costs. Indeed, many have come to believe that scientific progress will be achieved only by the establishment of large specialized USDA-operated laboratories. Yet many of these same administrators expect the agricultural colleges to "produce" for them high-quality, well-trained talent to man the research and action organs of the Department. They refuse to believe they have any responsibility for the human investment process from which they draw much of their trained personnel.

3. Most Secretaries of Agriculture tend to view the Cooperative Extension Service as their personal field staff for *selling* new policies and action programs. Since Extension must (or should) maintain the politically neutral position of an educational agency, this expectation can only lead to frustration and recrimination.

4. There is another set of attitudes that is eroding the once close relationship of the colleges and the Department. Originally the Extension Services of the land grant colleges were intimately associated with their state Farm Bureaus. In more recent decades in practically all states this direct linkage has been broken or substantially weakened. At the same time agricultural politics has become polarized and the American Farm Bureau has aligned itself with the conservatives on all issues and with the Republican Party on most political matters. The USDA, however, whether run by Democrats or Republicans, continues generally to regard the colleges as a monolith of conservatism and often the personal property of the Republican Party. The general farm organizations share this attitude toward the colleges, and the more liberal organizations either refuse to support or directly attack the colleges of agriculture. While this characterization of the colleges is accurate for some states it is not true for the system as a whole. Rarely do the farm organizations or the USDA recognize that changes have occurred or that the states and their colleges vary in their behavior, nor do they bother to test the colleges' current patterns of behavior. This attitude has had unfortunate effects on many actions of the Department. Where the colleges and their extension services actually commit themselves to a partnership with any political party or even to a distinct political philosophy,

they discredit themselves and destroy the national character of the Extension system. . . .

The land grant university is no longer linked exclusively to rural institutions at either the state or the Federal level. Research, teaching, and extension funds come from many sources today and not even the federal relations of the colleges of agriculture are predominately or exclusively with the Department of Agriculture and the agriculture committees of Congress. The land grant university is broadening its old functions of education and service to rural America to service and education for the whole of society. The USDA has been forced to narrow its function to service for commercial agriculture alone. The colleges of agriculture, whether they like it or not, are being forced to move in both directions simultaneously and are having a very bad time of it.

The USDA to an even greater degree than the college of agriculture, is no longer the master of its own house to the extent that it was in the 1920's and 1930's—when it was primarily a research and educational institution. Now that it is an action agency dispensing vast sums of money which directly affect the incomes and welfare of farmers, the agricultural committees of Congress, acting as agents of the commercial interests of agriculture, have taken over a substantial portion of the Department's executive function. Until very recently the committees exercised these functions with little concern for the desires of the Secretary of Agriculture or even the President of the United States.

No Secretary of Agriculture in modern times has really had effective control of the Department of Agriculture. This frustration of the Secretary's function is a consequence of the near monopoly of power in agriculture exercised by commercial agricultural interests (including nonfarm interests allied with farming) and focused primarily in specialized commodity organizations and the grass-roots farmer committee structures which extend to the Washington level. Operating through the committees of Congress, they have badly mauled the Department of Agriculture in the past when it has not behaved solely as the agent of the commercial and business interests in agriculture. This severely limits the Department's capacity for public consideration of broader rural interests or even the public interest in agriculture. That the USDA is made to behave so injures not only the Department, but commercial agriculture. It tends to give agriculture an image in government and in the rest of the society of little more than that of a powerful but narrow and badly behaved vested interest.

No executive department is as badly abused by those it serves as the Department of Agriculture. No other member of the President's Cabinet is subjected to the demeaning, public as well as private, political vituperation that is the daily fare of the Secretary of Agriculture—heaped upon him by the people he serves. His political usefulness is eroded in the vindictive crossfire leveled by the conflicting elements of the farm policy arena. He is held politically responsible for the design and execution of all policies by the very same brawling set of commercial agricultural interests who simultaneously attempt to deny him an effective role in the design of the same policies.

The result is that, in its efforts to limit or destroy the Secretary politically, commercial agriculture is destroying itself politically. This is not politics. Politics is the art of the possible—the compromise of conflicting interest. But in agriculture, many have forgotten what compromise is and are now engaged in a war, each to obtain his own ends, with no quarter given or expected and apparently with no concern for the long-run cost to agriculture—or to rural life, or to the Nation. Like the god of antiquity, Saturn, agriculture is devouring its own.

THE CHANGING POLITICAL POWER STRUCTURE
OF COMMERCIAL AGRICULTURE

What has been the effect of the successful economic development of farming upon the political structure of commercial agriculture? In the process of increasing their productivity, farmers specialized in the production of one or a few commodities. The farm supply and farm product marketing systems have become highly specialized. Similarly, entire farming regions have become specialized. Thus, there has developed within agriculture many narrow economic and political interests which often generate intense conflict. This has resulted in fragmentation of the political organization of agriculture and has transformed agricultural policy from legislation reasonably consistent with broad social purposes, generally supported by the society, into a hodge-podge of narrow special-interest legislation, the value of which is increasingly questioned by society.

Because of this fragmentation and the resultant political disorder, the power of political decision-making for agriculture is now drifting from the agriculture committees to other places in the Congress and to the Executive Branch. The disorder not only makes it nearly impossible to get a major decision in an agriculture committee but now makes agricultural legislation so politically expensive that legislation cannot be pushed through Congress without a political brawl or a major assist from the White House or both. Indeed agricultural legislation has grown to be the single most politically expensive part of any president's and his party's legislative program. Political capital used to push the farm program through represents a reduction in the amount of political capital available to push the rest of the program through. It would be remarkable in such a situation if the majority party and the White House did not desire a reduction both in budgetary and political costs of farm legislation. . . .

THE ROLE AND ORGANIZATION OF EXTENSION

Let us now look at a few of the more general problems of the two roles which both the colleges of agriculture and the USDA share in common, extension and research.

Arising out of the industrialization and urbanization of American life and the many problems thereby generated, is a great proliferation of extension-type organizations now being created or expanded, particularly by the Great Society programs. These range from the new general university extension monies generated under Title I of the Higher Education Act of 1965 and the industrial extension activities in the Commerce Department, through the Community Action Program and other activities financed by the Office of Economic Opportunity, the housing-associated educational programs in the new Department of Housing and Urban Development, to the Small Business Administration's outreach efforts. Where a few years ago Cooperative Extension was practically alone on the scene, it is presently one actor on a crowded stage. Few of these new organizations, it should be noted, have any meaningful and continuous relationship to a university. The potential in this proliferation of extension organizations for jurisdictional battles and organizational conflict is very great. When organizational conflict becomes too intense there follows an almost inevitable failure to obtain program objectives. Another common consequence is the tendency within a state or community to merge and centralize similar organizations or at least to create a powerful central organization to play the role of traffic cop and resource allocator at the state or community level. No matter how this problem is faced, it has great portent for the long-run future of Cooperative Extension.

It seems to me that there are two general organizational strategies open to Cooperative Extension. First, it can focus on commercial agriculture almost exclusively and become a highly specialized but increasingly smaller part of the whole extension scene. It is probable that this path will lead eventually to absorption into a larger state extension framework, although agricultural programs will probably retain a clear identity. A second organizational strategy would be to attempt to expand the cooperative extension role at least to all rural if not to major urban problems. Cooperative Extension has obvious skills and background of use in the solution of many urgent nonagricultural problems. Some Cooperative Extension organizations are well along in working on these nonagricultural problems of their state. Even in these cases we may end up as part of a larger extension framework, but at least we will have the satisfactions of greater social relevance and a far larger leadership role. In any case, the choice is difficult and involves many dilemmas.

Cooperative Extension could make a great contribution to this society over the next decade or so by transferring to others knowledge on how extension works. But this confronts one directly with an unusual and generally unrecognized problem, that is, the nearly universal failure to understand the real nature of extension. This failure is found not just among the urban people who are now attempting to create new extension-type organizations, but is endemic in agriculture and in Cooperative Extension as well. The number of obtuse or impossible statements about the nature or limits of extension that I have heard made by extension personnel and leadership are legion—and I have been listening carefully for several years now. Have you not heard your share? Have you ever seen, from any extension source, a cogent statement of the general principles of extension? Have you ever encountered a clear statement of what extension is in the abstract, separated from its immediate agricultural institutional arrangements, how it works, or more importantly, why it works? I don't think you have. There are few, if any, theorists of extension in the Cooperative Extension Service. Thus, we are not capable of generalizing from our own experience. When any conscious understanding of the concept of extension or "outreach" appears to be so limited in an organization that has been in the business for fifty years, one must face the question of how Cooperative Extension can possibly provide much leadership in transferring the extension concept to urban problems or even to the rest of rural life.[1]

The potential of the concept of extension in helping to solve the urgent problems of urban life is tremendous. But to realize our potential we must first overcome this endemic failure to understand the nature of extension. If we do not, it is highly likely that we shall see in urban life the same fifty-year period of pragmatic experimentation and failure before a core of people are built up who will, not by conscious intellect but by conditioned reflex, know how to organize and operate an extension activity. We do not have this much time to solve the already explosive problems of urban life. There is a grave danger that this lack of knowledge of extension will also lead to intense conflict in urban life between various types of "outreach" organizations and will result in a general failure to realize the goals of problem-solving programs. In any case, the leadership in agriculture must appreciate, above all, that the exciting future challenge in the application of the concept of extension to problem solving in this society lies not in agriculture but in the area of the unsolved problems of rural and urban life that lie outside of agriculture.

Finally, even within its own present mission, I would point out

1. I suppose it is fair to ask that one go on to expound one's own very tentative theory of extension, but that would require another whole paper and I must get on with this one.

another general problem, the apparent slowness of Cooperative Extension to rise to many of its modern challenges. Many of today's extension people refuse to take on certain problems because they believe that they should not be asked to challenge the power structure of their communities and of commercial agriculture. Direct confrontations are, I suppose, to be avoided, but extension has been transforming by indirect methods the attitude and organization of existing power structures in rural communities for decades. This is a major part of its primary skill. In many places the Cooperative Extension organization is quite satisfied with the way things are and with what it is doing. It responds sluggishly to challenge. Particularly, it responds slowly to what are now recognized as national or regional challenges (problems). . . .

Let me underline the fact that the problem of Cooperative Extension in rising as a national organization to many of its modern challenges is not just a problem of extension leadership. Other parts of the College of Agriculture and the University present obstacles. The complications of the political scene in some states greatly limit extension's decision-making flexibility. Where commercial agriculture insists on the status quo or demands and obtains a monopoly of the services of extension, even the best of our leadership is often immobilized. One of the obstacles is organizational arthritis. As Extension has grown larger and older many among its personnel have increasingly behaved like aging bureaucrats who find it much easier to do what has been done before than to take on new problems: In too many states efforts of Extension leadership to innovate and to face the modern problems of extension have been frustrated by nothing more than the inertia of an aging and complacent bureaucracy.

Despite all of its limitations and the difficulties encountered in facing these challenges, Cooperative Extension is working out its problems with persistence and often great skill. The question is, can we resolve these difficulties rapidly enough to retain command of our own organizational future? . . .

In any case, whatever our destiny in Extension, I see several immediate national needs in Cooperative Extension:

1. The first is the urgent necessity of a national command post capable of strong national leadership and of dealing on a daily

basis with the increasingly important events of the national scene. The states have never been willing to support this much organizational power or the necessary resources for the Federal Extension Service fully to perform this function. The states must have a strong well supported Washington command post in which they are intimately involved or many important matters will be resolved without Extension's involvement or knowledge. Even Extension's national committees have little decision-making power.

2. Extension needs to transform its training process so that extension personnel:

a. develop a far more realistic understanding of the rest of our society outside of agriculture and rural life.

b. develop a *conscious knowledge* of the operating principles of societal problem-solving.

c. develop a broader, more conscious philosophic outlook so that the admirable pragmatism of extension is not confined or injured in its imagination by anti-intellectualism and a particular set of (rural) values.

3. Extension needs urgently at the state and national level to expand productive dialogs and communications with the many new extension type organizations.

4. Extension needs to concern itself immediately with the nature of its organization as a national system. It must answer anew the question of how Extension should be organized to relate to the Federal government, to various elements of the national power structure and most particularly with the university itself.

RESEARCH POLICY AND ORGANIZATION

The manner in which we organize research in agriculture and indeed the present role of agricultural research both in the Department of Agriculture and in the Experiment Stations is in my judgment in grave jeopardy today. Let me identify three of the most general of the many problems which we face.

The first is the extreme isolation from their basic scientific disciplines of all biological, physical, or social science research in agriculture. This isolation has led to several things. While there are still many brilliant individual exceptions, we are slipping very badly in many of our (applied) agricultural sciences in maintaining a respectable command over our related basic scientific disciplines. The quality and even relevance of much of our research has deteriorated. This plus isolation *per se* leads to the low esteem with which agricultural scientists are held in the general scientific community. . . .

In our efforts to integrate research with other agricultural institutions, we have neglected the interface with science, which while we were busy has evolved a national power structure which we have ignored and from which we are excluded. It was not always so. But over the last seventy-five years, as we began to produce and hire our own Ph.D.'s and as we organized our own applied science professional associations and these became large and national, and as we were successful in creating quite adequate special agricultural research fund sources, and as commercial agriculture has grown more concerned for its monopoly of our services, we have become progressively more parochial, self-centered and self-satisfied. For all of its magnificent accomplishments, agricultural science today is an academic ghetto.

The second and related problem is that both the USDA and the Experiment Stations are bleeding to death. Each passing year sees greater losses of the most respected and promising of our scientists—to basic science departments, to the National Institutes of Health, the National Science Foundation, to private foundations, and others. Another decade or two of this erosion and many of our research institutions will be hollow shells.

Increasingly, to obtain resources adequate to sustain the high quality of scientific research, we are going to have to justify our agricultural research programs and organization to the general scientific community. This need runs into not only the two problems cited above, but also into a third problem, the vastly differing research-funding philosophies and consequent difference in pattern of control over decisions that prevail in the agricultural sciences and the general scientific community. In their dealings with universities to date, NIH, NSF, AEC, and NASA have all funded strictly on a project basis directly with the researcher or research team involved. Agricultural research funds are generated on an institutional basis, and in the case of the Experiment Stations distributed among states on a formula basis. The so-called project system in agriculture is a charade which has little or no effect on the volume of funds coming to an institution. . . .

Many experiment stations support commercial and semi-commercial activities as well as regulatory, testing, screening, demonstration and routine research activities that should be organized and financed elsewhere. The research that is done is often grossly duplicative and frequently devoted to relatively unimportant matters while research of far greater urgency to science or to society is simply not done. As long as these criticisms carry any element of truth (and they presently do), the general scientific community and the Federal decision makers whom they influence will continue with justice to question agricultural research funds and will attempt to tie restrictive conditions to their use. The Federal attempt to cut Hatch-Abernethy funds and the related creation of funds for direct grants to researchers is a reflection of just these sorts of criticisms which fill the atmosphere in which the USDA administrators annually must defend the USDA and experiment station research budgets.[2] The USDA may have approached the problem in an infuriating fashion but the colleges should reflect more thoughtfully on this experience than they yet appear to have.

The general scientific community is also in serious difficulty itself and is presently quite concerned about the effects upon academic institutions of its own exclusive use of a direct funding to individuals as a basis of research resource allocation. Issues (which I cannot pretend to judge) have been raised about research empires, interlocking directorates and various monopoloid practices which suggests that many problems are associated with the *exclusive* use of this approach to research funding. One University president, who is not prone to exaggeration, has said that direct grants to individual faculty are already well along in destroying the university as an effective organizational form. Since these research monies are attached to the individual researcher, when a well-established senior academic moves from an institution, a large slice of a department's research program, its junior faculty and its graduate students often leave with

2. It is well worth noting that within the U.S.D.A. a cut of $5.6 million in the research funds of the Agricultural Research Service was proposed in the 1967 budget.

him. . . .

The present special position of agricultural higher education and research in Federal legislation is not likely to continue indefinitely and if the colleges wish to survive as vital organizations they must make every effort to rejoin the general academic and scientific community. It behooves us greatly in agriculture to take a very serious look at the current problems of our research system and at the manner in which we approach our own research funding and to make every effort to move our own establishment in a direction that will allow us to function effectively within the framework towards which the general scientific community appears to be moving.

From this discussion of the extension and research roles of agricultural institutions let me draw a few general conclusions. The special status of agriculture in all its facets is becoming increasingly difficult to sustain. All of us, the USDA, the colleges, even commercial agriculture, need to develop greater rapport with and support from beyond agriculture. Thus, I suggest that we need to become more conventional members of the various communities to which we belong. The College of Agriculture must become a more conventional member of the university community and less a specially privileged enclave to which few of the rules of the rest of the university appear to apply. Similarly, the USDA must become a more conventional member of the Federal bureaucratic community. Both the colleges and the USDA research communities must rejoin the general scientific community. Even commercial agriculture must begin to conceive of itself as a reasonably conventional member of the broader industrial community of which it really is a part today. As it is politically expedient, and before they are taken from us, we should slowly eliminate most of our arguments and arrangements for special treatment and, depending upon the very considerable capacities of our system, simply fight for our share in the context of the general rules of the communities to which we belong.

We must relate ourselves to a far broader range of organizations within and without these communities of interest. And there is a corollary of this which all agricultural organizations must recognize if we are to survive as a developmental system, and that is, that we may not demand of each other a monopoly of the other's services or roles. Each organization must allow the other the freedom to work out its destiny in terms of the increasingly diverse conditions and roles being imposed upon us today.

The Implications of Changing
Political Power on Agriculture

DALE E. HATHAWAY

Dale E. Hathaway is Professor of Agricultural Economics, Michigan State University. In 1968 he was elected President of the American Agricultural Economics Association. In this paper, which he presented at the National Agricultural Credit Conference in November 1967, he discusses the effects of changes in political structure on agricultural institutions.

THERE HAS BEEN a great deal of talk in recent years, including several statements by the Secretary of Agriculture, about the rapid decline in the political power of agriculture. Such statements from the Secretary are not surprising, for Secretaries of Agriculture have never had political power commensurate with the responsibilities they have and the programs they run. I suspect that the demise of the political power of agriculture is being vastly exaggerated. What is happening is a series of *major shifts* in the political power base affecting agriculture, and it is some of these shifts that I want to discuss.

These shifts come from two directions. One is a change in the fundamental views that our population holds regarding the role of agriculture in our society. The other comes from a change in the economic and political system of the United States.

In the past a good deal of support for farm programs has come from nonfarm groups who believed that farm people made a special contribution to political, economic, and social stability, economic growth, and social justice in our society. It appears, however, that the long-standing ideas regarding agriculture's special contributions to the achievement of these values is rapidly being replaced by a radically different set of beliefs. The bitter struggle over civil rights, with its roots in the rural South, is convincing most people that rural people have no monopoly on justice or on concern for equality. The shameful treatment of

63

some migrant workers have confirmed these feelings. The difficulties of assimilating the rural migrants in large cities have con-
vinced many that the virtues of rural upbringing are hardly
sufficient to offset poor schools. And, the enthusiasm of numerous
rural areas for extreme right-wing political candidates has done
little to convince the general population that farmers add greatly
to the stability of our political system.

On the other side there appears to be a new and growing
understanding among nonfarm people regarding the importance
of a vigorous and productive agricultural industry. Whereas,
ten years ago many nonfarm leaders and writers were viewing
agriculture as a national disgrace and public scandal, some now
see it as one of our major national strengths. This change comes,
I believe, because of the almost chronic inability of the Com-
munists to achieve their agricultural goals and the increasing
attention given to the potential world food crisis highlighted by
the recent Indian crop difficulties. The short run world food
problem was overplayed, but it has caused many people to
realize for the first time that agriculture is still important.

These shifts increasingly cause farming to be regarded by nonfarmers primarily as an economic enterprise. It is regarded as a
crucial enterprise in the world economy, but not as one which
has special virtues that exempt it from social control or as one
which should be maintained at a particular size or structure
because of its special contributions to noneconomic values. . . .

These two important shifts in political attitudes would have
produced new shifts in farm policy if no other changes had
occurred. But, there have been other important political and
economic shifts also and they have added to the change in agricultural politics and will be even more important in the future.

GEOGRAPHICAL SHIFTS

Not many years ago it would have been only a slight exaggeration to say that the South dominated Congressional action,
and especially agricultural affairs, as a result of its one-party
structure and the institution of seniority in Congress. The southern dominance in agricultural affairs was reinforced by Republicans from the rural Midwest. Slowly this structure has been

eroded by reapportionment, population shifts, and the rise of the two-party system in the South. This has been dramatically illustrated in agricultural affairs with the defeat of Mr. Cooley [1] and the large turnover on the House Agricultural Committee in the 1966 election. The political power of the Southwest and West is rising nationally and in agricultural affairs as well. And, these geographic shifts in power appear to have important implications for agriculture.

One implication is for programs to serve the rural poor. However inadequate one may judge these programs that aid the low-income farmer to be, they have originated largely with representatives from the old South. This is to be expected since a majority of the rural poor were and are in the South. Programs of this type have never been of major concern to rural representatives from the Midwest, Great Plains, or West. Indeed, they and the farm organizations from these areas have often opposed such programs, perhaps viewing them as competitors for limited funds which might otherwise be used to improve the position of commercial farmers.

The current and future political support for federal programs in the poverty area is centered largely in the core of our largest metropolitan areas and are heavily oriented to nonwhites. The supporters of these programs indicate a deep interest in drastically altering local and national social and political structures, often in ways that are not attractive to commercial agricultural interests. But, to be effective over the long run, commercial agricultural interests must make some political accommodation with these groups just as they have dealt with the interests of the rural poor over the past four decades. . . .

As a result of [recent] trends, old political alliances no longer will be effective, old political powers are no longer powerful. This is especially true for agriculture where political power has rested on the twin base of regional power in Congress, the rural South and the Midwest, and special pressure groups—the general farm organizations and co-ops. The system was interlocking so that when the regional power in Congress shifted, the farm

1. [Mr. Cooley, former Congressman from North Carolina, was Chairman of the House Agriculture Committee.—*Editor*]

organizations lost most of their effectiveness as national political powers.

As the old structures have weakened there has been a perceptible move by the farm organizations toward partisanship, with the National Grange and National Farmers Union supporting almost anything the Democratic party has proposed in farm policy and the American Farm Bureau Federation opposing almost anything the Democrats put forth.

This is likely to be a temporary situation, however, because the national parties are finding their historic power bases as badly eroded as all other groups by the changes I have described. For instance, can the Democrats hold the coalition of the rural South and the northern minority groups in the central cities? Or can the Republicans put together a working majority from the suburbs, the rural Midwest, and the conservative South? I doubt it, so both parties will be anxiously seeking the support of groups which offer promise of a majority. In such a fluid situation, well-organized economic blocs or regional interests may find they have political power far beyond their absolute size. As yet agricultural leaders do not appear to have realized this, or if they have realized it, have been too committed to the old ways of doing political business to make a change.

AGRI-BUSINESS

Much—too much—has been written about the decline in political power among farmers as their numbers decline. What is rarely mentioned is that the very forces that bring a decline in the number of farmers create new, and perhaps more powerful, political forces in agriculture. These forces are the large agricultural input producing and marketing industries which did not exist when our farm organizations, Department of Agriculture, or Colleges of Agriculture were formed. These older institutions bemoan the reduction in the number of farmers as if farmers were the only ones with economic interests and political power in modern commercial agriculture.

I can assure you it was not political pressure from a group of small family farmers that precipitated the "chicken war" of a few years back. It was a group of large integrated broiler producers. Nor is the main public push for our recent "feed the world" enthusiasm coming primarily from county farm organizations. It comes largely from the nonfarm producers of chemicals, fertilizers, and owners of storage and shipping facilities.

It is doubtful if the biggest political problem of commercial farmers, now or in the future, lies in the shortage of potential political allies with substantial influence. These agri-business complexes can and will be major political forces in the future, but not necessarily always in the interests of the farm producers. Do not expect that this political marriage of farming and agri-business will always be a happy one. In fact, some beautiful feuds are in the cards—over legislation relating to farmer bargaining and legislation to restrict vertical integration into farm production. . . .

Another important development in agriculture with political significance for the future is the steady entry of large quantities of nonfarm capital and management directly into farm production. We have seen it in the poultry and egg industry and it is well under way in cattle feeding and dairying. I hear of plans for entry into large-scale crop farming by large nonfarm corporations. To believe that these organizations do not have and will not exercise political power to protect their economic interests, as they see them, is to not understand our political system.

It seems to me, however, that a political alliance of farm producers and agri-business may have some different political positions than the farmers alone might take. One, for instance, relates to price and production policy; and I would anticipate more programs based upon a high-production, low-margin agriculture with little or no effort at effective production controls.

The recent report of the President's Food and Fiber Commission is an interesting illustration of this point. It calls for more market orientation for agriculture, expanded markets, less government intervention, a freer trade. Then the majority, having followed their logical interests and beliefs, endorsed the most liberal proposals that I have seen for low-income rural people. It remains to be seen as to whether the various interests represented will really do political battle for these latter programs, but their interest in the former ones is quite clear.

My conclusion, then, is that the political power of agriculture is not disappearing; it is changing. It is disappearing as far as some persons in the old power structure are concerned, for they are no longer going to play a major role in exercising the new political power of agriculture. But, there will be new coalitions which will be effective and which will be able to protect certain political interests of agriculture.

The new political power will focus heavily upon the interests of commercial agriculture. It will be oriented toward expanding markets and efficient producers. It will be subject to more influence from outside the rural community, and in fact will leave little interest in the rural communities as such.

The old power structure based upon local and county units of general farm organizations, local and district political parties, was concerned with the quality of rural living as well as with the prices and markets for commodities. As such it was an integrative force that tied together the multitude of national, state, and local programs relating to farm people. The new political structure that I have outlined contains no such integrative political force. Thus, it is possible that we may find increasingly prosperous and politically potent commercial farms in the midst of an increasingly disorganized rural society, where they have power to influence their prices and markets but not their roads, schools, and social institutions.

PART TWO Price and Income Policy
for Commercial Agriculture

Programs for Agriculture, 1933–1965
WAYNE D. RASMUSSEN and GLADYS L. BAKER

The authors are members of the Agricultural History Branch of the Economic Research Service, U.S. Department of Agriculture. Their article, published in Agricultural Economics Research, July 1966, *traces the lineage of U.S. farm policy from the Depression years up to the programs now in force.*

MANY PROGRAMS of the U.S. Department of Agriculture, particularly those concerned with supporting the prices of farm products and encouraging farmers to adjust production to demand, are the result of a series of interrelated laws passed by the Congress from 1933 to 1965.

The unprecedented economic crisis which paralyzed the nation by 1933 struck first and hardest at the farm sector of the economy. Realized net income of farm operators in 1932 was less than one-third of what it had been in 1929. Farm prices fell more than 50 percent, while prices of goods and services farmers had to buy declined 32 percent. The relative decline in the farmers' position had begun in the summer of 1920. Thus, farmers were caught in a serious squeeze between the prices they received and the prices they had to pay.

Farm journals and farm organizations had, since the 1920's, been advising farmers to control production on a voluntary basis. Attempts were made in some areas to organize crop-withholding movements on the theory that speculative manipulation was the cause of price declines. When these attempts proved unsuccessful, farmers turned to the more formal organization of cooperative marketing associations as a remedy. The Agricultural Marketing Act of 1929, establishing the Federal Farm Board, had been enacted on the theory that cooperative marketing organizations aided by the Federal Government could provide a solution to the problem of low farm prices. To supplement this method the Board was also given authority to make loans to stabilization corporations for the purpose of controlling any surplus through purchase operations. By June 30, 1932, the Federal Farm Board stated that its efforts to stem the disastrous decline in farm prices had failed. In a special report to Congress in December 1932, the Board recommended legislation which would "provide an effective system for regulating acreage or quantities sold, or both." The Board's recommendation on control of acreage or marketing was a step toward the development of a production control program.

Following the election of President Franklin D. Roosevelt, who had committed himself to direct Government action to solve the farm crisis, control of agricultural production became the primary tool for raising the prices and incomes of farm people.

THE AGRICULTURAL ADJUSTMENT ACT OF 1933

The Agricultural Adjustment Act was approved on May 12, 1933. Its goal of restoring farm purchasing power of agricultural commodities to the prewar 1909–14 level was to be accomplished through the use, by the Secretary of Agriculture, of a number of methods. These included the authorization (1) to secure voluntary reduction of the acreage in basic crops through agreements with producers and use of direct payments for participation in acreage control programs; (2) to regulate marketing through voluntary agreements with processors, associations of producers, and other handlers of agricultural commodities or products; (3) to license processors, associations of producers, and others handling agricultural commodities to eliminate unfair practices or charges; (4) to determine the necessity for and the rate of processing taxes; and (5) to use the proceeds of taxes and appropriate funds for the cost of adjustment operations, for the expansion of markets, and for the removal of agricultural surpluses. Congress declared its intent, at the same time, to protect the consumers' interest. Wheat, cotton, field corn, hogs, rice, tobacco, and milk and its products were designated as basic commodities in the original legislation. Subsequent amendments in 1934 and 1935 expanded the list of basic commodities to include the following: rye, flax, barley, grain sorghums, cattle, peanuts, sugar beets, sugarcane, and potatoes. However, acreage allotment programs were only in operation for cotton, field corn, peanuts, rice, sugar, tobacco, and wheat.

The acreage reduction programs, with their goal of raising farm prices toward parity (the relationship between farm prices and costs which prevailed in 1909–14), could not become effective until the 1933 crops were ready for market. As an emergency measure during 1933, programs for plowing under portions of planted cotton and tobacco were undertaken. The serious financial condition of cotton and corn-hog producers led to demands in the fall of 1933 for price fixing at or near parity levels. The Government responded with nonrecourse loans for cotton and corn. The loans were initiated as temporary measures to give farmers in advance some of the benefits to be derived from controlled production and to stimulate farm purchasing power as a part of the overall recovery program. The level of the first cotton loan, in 1933, at 10 cents a pound, was at approximately 69 percent of parity. The level of the first corn loan, at 45 cents per bushel, was at approximately 60 percent of parity. The loans were made possible by the establishment of the Commodity Credit Corporation on October 17, 1933, by Executive Order 6340. The funds were secured from an allocation authorized by the National Industrial Recovery Act and the Fourth Deficiency Appropriation Act.

The Bankhead Cotton Control Act of April 21, 1934, and the Kerr Tobacco Control Act of June 28, 1934, introduced a system of marketing quotas by allotting to producers quotas of tax-exemption certificates and tax-payment warrants which could be used to play sales tax imposed by these acts. This was equivalent to allotting producers the quantities they could market without being taxed. These laws were designed to prevent growers who did not participate in the acreage reduction program from sharing in its financial benefits. These measures introduced the mandatory use of referendums by requiring that two-thirds of the producers of cotton, or growers controlling three-fourths of the acreage of tobacco, had to vote for a continuation of each program if it was to be in effect after the first year of operation.

Surplus disposal programs of the Department of Agriculture were initiated as an emergency supplement to the crop control programs. The Federal Surplus Relief Corporation, later named the Federal Surplus Commodities Corporation, was established on October 4, 1933, as an operating agency for carrying out cooperative food purchase and distribution projects of the Department and the Federal Emergency Relief Administration. Processing tax funds were used to process heavy pigs and sows slaughtered during the emergency purchase program, which was part of the corn-hog reduction campaign begun during November 1933. The pork products were distributed to unemployed families. During 1934 and early 1935, meat from animals purchased with special drought funds was also turned over to relief distribution. Other food products purchased for surplus removal and distribution in relief channels included butter, cheese, and flour. Section 32 of the amendments of August 24, 1935, to the Agricultural Adjustment Act set aside 30 percent of the customs receipts for the removal of surplus farm products.

Production control programs were supplemented by marketing agreement programs for a number of fruits and vegetables and for some other nonbasic commodities. The first such agreement, covering the handling of fluid milk in the Chicago market, became effective August 1, 1933. Marketing agreements raised producer prices by controlling the timing and the volume of the commodity marketed. Marketing agreements were in effect for a number of fluid milk areas. They were also in operation for a short period for the basic commodities of tobacco and rice, and for peanuts before their designation as a basic commodity.

On August 24, 1935, amendments to the Agricultural Adjustment Act authorized the substitution of orders issued by the Secretary of Agriculture, with or without marketing agreements, for agreements and licenses.

The agricultural adjustment program was brought to an abrupt halt on January 6, 1936, by the Hoosac Mills decision of the Supreme Court, which invalidated the production control provisions of the Agricultural Adjustment Act of May 12, 1933.

Farmers had enjoyed a striking increase in farm income during the period the Agricultural Adjustment Act had been in effect. Farm income in 1935 was more than 50 percent higher than farm income during 1932, due in part to the farm programs. Rental and benefit payments contributed about 25 percent of the amount by which the average cash farm income in 1933–35 exceeded the average cash farm income in 1932.

THE SOIL CONSERVATION AND DOMESTIC ALLOTMENT ACT OF 1936

The Supreme Court's ruling against the production control provisions of the Agricultural Adjustment Act presented the Congress and the Department with the problem of finding a new approach before the spring planting season. Department officials and spokesmen for farmers recommended to Congress that farmers be paid for voluntarily shifting acreage from soil-depleting surplus crops into soil-conserving legumes and grasses. The Soil Conservation and Domestic Allotment Act was approved on February 29, 1936. This Act combined the objective of promoting soil conservation and profitable use of agricultural resources with that of reestablishing and maintaining farm income at fair levels. The goal of income parity, as distinguished from price parity, was introduced into legislation for the first time. It was defined as the ratio of purchasing power of the net income per person on farms to that of the income per person not on farms which prevailed during August 1909–July 1914.

President Roosevelt stated as a third major objective "the protection of consumers by assuring adequate supplies of food and fibre." Under a program launched on March 20, 1936, farmers were offered soil-conserving payments for shifting acreage from soil-depleting crops to soil-conserving crops. Soil-building payments for seeding soil-building crops on cropland and for carrying out approved soil-building practices on cropland or pasture were also offered.

Curtailment in crop production due to a severe drought in 1936 tended to obscure the fact that planted acreage of the crops which had been classified as basic increased despite the soil conservation program. The recurrence of normal weather, crop surpluses, and declining farm prices in 1937 focused attention on the failure of the conservation program to bring about crop reduction as a byproduct of better land utilization.

AGRICULTURAL ADJUSTMENT ACT OF 1938

Department officials and spokesmen for farm organizations began working on plans for new legislation to supplement the Soil Conservation and Domestic Allotment Act. The Agricultural Adjustment Act of 1938, approved February 6, 1938, combined the conservation program of the 1936 legislation with new features designed to meet drought emergencies as well as price and income crises resulting from surplus production. Marketing control was substituted for direct production control, and authority was based on Congressional power to regulate interstate and foreign commerce. The new features of the legislation included mandatory nonrecourse loans for cooperating producers of corn, wheat, and cotton under certain supply and price conditions—if marketing quotas had not been rejected—and loans at the option of the Secretary of Agriculture for producers of other commodities; marketing quotas to be proclaimed for corn, cotton, rice, tobacco, and wheat when supplies reached certain levels; referendums to determine whether the marketing quotas proclaimed by the Secretary should be put into effect; crop insurance for wheat; and parity payments, if funds were appropriated, to producers of corn, cotton, rice, tobacco, and wheat in amounts which would provide a return as nearly equal to parity as the available funds would permit. These payments were to supplement and not replace other payments. In addition to payments authorized under the continued Soil Conservation and Domestic Allotment Act for farmers in all areas, special payments were made in ten States to farmers who cooperated in a program to retire land unsuited to cultivation as part of a restoration land program initiated in 1938. The attainment, insofar as practicable, of parity prices and parity income was stated as a goal of the legislation. Another goal was the protection of consumers by the maintenance of adequate reserves of food and fiber. Systematic storage of supplies made possible by nonrecourse loans was the basis for the Department's Ever-Normal Granary plan.

Department officials moved quickly to activate the new legislation to avert another depression which was threatening to engulf agriculture and other economic sectors in the Nation. Acreage allotments were in effect for corn and cotton harvested in 1938. The legislation was too late for acreage allotments to be effective for wheat harvested in 1938, because most of this wheat had been seeded in the fall of 1937. Wheat allotments were used only for calculating benefit payments. Marketing quotas were in effect during 1938 for cotton and for flue-cured, burley, and dark tobaccos. Marketing quotas could not be applied to wheat since the Act prohibited their use during the 1938-39 marketing year, unless funds for parity payments had been appropriated prior to May 15, 1938. Supplies of corn were under the level which required proclamation of marketing quotas.

The agricultural adjustment program became fully operative in the 1939-40 marketing year, when crop allotments were available to all farmers before planting time. Commodity loans were available in time for most producers to take advantage of them.

On cotton and wheat loans, the Secretary had discretion in determining the rate at a level between 52 and 75 percent of parity. A loan program was mandatory for these crops if prices fell below 52 percent of parity at the end of the crop year, or if production was in excess of a normal year's domestic consumption and exports. A more complex formula regulated corn loans with the rate graduated in relation to the expected supply, and with 75 percent of parity loans available when production was at or below normal as defined in the Act. Loans for commodities other than corn, cotton, and wheat were authorized, but their use was left to the Secretary's discretion.

Parity payments were made to the producers of cotton, corn, wheat, and rice who cooperated in the program. They were not made to tobacco producers under the 1939 and 1940 programs because tobacco prices exceeded 75 percent of parity. Appropriation language prohibited parity payments in this situation.

Although marketing quotas were proclaimed for cotton and rice, and for flue-cured, burley, and dark air-cured tobacco for the 1939-40 marketing year, only cotton quotas became effective. More than a third of the rice and tobacco producers participating in the referendums voted against quotas.

Without marketing quotas, flue-cured tobacco growers produced a recordbreaking crop and, at the same time, the growers faced a sharp reduction in foreign markets due to the withdrawal of British buyers about five weeks after the markets opened. The loss of outlets caused a shutdown in the flue-cured tobacco market. During the crisis period, growers approved marketing quotas for their 1940–41 crop, and the Commodity Credit Corporation, through a purchase and loan agreement, restored buying power to the market.

In addition to tobacco, marketing quotas were in effect for the 1941 crops of cotton, wheat, and peanuts. Marketing quotas for peanuts had been authorized by legislation approved on April 3, 1941.

Acreage allotments for corn and acreage allotments and marketing quotas for cotton, tobacco, and wheat reduced the acreage planted during the years they were in effect. For example, the acreage of wheat seeded dropped from a high of almost 81 million acres in 1937 to around 63 million in 1938; it remained below 62 million acres until 1944. Success in controlling acreage, which was most marked in the case of cotton, where marketing quotas were in effect every year until July 10, 1943, and where long-run adjustments were taking place, was not accompanied by a comparable decline in production. Yield per harvested acre began an upward trend for all four crops. The trend was most marked for corn, due largely to the use of hybrid seed.

High farm production after 1937, at a time when nonfarm income remained below 1937 levels, resulted in a decline in farm prices of approximately 20 percent from 1938 through 1940. The nonrecourse loans and payments helped to prevent a more drastic decline in farm income. Direct Government payments reached their highest levels in 1939 when they were 35 percent of net cash income received from sales of crops and livestock. They were 30 percent in 1940, but fell to 13 percent in 1941 when farm prices and incomes began their ascent in response to the war economy.

In the meantime, the Department had been developing new programs to dispose of surplus food and to raise the nutritional level of low-income consumers. The direct distribution program, which began with the distribution of surplus pork in 1933, was supplementary by a nationwide school lunch program, a low-cost milk program, and a food stamp program. The number of schools participating in the school lunch program reached 66,783 during 1941. The food-stamp program, which reached almost 4 million people in 1941, was discontinued on March 1, 1943 because of the wartime development of food shortages and relatively full employment.

WARTIME MEASURES

The large stocks of wheat, cotton, and corn resulting from price-supporting loans, which had caused criticism of the Ever-Normal-Granary, became a military reserve of crucial importance after the United States entered World War II. Concern over the need to reduce the buildup of Government stocks—a task complicated by legislative barriers such as the minimum national allotment of 55 million acres for wheat, the restrictions on sale of stocks of the Commodity Credit Corporation, and the legislative definition of farm marketing quotas as the actual production or normal production on allotted acreage—changed during the war and postwar period to concern about attainment of production to meet war and postwar needs.

On December 26, 1940, the Department asked farmers to revise plans and to have at least as many sows farrowing in 1941 as in 1940. Following the passage of the Lend-Lease Act on March 11, 1941, Secretary of Agriculture Claude R. Wickard announced, on April 3, 1941, a price-support program for hogs, dairy products, chickens, and eggs at a rare above market prices. Hogs were to be supported at not less than $9 per hundredweight.

Congress decided that legislation was needed to insure that farmers shared in the profits which defense contracts were bringing to the American economy and as an incentive to war-time production. It passed legislation, approved on May 26, 1941, to raise the loan rates of cotton, corn, wheat, rice, and tobacco, for which producers had not disapproved marketing quotas, up to 85 percent of parity. The loan rates were available on the 1941 crop and were later extended to subsequent crops of cotton, corn, wheat, peanuts rice, and tobacco.

Legislation raising the loan rates for basic commodities was followed by the "Steagall Amendment" on July 1, 1941. This Amendment directed the Secretary to support at not less than 85 percent of parity the prices of those nonbasic commodities for which he found it necessary to ask for an increase in production.

The rate of support was raised to not less than 90 percent of parity for corn, cotton, peanuts, rice, tobacco, and wheat, and for the Steagall nonbasic commodities, by a law approved on October 2, 1942. However, the rate of 85 percent of parity could be used for any commodity if the President should determine the lower rate was required to prevent an increase in the cost of feed for livestock and poultry and in the interest of national defense. This determination was made for wheat, corn, and rice. Since the price of rice was above the price support level, loans were not made.

The legislation of October 2, 1942, raised the price-support level to 90 percent of parity for the nonbasic commodities for which an increase in production was requested. The following were entitled to 90 percent of parity by the Steagall Amendment: manufacturing milk, butterfat, chickens, eggs, turkeys, hogs, dry peas, dry beans, soybeans for oil, flaxseed for oil, peanuts for oil, American Egyptian cotton, Irish potatoes, and sweetpotatoes.

The price-support rate for cotton was raised to 92½ percent of parity and that for corn, rice, and wheat was set at 90 percent of parity by a law approved on June 30, 1944. Since the price of rice was far above the support level for rice, loan rates were not announced. The Surplus Property Act of October 3, 1944 raised the price support rate for cotton to 95 percent of parity with respect to crops harvested after December 31, 1943 and those planted in 1944. Cotton was purchased by the Commodity Credit Corporation at the rate of 100 percent of parity during 1944 and 1945.

In addition to price-support incentives for the production of crops needed for lend-lease and for military use, the Department gradually relaxed penalties for exceeding acreage allotments, provided the excess acreage was planted to war crops. In some areas during 1943, deductions were made in adjustment payments for failure to plant at least 90 percent of special war-crop goals. Marketing quotas were retained throughout the war period on burley and flue-cured tobacco to encourage production of crops needed for the war. Marketing quotas were retained on wheat until February 1943. With the discontinuance of marketing quotas, farmers in spring wheat areas were urged to increase plantings whenever the increase would not interfere with more vital war crops. Quotas were retained on cotton until July 10, 1943, and on fire-cured and dark air-cured tobacco until August 14, 1943. With controls removed, the adjustment machinery was used to secure increased production for war requirements and for postwar needs of people abroad who had suffered war's destruction.

POSTWAR PRICE SUPPORTS

With wartime price supports scheduled to expire on December 31, 1948, price support levels for basic commodities would drop back to a range of 52 to 75 percent of parity as provided in the Agricultural Adjustment Act of 1938, with only discretionary support for non-basic commodities. Congress decided that new legislation was needed, and the Agricultural Act of 1948, which also contained amendments to the Agricultural Adjustment Act of 1938, was approved on July 3, 1948. The Act provided mandatory price support at 90 percent of parity for the 1949 crops of wheat, corn, rice, peanuts marketed as nuts, cotton, and tobacco marketed before June 30, 1950, if producers had not disapproved marketing quotas. Mandatory price support at 90 percent of parity or comparable price was also provided for Irish potatoes harvested before January 1, 1949; hogs; chickens over $3\frac{1}{2}$ pounds live weight; eggs; and milk and its products through December 31, 1949. Price support was provided for edible dry beans, edible dry peas, turkeys, soybeans for oil, flaxseed for oil, peanuts for oil, American Egyptian cotton, and sweetpotatoes through December 31, 1949, at not less than 60 percent of parity or comparable price nor higher than the level at which the commodity was supported in 1948. The Act authorized the Secretary of Agriculture to require compliance with production goals and marketing regulations as a condition of eligibility for price support to producers of all nonbasic commodities marketed in 1949. Price support for wool marketed before June 30, 1950, was authorized at the 1946 price support level, an average price to farmers of 42.3 cents per pound. Price support was authorized for other commodities through December 31, 1949, at a fair relationship with other commodities receiving support, if funds were available.

The parity formula was revised to make the pattern of relationships among parity prices dependent upon the pattern of relationships of the market prices of such commodities during the most recent moving ten-year period. This revision was made to adjust for changes in productivity and other factors which had occurred since the base period 1909–14.

Title II of the Agricultural Act of 1948 would have provided a sliding scale of price support for the basic commodities (with the exception of tobacco) when quotas were in force but it never became effective. The Act of 1948 was superseded by the Agricultural Act of 1949 on October 31, 1949.

The 1949 Act set support prices for basic commodities at 90 percent of parity for 1950 and between 80 percent and 90 percent for 1951 crops, if producers had not disapproved marketing quotas or (except for tobacco) if acreage allotments or marketing quotas were in effect. For tobacco, price support was to continue after 1950 at 90 percent of parity if marketing quotas were in effect. For the 1952 and succeeding crops cooperating producers of basic commodities—if they had not disapproved marketing quotas—were to receive support prices at levels varying from 75 to 90 percent of parity, depending upon the supply.

Price support for wool, mohair, tung nuts, honey, and Irish potatoes was mandatory at levels ranging from 60 to 90 percent of parity. Whole milk and butterfat and their products were to be supported at the level between 75 and 90 percent of parity which would assure an adequate supply. Wool was to be supported at such level between 60 and 90 percent of parity as was necessary to encourage an annual production of 360 million pounds of shorn wool.

Price support was authorized for any other nonbasic commodity at any level up to 90 percent of parity, depending upon the availability of funds and other specified factors, such as perishability of the commodity and ability and willingness of producers to keep supplies in line with demand.

Prices of any agricultural commodity could be supported at a level higher than 90 percent of parity if the Secretary determined, after a public hearing, that the higher price support level was necessary to prevent or alleviate a shortage in commodities essential to national welfare, or to increase or maintain production of a commodity in the interest of national security.

The Act amended the modernized parity formula of the Agricultural Act of 1948 to add wages paid hired farm labor to the parity index and to include wartime payments made to producers in the prices of commodities and in the index of prices received. For basic commodities, the effective parity price through 1954 was to be the "old" or the "modernized," whichever was higher. For many nonbasic commodities, the modernized parity price became effective in 1950. However, parity prices for individual commodities under the modernized formula, provided in the Act of 1948, were not to drop more than 5 percent a year from what they would have been under the old formula.

The Act provided for loans to cooperatives for the construction of storage facilities and for certain changes with respect to acreage allotment and marketing quota provisions, and directed that Section 32 funds be used principally for perishable, nonbasic commodities. The Act added some new provisions on the sale of commodities held by the Commodity Credit Corporation. Prices were to be supported by loans, purchases, or other operations.

Under authority of the Agricultural Act of 1949, price support for basic commodities was maintained at 90 percent of parity through 1950. Supports for nonbasic commodities were generally at lower levels during 1949 and 1950 than in 1948 whenever this was permitted by law. Price supports for hogs, chickens, turkeys, long-staple cotton, dry edible peas, and sweetpotatoes were discontinued in 1950.

THE KOREAN WAR

The flexible price support provisions of the Agricultural Act of 1949 were used for only one basic commodity during 1951. Secretary Charles F. Brannan used the national security provision of the Act to keep price support levels at 90 percent of parity for all of the basic commodities except peanuts. The price support rate for peanuts was raised to 90 percent for 1952. The outbreak of the Korean War on June 25, 1950, made it necessary for the Department to adjust its programs to secure the production of sufficient food and fiber to meet any eventuality. Neither acreage allotments nor marketing quotas were in effect for the 1951 and 1952 crops of wheat, rice, corn, or cotton. Allotments and quotas were in effect for peanuts and most types of tobacco.

Prices of oats, barley, rye, and grain sorghums were supported at 75 percent of parity in 1951 and 80 percent in 1952. Naval stores, soybeans, cottonseed, and wool were supported both years at 90 percent, while butterfat was increased to 90 percent for the marketing year beginning April 1, 1951. Price support for potatoes was discontinued in 1951 in accordance with a law of March 31, 1950, which prohibited price support on the 1951 and subsequent crops unless marketing quotas were in effect. Congress never authorized the use of marketing quotas for potatoes.

The Korean War strengthened the case of Congressional leaders who did not want flexible price supports to become effective for basic commodities. Legislation of June 30, 1952, to amend and extend the Defense Production Act of 1950 provided that price support loans for basic crops to cooperators should be at the rate of 90 percent of parity, or at higher levels, through April 1953, unless producers disapproved marketing quotas.

The period for mandatory price support at 90 percent of parity for basic commodities was again extended by legislation approved on July 17, 1952. It covered the 1953 and 1954 crops of basic commodities if the producers had not disapproved marketing quotas. This legislation also extended through 1955 the requirement that the effective parity price for the basic commodities should be the parity price computed under the new or the old formula, whichever was higher. Extra long staple cotton was made a basic commodity for price support purposes.

LEVELS OF PRICE SUPPORT—FIXED OR FLEXIBLE

The end of the Korean War in 1953 necessitated changes in price support, production control, and related programs. For the next eight years, controversy over levels of support—high, fixed levels versus a flexible scale—dominated the scene.

Secretary of Agriculture Ezra Taft Benson proclaimed marketing quotas for the 1954 crops of wheat and cotton on June 1, 1953, and October 9, 1953, respectively. The major types of tobacco and peanuts continued under marketing quotas. However, quotas were not imposed on corn. The Secretary announced on February 27, 1953, that dairy prices would be supported at 90 percent of parity for another year beginning April 1, 1953. Supports were continued at 90 percent of parity for basic crops during 1953 and 1954, in accordance with the legislation of July 17, 1952.

The Agricultural Trade Development and Assistance Act, better known as Public Law 480, was approved July 10, 1954. This Act, which served as the basic authority for sale of surplus agricultural commodities for foreign currency, proved to be of major importance in disposing of farm products abroad.

The Agricultural Act of 1954, approved August 28, 1954, established price supports for the basic commodities on a flexible basis, ranging from 82.5 percent of parity to 90 percent for 1955 and from 75 percent to 90 percent thereafter; an exception was tobacco, which was to be supported at 90 percent of parity when marketing quotas were in effect. The transition to flexible supports was to be eased by "set asides" of basic commodities. Not more than specified maximum nor less than specified minimum quantities of these commodities were to be excluded from the "carryover" for the purpose of computing the level of support. Special provisions were added for various commodities. One of the most interesting, under the National Wool Act, required that the price of wool be supported at a level between 60 and 110 percent of parity, with payments to producers authorized as a method of support. This method of support has continued in effect.

THE SOIL BANK

The Soil Bank, established by the Agricultural Act of 1956, was a large-scale effort, similar in some respects to programs of the 1930's, to bring about adjustments between supply and demand for agricultural products by taking farmland out of production. The program was divided into two parts—an acreage reserve and a conservation reserve. The specific objective of the acreage reserve was to reduce the amount of land planted to allotment crops—wheat, cotton, corn, tobacco, peanuts, and rice. Under its terms, farmers cut land planted to these crops below established allotments, or, in the case of corn, their base acreage, and received payments for the diversion of such acreage to conserving uses. In 1957, 21.4 million acres were in the acreage reserve. The last year of the program was 1958.

All farmers were eligible to participate in the conservation reserve by designating certain crop land for the reserve and putting it to conservation use. A major objection to this plan in some areas was that communities were disrupted when many farmers placed their entire farms in the conservation reserve. On July 15, 1960, 28.6 million acres were under contract in this reserve.

The Agricultural Act of August 28, 1958, made innovations in the cotton and corn support programs. It also provided for continuation of supports for rice, without requiring the exact level of support to be based on supply. Price support for most feed grains became mandatory.

For 1959 and 1960, each cotton farmer was to choose between (a) a regular acreage allotment and price support, or (b) an increase of up to 40 percent in allotment with price support 15 points lower than the percentage of parity set under (a). After 1960, cotton was to be under regular allotments, supported between 70 and 90 percent of parity in 1961 and between 65 and 90 percent after 1961.

Corn farmers, in a referendum to be held not later than December 15, 1958, were given the option of voting either to discontinue acreage allotments for the 1959 and subsequent crops and to receive supports at 90 percent of the average farm price for the preceding three years but not less than 65 percent of parity, or to keep acreage allotments with supports between 75 and 90 percent of parity. The first proposal was adopted for an indefinite period in a referendum held November 25, 1958.

FARM PROGRAMS IN THE 1960s

President John F. Kennedy's first executive order after his inauguration on January 20, 1961, directed Secretary of Agriculture Orville L. Freeman to expand the program of food distribution to needy persons. This was done immediately. A pilot food stamp plan was also started. In addition, steps were taken to expand the school lunch program and to make better use of American agricultural abundance abroad.

The new Administration's first law dealing with agriculture, the Feed Grain Act, was approved March 22, 1961. It provided that the 1961 crop of corn should be supported at not less than 65 percent of parity (the actual rate was 74 percent), and established a special program for diverting corn and grain sorghum acreage to soil-conserving crops or practices. Producers were eligible for price supports only after retiring at least 20 percent of the average acreage devoted to the two crops in 1959 and 1960.

The Agricultural Act of 1961 was approved August 8, 1961. Specific programs were established for the 1962 crops of wheat and feed grains, aimed at diverting acreage from these crops. The Act authorized marketing orders for peanuts, turkeys, cherries and cranberries for canning or freezing, and apples produced in specified States. The National Wool Act of 1954 was extended for 4 years, and Public Law 480 was extended through December 31, 1964.

The Food and Agriculture Act of 1962, signed September 27, 1962, continued the feed grain program for 1963. It provided that price supports would be set by the Secretary between 65 and 90 percent of parity for corn and related prices for other feeds. Producers were required to participate in the acreage diversion as a condition of eligibility for price support.

The Act of 1962 provided supports for the 1963 wheat crop at $1.82 a bushel (83 percent of parity) for farmers complying with existing wheat acreage allotments, and offered additional payments to farmers retiring land from wheat production.

Under the new law beginning in 1964, the 55-million-acre minimum national allotment of wheat acreage was permanently abolished, and the Secretary could set allotments as low as necessary to limit production to the amount needed. Farmers were to decide between two systems of price supports. The first system provided for the payment of penalties by farmers over-planting acreage allotments and provided for issuance of marketing certificates based on the quantity of wheat estimated to be used for domestic human consumption and a portion of the number of bushels estimated for export. The amount of wheat on which farmers received certificates would be supported between 65 and 90 percent of parity; the remaining production would be set at a figure based upon its value as feed. The 15-acre exemption was also to be cut. The second system imposed no penalties for overplanting, but provided that wheat grown by planters complying with allotments would be supported at only 50 percent of parity.

The first alternative was defeated in a referendum held on May 21, 1963, but a law passed early in 1964 kept the second alternative from becoming effective.

On May 20, 1963, another feed grain bill permitted continuation in 1964–65, with modifications, of previous legislation. It provided supports for corn for both years at 65 to 90 percent of parity, and authorized the Secretary to require additional acreage diversion.

The most important farm legislation in 1964 was the Cotton-Wheat Act, approved April 11, 1964. The Secretary of Agriculture was authorized to make subsidy payments to domestic handlers or textile mills in order to bring the price of cotton consumed in the United States down to the export price. Each cotton farm was to have a regular and a domestic cotton allotment for 1964 and 1965. A farmer complying with his regular allotment was to have his crop supported at 30 cents a pound (about 73.6 percent of parity). A farmer complying with his domestic allotment would receive a support price up to 15 percent higher (the actual figure in 1964 was 33.5 cents a pound).

The Cotton-Wheat Act of 1964 set up a voluntary wheat-marketing certificate program for 1964 and 1965, under which farmers who complied with acreage allotments and agreed to participate in a land-diversion program would receive price supports, marketing certificates, and land-diversion payments, while noncompliers would receive no benefits. Wheat food processors and exporters were required to make prior purchases of certificates to cover all the wheat they handled. Price supports, including loans and certificates, for the producer's share of wheat estimated for domestic consumption (in 1964, 45 percent of a complying farmer's normal production) would be set from 65 to 90 percent of parity. The actual figure in 1964 was $2 a bushel, about 79 percent of parity. Price supports, including loans and certificates, on the production equivalent to a portion of estimated exports (in 1964, also 45 percent of the normal production of the farmer's allotment) would be from 0 to 90 percent of parity. The export support price in 1964 was $1.55 a bushel, about 61 percent of parity. The remaining wheat could be supported from 0 to 90 percent of parity; in 1964 the support price was at $1.30, about 52 percent of parity. Generally, price supports through loans and purchases on wheat were at $1.30 per bushel in 1964, around the world market price, while farmers participating in the program received negotiable certificates which the Commodity Credit Corporation agreed to purchase at face value to make up the differences in price for their share of domestic consumption and export wheat. The average national support through loans and purchases on wheat in 1965 was $1.25 per bushel.

The carryover of all wheat on July 1, 1965, totaled 819 million bushels, compared with 901 million bushels in 1964 and 1.3 billion bushels in 1960.

THE FOOD AND AGRICULTURE ACT OF 1965

Programs established by the Food and Agriculture Act of 1965, approved November 3, 1965, are to be in effect from 1966 through 1969. After approval of the plan in referendum, each dairy producer in a milk marketing area is to receive a fluid milk base, thus permitting him to cut his surplus production. The Wool Act of 1954 and the voluntary feed grain program begun in 1961 are extended through 1969.

The market price of cotton is to be supported at 90 percent of estimated world price levels, thus making payments to mills and export subsidies unnecessary. Incomes of cotton farmers are to be maintained through payments based on the extent of their participation in the allotment program, with special provisions for protecting the income of farmers with small cotton acreages. Participation is to be voluntary (although price support eligibility generally depends on participation) with a minimum acreage reduction of 12.5 percent from effective farm allotments required for participation on all but small farms.

The voluntary wheat certificate program begun in 1964 is extended through 1969 with only limited changes. The rice program is to be continued, but an acreage diversion program similar to wheat is to be effective whenever the national acreage allotment for rice is reduced below the 1965 figure.

The Act established a cropland adjustment program. The Secretary is authorized to enter into 5- to 10-year contracts with farmers calling for conversion of cropland into practices or uses which will conserve water, soil, wildlife, or forest resources, or establish or protect or conserve open spaces, national beauty, wildlife or recreational resources, or prevent air or water pollution. Payments are to be not more than 40 percent of the value of the crop that would have been produced on the land. Contracts entered into in each of the next four fiscal years may not obligate more than $225 million per calendar year.

The Food and Agriculture Act of 1965, which offers farmers a base for planning for the next four years, continues many of the features which have characterized farm legislation since 1933. For a third of a century, price support and adjustment programs have had an important impact upon the farm and national economy. Consumers have consistently had a reliable supply of farm products, but the proportion of consumers' income spent for these products has declined. The legislation and resulting programs have been modified to meet varying conditions of depression, war, and prosperity, and have sought to give farmers, in general, economic equality with other segments of the economy.

A Cartoonist's View of Parity

"*What IS parity?*"

89

Parity Price

F. L. THOMSEN and R. J. FOOTE

Most people find the concept of parity prices an elusive one. This lucid description of parity prices as applied to U.S. agriculture appeared in the authors' book, Agricultural Prices, *published in 1952.*

PARITY PRICE

The term "parity price" came into vogue with the passage of the Agricultural Adjustment Act. A parity price is one that will buy the same quantity of other products as it would during some specified base period. The exact methods used to calculate parity prices have changed considerably since the concept was first introduced, but the basic purpose remains the same, namely, to provide a yardstick designed to represent a "fair" price for the commodities which farmers produce in relation to the price of the commodities which they buy.

The first step in computing parity prices is to determine the level of the "parity index." This is an index number with the period 1910–1914 as a base which includes the following cost items: the general level of prices for articles and services that farmers buy, wages of hired farm labor, interest on farm indebtedness secured by farm real estate, and taxes on farm real estate. This index is computed monthly by the Economic Research Service and is published in the monthly report entitled *Agricultural Prices.*

The second series needed for the parity price computation is an index number of prices received by farmers for all agricultural commodities, including any wartime subsidy payments. The same general methods are used in computing this index as are used for the prices-paid index.

The ratio of these two index numbers is frequently referred to as the "parity ratio." It represents the percent which agricultural prices in general are of parity. The two index numbers are shown in the upper half of Figure 1, and the parity ratio is shown in the lower half. It will be noted that the parity ratio was relatively low during the early 1930's. This was the period when the parity concept first became popular.

The "adjusted base price" is next required. This equals the average price received for a particular commodity, including any wartime subsidy payments, for the ten-year period ending on the thirty-first of December prior to the date of computation divided by the average index number of prices received by farmers for all commodities for the same ten-year period. The parity price for the particular commodity is then obtained by multiplying the adjusted base price by the parity index.

An example will help to make the meaning clearer. The average price received by farmers for eggs for the 120 months, January, 1940–December, 1949, was 36.6 cents per dozen. The index of prices received by farmers during the same period averaged 202 percent of its 1910–14 base period. The adjusted base price of 18.1 cents is obtained by dividing the 36.6 cents by 2.02. The index of prices paid, including interest, taxes, and wage rates

FIG. 1. *Prices Received by Farmers,
Parity Index, and Parity Ratio*

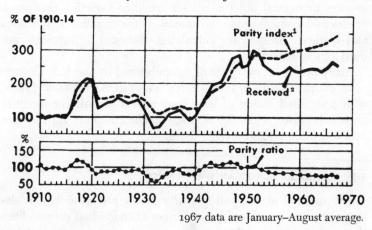

1967 data are January–August average.

1. Prices paid, interest, taxes, and farm wage rates.
2. Prices received for all farm products.
SOURCE: USDA

(the parity index) for March 15, 1950, was 250 percent of its 1910–14 average. Multiplying the adjusted base price by the parity index (18.1 times 2.50), we obtain 45.2 cents per dozen as the parity price of eggs as of March 15, 1950.

This method of computing parity prices became effective on January 1, 1950, as a result of amendments to the Agricultural Adjustment Act of 1938 contained in the agricultural acts of 1948 and 1949. So-called "transitional parity prices" were provided, so that there would not be a sharp change from the old parity price to the new one. Under these acts, the new formula now is applicable to all commodities. The new formula is designed to keep the same ratio between prices received by farmers for all commodities and prices paid by farmers as in the period 1910–1914, but to permit price relationships between individual commodities to be as they were in the most recent ten years.

Parity prices apply to the local markets in which farmers normally sell their produce. They thus represent an average of all classes and grades of the commodity as sold by all farmers in the United States, except as otherwise specified. Special base periods are used for certain commodities, and other special formulas are used from time to time, particularly for commodities covered by marketing agreements or orders. Where necessary, average or normal differentials for specified varieties, classes, or grades and average or normal spreads between different locations and methods of sale are calculated. Seasonal adjustments are used for a few items.

Parity prices for major items are published by the U.S. Department of Agriculture in the monthly issues of *Agricultural Prices*, with a detailed listing at least once a year for all commodities on which parity prices are computed. The complete list includes over one hundred and seventy items.

THE ECONOMIC SIGNIFICANCE OF PARITY

The method of computing parity prices just described is designed to give a series of parity prices of individual commodities that represent a weighted average purchasing power, in terms of the items making up the parity index, equal to that of 1910–1914. In this respect, the new parity computation serves the same

purpose as the old, under which the average price of each individual product in the base period was multiplied by the current
index of prices paid by farmers for commodities used in living
and production.

The new method of allowing for changes in the *relative* prices
of individual farm products composing the index of prices received by farmers recognizes the obvious fact that changes occur
in relative costs of production, supply, and demand and that it
would be undesirable to perpetuate relationships existing in
1910–1914 but now outmoded. For example, the use of hybrid
seed corn and modern corn-harvesting machinery, as well as
other conditions, has lowered the relative costs of producing corn
and increased the willingness of farmers to produce corn at any
given relative price. To retain the higher 1910–1914 relationships
in computing parity prices for corn and other farm products
would result in unduly high government loan values and other
provisions affecting corn, in relation to those for other commodities, and disrupt feed-livestock price relations and producing operations. The new method of computing parity is intended to
avoid this dilemma by using relative prices of the different commodities over the most recent ten-year period.

This correction is only partially effective, however, owing partly
to the fact that prices of the several commodities have not been
permitted to seek their own supply-and demand levels during
the past decade but have been greatly influenced, but absolutely
and relatively, by price support or control operations linked to
the old parity computation. This situation sets up a circular chain
of influence that will never be avoided so long as government
programs substantially affect prices. Despite this difficulty, however, the principle of the new method is much superior to that
of the old.

The concept of parity price has become a part of the economic
faith of farmers, accepted without question as an objective measure of a "fair" price. Actually, it is merely a mathematical ex-
pression of somebody's idea of what is fair. There is no possible
objective measure of fairness or equity, which is entirely a subjective concept. The completely arbitrary nature of the parity
measure becomes obvious when we consider the factors relating
to choice of a base period and the items included in the parity

index.

We have seen that the years 1910–1914 represent a period in which prices of farm products, relative to those of other commodities, were in the most favorable position they have enjoyed over a century and a half except for brief periods during and following World Wars I and II. To use this as the basis for parity is equivalent in principle, although not in degree, to accepting the earnings of a munitions manufacturer at the height of preparation for war as a measure of "fair" earnings in the future.

Since 1910–1914, many events have occurred to change the costs of producing farm products. Farm machinery, hybrid seed corn, the increased use of fertilizers, more efficient livestock-feeding methods, and many other developments have contributed to higher yields and reduced costs. Yet, when revision of the parity index was under consideration over the years, there were no proposals from the farm group to include measures of this kind in the index; only a combination of items that would *raise* the parity index was suggested.

Before the new method of computing parity prices was enacted into law, including these parity-raising items and raising relative parities for certain commodities, base periods other than 1910–1914 were used in computing parity prices for these commodities for which the standard computation resulted in "too low" a parity. In other words, the old parity was "equitable" only when it resulted in computation of prices higher than current prices in most years.

Parity, therefore, is merely an arithmetical rationalization of prices that farmers, farm leaders, and politicians consider high enough to be satisfactory. If, in the future, such prices should become unsatisfactory because supply and demand permit substantially higher prices for farm products relative to prices of nonagricultural products, the concept of parity undoubtedly will be dropped like a hot potato, or some change made in it to raise the parity level. At least, this will be done if farmers retain their Congressional voting power.

These considerations do not necessarily indicate that parity prices are not fair or do not represent desirable goals of agricultural policy. That is purely a matter of subjective opinion, and one voter's idea is just as good as another's. But a straw poll of voters' opinion cannot be taken each month to determine what price for each commodity is considered "fair"; so it may be desirable to have some standard such as parity. If parity prices as now computed become far out of line with the voters' opinions, as expressed through legislative channels, the method will be changed. It is highly desirable, however, that students of agricultural prices understand the subjective nature of the parity concept and do not confuse arithmetic with equity.

Parity: New Concept Needed

NATIONAL ADVISORY COMMISSION ON
FOOD AND FIBER

As a tool for measuring the economic well-being of farmers, parity prices can be quite deceptive. Agricultural economists and others have long argued for the adoption of "parity income" as the yardstick for these measurements. This excerpt from the 1967 report of the National Advisory Commission on Food and Fiber, entitled Food and Fiber for the Future, *summarizes the arguments in favor of the "parity income" concept.*

THE COMMODITY purchasing power concept of the parity price formula, based on a historical relationship and its maintenance over a period of time, is not a true test of equitable prices in a changing economy. "Equitable prices" means prices that will result from free competitive interplay in the market of the forces of supply and demand.

The price of a commodity should change with supply and demand. Second, when science, technology, or management improve, the farmer can sell his product for less and might still earn the same rate—or better—on the resources he has invested.

In terms of the parity ratio, when farm productivity rises faster than productivity in the rest of the economy, the ratio can be expected to decline. It does not mean that the farmer is no longer getting a "fair" return for his product. It merely means that the relative cost of producing the product has gone down.

The fundamental shortcoming of the parity price index for measuring changes in net farm income is its failure to adequately reflect the considerable changes in capital requirements and productivity of modern farming. For example, farm productivity *rose* 32 percent from 1950 to 1965; but the parity ratio *declined* from 101 to 77 or 24 percent during the same period. Net income of farmers is the critical measurement, and even though capital requirements have been increasing rapidly, the productivity and the scale advantages are such that farmers who are in a position to exploit the opportunities through modern technology are increasingly better off.

As an example of these phenomena, while the parity ratio was only 77 in 1965, farms in the sales groups above $20,000 averaged parity of income. They represented 65 percent of all sales, but only 15 percent of all farms. Moreover, the number of farms in the size group achieving such parity of income will increase substantially as net farm income increases. By 1970, USDA estimates that most or all of the family farms in the $10,000 sales group and above will have achieved parity of income.

From this and other evidence, it is clear that there is no longer any close relationship between the parity price index and parity of income to a growing number and proportion of farmers.

The parity price index should be discarded as a device for measuring and evaluating changes in net farm income. Prices for farm commodities should be evaluated by the same criteria as any other prices in the economy; that is, relating changes in price to productivity and matching the returns to capital, labor and management against returns to similar factors in other businesses.

Farm income is determined by a complex of forces including the size and nature of operations, the technology used, the adaptation of resources and production to market prices, and the managerial adaptiveness of the operator. Farm income is a function of these things, as well as of the level of prices. Hence, the economic position of farmers, or particular groups within agriculture, cannot be adequately reflected in a simple measure such as the parity price ratio. This concept is inflexible and doesn't adequately express the differential lag or thrust of consumer demand and farm productivity gains among different commodities.

The incomes of farmers do not come neatly packaged in compartments labeled "return to capital" and "return for labor." Farmers receive gross income, including noncash income. They pay production expenses, including pay for hired labor and pay for the use of capital owned by others. The net income which remains is a payment for the farmer's current return for his own capital, and for his and unpaid family labor, and for management. In addition to annual income, capital gains or losses have an important impact on the financial position of farm operators and their families.

To reflect income parity of farmers—as distinct from parity prices—we must consider first, the actual income of farmers, including current income and changes in net worth; and, second, what the resources of farmers could earn outside farming. Comparing these two would give a better indication of equitable income or return.

A new concept of parity for farmers should be developed and put into use. This concept should be predicated on the idea of comparing the rate of return to the labor, capital, and management used in farm production with the rate of return on such resources employed in other parts of the economy.

This concept of parity should be designed to take into consideration the changing capital, labor, and management requirements of modern farming and it should take account of the variation of income among economic classes of farms and between types of farms, in order to provide a really useful comparison between farm and nonfarm returns.

This new concept of parity should be conceived as an analytical tool rather than as a guide to prices that should prevail for farm products. It should be conceived in terms of income rather than of prices. Parity, then, would be thought of as income standards which measure performance of resource combinations and in a fully market-oriented economy it would not be used as a justification to interfere with price movements of farm commodities.

Commodity Programs for Agriculture

LUTHER G. TWEETEN

A generation of agricultural economists has studied the operation and economic impacts of both existing and proposed farm programs—including a full return to free markets. In this article, first published in 1967 in volume 5 of the Technical Papers *of the National Advisory Commission on Food and Fiber, Professor L. G. Tweeten of the Agricultural Economics Department at Oklahoma State University draws together the highlights of many of these studies.*

THE GOVERNMENT has administered commodity programs to raise farm prices and income since 1933. This paper reviews the research that has been done (almost all of it since 1960) on the total effect of these commodity programs on the farm economy.

These government programs have involved much more than production controls and land withdrawal. There have been storage programs and attempts to build greater demand through exports, advertising, and research on new uses for farm commodities. The paper attempts to put all of these diverse programs into perspective.

IMPLICATIONS OF A FREE MARKET FOR AGRICULTURE

Government involvement—in collection and publishing of agricultural data, basic research and education, soil conservation, and numerous measures such as establishing grades and standards to improve the functioning of the market for farm products—is widely supported and in the following studies is assumed to continue. I include a brief description of additional assumptions made in each study. Major emphasis is given to farm prices and income that have been estimated in the numerous studies reported.

Studies Projecting Yields and Demand · In a report published

in 1960, Iowa State University economists projected the impact
on the farm economy from 1960 to 1963 if price supports and
production controls were terminated on all major farm commodities, except tobacco. Storage stocks would be held stable; export
subsidies would terminate, but sales for barter and foreign cur-
rencies would continue. Long term land retirement (Conservation
Reserve) would remove 28 million acres from production in 1960,
but old contracts would not be renewed thereafter, releasing
about one million acres annually for production.

Based on these assumptions Geoffrey Shepherd, *et. al.* estimated
that the price of hogs would decline from $.14 per pound in 1959
to $.11 per pound in 1963. The price of beef cattle, $.23 per
pound in 1959, would fall to $.12 per pound by 1963. Prices of
corn and wheat averaged $1.04 and $1.76 per bushel in 1959,
respectively. According to the study, by 1963 prices would fall
to $.66 per bushel for corn and $.74 per bushel for wheat. Estimated gross receipts from livestock would decline 22 percent
below the 1957–1958 level. Net income from livestock would fall
50 percent.

In what is generally called the "Ellender Report", the technical
staff of the United States Department of Agriculture in conjunction with the Interregional Committee on National Policies for
Agriculture (IRM–1), in 1960 projected farm prices and income
to 1965. The study was based on the assumption that all production controls, except those on tobacco, would be withdrawn, that
Public Law 480 and Section 32 export programs would continue
and that the school lunch, Sugar Act, Wool Act, and marketing
order programs would remain unchanged. The Conservation
Reserve Program would withdraw 30 million acres from production; and commodity stocks would not be allowed to accumulate
in storage.

The projected increase in total farm output from the period
1955–1957 to 1965 was 20 percent, a gain of approximately 2
percent per year. Growth in livestock output was projected to
reduce feed grain stocks by 7 million tons annually. The rise
in marketings was projected to decrease the average farm price
of wheat to $.90 per bushel, corn to $.80 per bushel, beef cattle
to $.15 per pound, and hogs to $.11 per pound. The larger volume
of output tends to compensate for lower prices, leaving gross

receipts at nearly the 1955–1957 level. However, rising production expenses would reduce net farm income from $11.5 billion to $7 billion in 1965—a 40 percent reduction. The provisions for a larger Conservation Reserve, export subsidy, and some price support make the economic repercussions in the "Ellender Report" less severe than those in the Iowa State University study.

K. L. Robinson, an economist at Cornell University, estimated the change in farm output, price and income between 1959 and 1965 under assumptions similar to those of the "Ellender Report." His estimates were based on elimination of direct price supports and acreage controls but continuation of programs for exports, schools lunches, research, extension, soil conservation, marketing orders for milk, fruits and vegetables, and a Conservation Reserve of 30 million acres. He estimated that by 1965 beef would decline to $.15 per pound, or 34 percent below the 1959 level. Hog prices were projected to drop to $.14 per pound, a 1 percent decline from the 1959 level. The projected unsupported corn and wheat prices were, respectively, $.98 and $1.18 per bushel. Gross farm income was projected to decline by only 6 percent; but because production expenses are highly stable and unresponsive to lower prices, net farm income would fall 19 percent from 1959 to 1965. Robinson's projections are somewhat less extreme than those of the Shepherd and Ellender studies. The free market program would reduce annual government outlays for farm programs up to $2 billion per year in the short run and to a maximum of $3.5 billion in the long run, according to the study. This saving would represent about 2 percent of the federal budget. In the long run, Robinson estimated that savings from removal of direct farm price support programs would amount to 4 percent of the federal budget.

In a 1960 study, George E. Brandow estimated the impact of removing production restrictions and price supports after 1960 but with continuation of the sugar, Conservation Reserve, agricultural conservation, and limited P.L. 480 export programs. In 1961 prices received by farmers would be 22 percent below the 1959 level, and net income would fall to $6.1 billion (45 percent of the 1959 level). By 1965 prices would recover slightly, and net farm income would rise to $7.2 billion. For 1965 the projected corn price was $.80 per bushel, wheat $.90 per bushel, cattle

$17.06 per cwt., and hogs $10.88 per cwt. Despite certain differences in underlying assumptions, it is apparent that this study provided results similar to the "Ellender Report."

In a more recent Pennslyvania State University study, James Herendeen projected the implications of removing production controls and price supports on the major commodities. "Minor farm programs" including the conservation program, sugar program, wool program, Conservation Reserve, and P.L. 480 wheat exports were assumed to continue. Compared with 1960, the result would be a decline by 1965 of 15 percent in price received by farmers and 4 percent in gross farm income. Net farm income would fall to $7.4 billion in 1965, 34 percent below the 1960 level.

The center for Agricultural and Economic Development and Oklahoma State University published in 1963 the implications of terminating government price and production control programs for feed grains and wheat. Additional assumptions were that beginning with 1964 Conservation Reserve contracts would not be renewed as they expire, and P.L. 480 programs would maintain wheat exports at 600 million bushels. Programs for conservation, wool, rice, cotton, tobacco, and dairy would remain in effect. Allowing for some production cutback by farmers in response to lower prices, the 1967 estimated gross farm income dropped 15 percent from 1962. Net income was down 37 percent from 1962—to $7.6 billion. Prices of corn and wheat, respectively, were $.85 per bushel and $.94 per bushel in 1967. The price of cattle and calves was $15.80 per cwt., and of hogs was $13.50 per cwt. in 1967 according to the study.

Historical Studies · The results of the above studies can be criticized on several grounds. First, they are based on predicted future yields when in fact yields fluctuate with weather and technology. Second, shortrun domestic demand conditions can be estimated with considerable reliability, but it is very difficult to forecast foreign demand for U.S. farm commodities.

The following studies were made from known conditions for past years, looking backward to estimate the results if government price supports and production controls had not been in operation.

Brandow estimated the effect on farm prices and income if supplies diverted for the government from the market in the

1955–1957 period had been placed on the market. His results suggest that livestock prices would have averaged 11 percent lower and crop prices 20 percent lower. Because of the small decline in production expenses, the realized net income of farm operators would have decreased 35 percent below actual 1955–1957 in income. The drop in retail food prices would have been 4.67 percent, but the consumer price index would have dropped only 1.5 percent.

Using a similar approach, Shepherd, *et. al.*, predicted that if wheat and feed grain stocks had been held constant from 1952 to 1958 and surplus production marketed rather than put into storage, then total net cash income from farming would have decreased 34 percent. The authors estimated that the average price of beef cattle would have been $.17 per pound and of hogs $.13 to $.15 per pound. The actual prices averaged $.18 per pound for both hogs and beef during the period. The actual average corn price was $1.32 per bushel during the 1952–1958 period, but without government stock accumulation the corn price would have been from $1.13 and $.97 per bushel according to their estimates.

Based on a comparatively recent USDA estimate, farm prices would have averaged 22 percent lower, cash farm receipts 16 percent lower, and realized net farm income 52 percent lower without government price and income support programs from 1961 to 1963. The estimated reduction in farm production expenses, 2.4 percent, would not have provided much cushion against falling receipts; this accounts for the sharp shortrun decline in net farm income.

Most studies have focused on price and production of individual commodities with less government involvement in the farm economy. This degree of detail can be misleading, however, because (a) the supply response of individual commodities to lower prices has not yet been reliably determined by economists, and (b) there may be substantial substitution in production of one commodity for another on farms without much impact on aggregate incomes. After working with the foregoing types of analysis for some years, I favor the following approach of emphasizing the "simple," more easily understood and estimated aggregate effects; and giving less emphasis to the individual commodity effects which cannot be estimated with a practical degree of reliability.

The first measure of excess capacity (government diversions divided by production) in Table 1 includes only commodities diverted from the market primarily by (a) CCC commodity stock accumulation, and (b) land withdrawal. These two activities might be the first to be terminated under free market conditions and would have increased commercial marketings by approximately 3.5 percent as an average for the 1955–1962 period.

If a free market also would have meant a drop of 40 percent in government subsidized exports, then estimate (b) in Table 1 is appropriate and indicates that marketings would have been 7 percent greater in recent years. This may be the most realistic of the three estimates in Table 1.

Finally, if *all* government export programs along with acreage controls and stock accumulation were curtailed, then over 10 percent more farm commodities would have gone through price setting markets in recent years (estimate (c), Table 1).

TABLE 1. *Excess Capacity in U.S. Agriculture, Measured by the Percentage of Production Diverted from Price Setting Markets by Government Programs*

Year	Government diversions as percent of potential production at existing prices		
	a Percent	b Percent	c Percent
1955–1956	3.8	6.4	8.1
1956–1957	0	5.3	8.9
1957–1958	4.4	9.1	12.3
1958–1959	7.7	11.2	13.5
1959–1960	4.3	9.1	12.4
1960–1961	1.8	7.1	10.6
1961–1962	2.8	7.4	10.4

a Net purchases of farm commodities by the CCC plus estimated production on land diverted from production by land withdrawal programs divided by actual farm output plus anticipated production on diverted areas.

b Same as (a), but including as government diversion 40 percent of subsidized exports with net stock accumulation by CCC and land withdrawal.

c Same as (b), but including as government diversion *all* subsidized exports, net stock accumulation by CCC and land withdrawal.

source: Fred Tyner and Luther Tweeten, "Excess Capacity in U.S. Agriculture," *Agricultural Economics Research*, Vol. 16, No. 1, Jan. 1964, pp. 23–31.

Expansion in farm production capacity has been substantial since the Korean War. Yet excess capacity appears to have fallen since 1959 according to Table 1. The reason is that aggressive policies to expand markets, especially exports, have compensated for rising production, and have stabilized at least temporarily the tendency to create excess capacity.

Based on a widely used estimate, $-.25$, of the price elasticity of demand for farm commodities in aggregate, each 1 percent increase in farm production placed on the market depresses farm prices 4 percent, gross receipts 3 percent, and net farm income 9 percent in the short run. It is reasonable to conclude that termination of government programs would release at least an additional 5 percent of farm production to the market. The effect would be to depress farm prices 20 percent, gross commodity receipts 15 percent, and net farm income 45 percent. These results are consistent with Table 1 and the findings of studies cited above. Net income falls sharply because farmers tend to continue high production and thereby maintain production expenses.

In a longer run period, a downward adjustment in resource use would occur in response to lower prices. Based on an extensive economic study of farm labor, machinery, and other input markets by Earl O. Heady and the author, results indicate that in four years farm prices, gross income, and net income respectively would recover to 90, 93, and 88 percent of the initial level that held before release of 5 percent more commodities on the market. A net increase in labor outmovement of 7 percent could be anticipated in response to lower prices in four years. Since net income to pay labor would fall farther than labor input, earnings per worker would be lower after this period of adjustment.

Summary and Critique of Above Studies · The foregoing studies clearly established that farm prices, receipts, and net income would have been lower without government support programs since 1955. In summary, prices received by farmers would have been 10 to 20 percent lower, gross receipts 5 to 15 percent lower, and net farm income 25 to 50 percent lower in recent years in the absence of government supports. There is a surprising degree of agreement among the studies, despite the fact that many were performed independently by economists with a considerable range of approaches. This consistency leads credence to the results.

The findings also tell us that farm prices and incomes likely would fall substantially in the near future if major government support programs were terminated. Thus movement toward freer markets must be accompanied by measures to cushion the shock to farmers and to other elements of the economy while the process of adjustment is taking place. Some suggested recent programs have taken this fact into account.

What the above studies fail to establish is the *longrun* market and price situation for farm commodities under free markets. Economists are not at all certain about longrun demand elasticities for U.S. farm commodities, especially those sold abroad. They are not in agreement on the longrun level of farm prices and income under a free market. We do have some clues, however. Production controls on land have been the principal instrument used to raise farm income. A farmer can afford to pay additional interest on land equal to the monetary benefits of allotments and be just as well off as the farmer who has no allotment. As land changes hands over time, the intended income benefits of farm programs are lost through this method of capitalization. A recent study estimates that up to one-third of the land value gains since 1950 are imputed to farm programs. Discounted at 10 percent, this $30 billion represents a perpetual income stream of $3 billion per year. The latter figure may not be an unreasonable estimate of the long-term expected annual contribution of programs to net farm income. In the longrun the benefit goes to the past generation of landowners and is lost to the new generation of farmers. Government programs thus lose much of their intended income effect over time.

Then why have government support programs? Would not the price mechanism restore equilibrium to agriculture so that farm resources would earn satisfactory returns in the long run? The problem is the slow adjustment in farm labor. A recent study at Oklahoma State University shows the free market equilibrium (least cost mix, at opportunity cost earnings) of nine resources from 1951 to 1962. If farm labor had earned 85 percent of the nonfarm factory wage, if real estate were fixed in supply, and if all seven capital resources earned their cost of purchase, then the most efficient United States aggregate resource level would have been 12.5 percent below the actual level. Equilibrium output would have been 6.6 percent less than actual output, and the equilibrium parity price ratio 93 (1910–14 = 100). Input cost would have been minimized by a 40 percent reduction in farm labor and a 17 percent average increase in capital items. The important implication is that this longrun free market equilibrium is impossible to achieve because farm labor adjusts slowly. By the time the current disequilibrium is eliminated by resource adjustments, a new gap will have emerged.

There are at least three reasons why farm programs are beneficial even if, as argued above, they are less than effective in raising farm income over the long pull. Government programs stabilize income and remove some of the risk and uncertainty that farmers increasingly are unwilling and unable to absorb. I am referring here to variation in weather and demand which gives rise to annual market instability. From 1955 to 1964, the range in net farm income was $11.6 to $13.5 billion. There is no previous period in modern times when American farmers realized this degree of economic stability.

Second, Government programs cushion the effect of a long term, sizeable shift in demand or supply. Since 1950, productivity of agriculture has increased approximately 30 percent. The increased productivity means that demands for food and fiber can be met with fewer resources, and the price mechanism signals this through sharp price reductions. Farm programs buy time for farmers to make necessary adjustments and find jobs elsewhere. Still these programs did not appreciably slow labor adjustments. Farm population and labor force have been cut nearly in half since 1950! In many instances price supports gave farmers the security they needed to increase efficiency through specialization and large scale production and through purchase of highly productive new capital inputs. Each U.S. farm worker supplied 15 persons with farm products in 1950; in 1964 he supplied 33 persons.

A third reason for government programs is insurance for national emergencies. Excess production capacity in agriculture and excess CCC commodity stocks have been highly valuable emergency stockpiles in time of war and drought in the past—and they may be again in the future. But the economic structure of agriculture places a heavy burden on farmers if they are to carry the strategic reserve in the form of excess production capacity with no government assistance.

IMPLICATIONS OF PROGRAMS OTHER THAN FREE MARKET

A wide array of public programs to raise farm incomes can be suggested. A number of these are discussed in this section. Each program is briefly described, and certain advantages and disadvantages are stated.

Long Term Land Retirement · Programs in this category include the Conservation Reserve, Cropland Conversion, and Cropland Adjustment. Whole or part farms are retired from crop production by long term contracts. The advantage of the method is that if run "efficiently" (through use of sealed bids, whole farms, ten-year contracts, etc.), it removes more farm production per government dollar than any other voluntary program. Without unduly stimulating land prices, it makes government dollars go far to raise farm income. The USDA estimated that under the Conservation Reserve Program each $100 of rental payments reduced production $292 from 1957 to 1960. The program also increases farming efficiency by encouraging movement of farm resources, including workers and marginal land, to uses more favorable by society. It leaves to farmers a high degree of freedom in production and in marketing decisions. Disadvantages arise when this long term land retirement program is administered efficiently, however. Its concentration in marginal farming acres creates large adjustment problems not only for farmers but also for people who formerly supplied inputs to the "retired" farms. Another disadvantage is that it is inflexible since the long term contracts cannot be changed rapidly to correct for a new supply-demanded balance. It is estimated that up to 80 million acres would need to be retired to bring supply in line with demand at acceptable prices.

Short Term Land Retirement · Acreage diversion and related programs in recent years have been effective in curtailing production of specific crops as corn and wheat. These have been the "bread-and-butter" programs of the past two administrations in Washington. Like the land retirement program, they have a double-barrel effect on farm income and make government dollars go far to raise farm earnings. Farmers increase their income first by receiving a cash payment to remove land from production. Second, by reducing production over many farms, farmers reduce aggregate output and get better prices in the market. The USDA estimates that each $100 spent on the Feed Grain Program in recent years has increased farm income $186.

Because acreage diversion is oriented to better land than long term land retirement, it reduces output with a smaller acreage withdrawal. From 1961 to the present, 14 to 29 million acres of long term retirement land plus 25 to 50 million acres under acreage diversion programs have brought production in line with utilization (Table 2).

Disadvantages of acreage diversion are that farmers learn to reduce the effectiveness and increase the cost of the control program by substituting fertilizers for land and by diverting inferior acres. Also, the program is not as effective as the whole-farm land retirement program in inducing movement of farm workers and marginal land to uses higher in the public interest.

Commodity Storage Programs · One way to raise farm income is for the CCC to purchase and store commodities. The advantages of storage are that it gives flexibility to price support programs,

TABLE 2. *Cropland Diverted Under Government Programs,*[a] *1960–1965 (thousands of acres)*

		Program			
Year	Conservation reserve	Feed grain	Wheat	Crop conversion	Total
1960	28,660.7				28,660.7
1961	28,511.5	25,215.1			53,726.6
1962	25,804.6	28,211.1	10,699.2		64,714.9
1963	24,255.7	24,466.6	7,161.0	129.0	56,012.3
1964	17,437.4	32,435.2	5,123.0	129.0	55,124.6
1965[b]	13,979.7	34,600.0	7,457.0	453.0	56,489.7

[a] Data from Economic Research Service, USDA.
[b] Preliminary.

stabilizes farm prices, and provides insurance against unforeseen droughts, war, and foreign needs such as now experienced in India. The disadvantage is that strong political pressures exist to raise stocks above reasonable needs. The optimum carryover may be approximately 600 million bushels of wheat and 40 million tons of feed grains. A "free market" carryover is perhaps about half these levels, hence a goodly portion of the "optimum" represents a "strategic" stockpile. The government finds it politically popular to increase storage to stabilize falling prices, but meets strong resistance to release of stocks to stabilize rising prices. Yet the stabilization function can only be effective if stocks can also be released.

Multiple Pricing · Multiple pricing has been used for several farm commodities including feed grains in recent years, but has its principle application to wheat. It uses the principle of market separation with the higher price in the market where quantity is unresponsive to price, and the lower price in the market where receipts are expanded by a low price. The system effectively raises farm income above free market levels at minimum treasury cost where (a) markets are markedly different in elasticities, (b) can be separated, and (c) no good substitutes in the high priced market will erode the gains over time. The two-price approach has had many backers since the McNary-Haugen era in the 1920's, but it can be applied usefully to few farm commodities. This is because there are good substitutes for most farm commodities, consumers or processors in the high-price market resist the program, or the needed administrative mechanisms are not available to divide markets.

Direct Payments Without Controls · Direct payments or grants to farmers have considerable appeal to economists because they potentially provide free-market pricing, output, freedom, and efficiency, while at the same time correct some of the inequitable income distribution within farming and between farm and other groups. These advantages, plus the flexibility of direct payments, have led to growing use of the method until currently it is an important component of several commodity programs including feed grains.

There are several disadvantages of direct payments. Direct transfer payments do not get the "double barrel" income effect described earlier for control programs. Hence, they are costly to taxpayers. If free market net income were $7 billion (a frequent estimate in the studies cited earlier), then farm income can be brought to $13 billion by a government payment of $6 billion (government costs of income supports have averaged about $4 billion annually in recent years). Taxpayers are not pleased with this high cost of a farm program, but consumers do get abundant, low-priced food.

A second disadvantage is that direct payments without controls stimulate farm production even beyond the free market level because of security and capital farmers get from the program. A third disadvantage is that farmers do not like outright subsidies. This drawback can be avoided by making the payment contingent on the farmer doing something, even though small, to "deserve" the payment.

A final disadvantage is the difficulty of establishing equitable payment procedures: If payments are proportional to sales, the big farmers receive the lion's share and the income transfer often is from a low-income taxpayer to a more well-to-do farmer. If it is a flat payment per person in farming, then it may be argued that the small farmer is encouraged to stay in farming when he might have otherwise improved his economic position with a nonfarm job. If the payment is cut off for the large producer, it is said that, "he is penalized for being efficient." And finally, direct payments used to induce production controls are likely to be ineffective if they omit large farms which produce a high proportion of farm output.

Other Land Control Instruments · Several methods for withdrawing land from crop production could be used in addition to those already tried. One is outright purchase of land by the government. The total cost of USDA programs to stabilize farm prices and incomes was $18 billion from 1933 through 1959 and $18 billion since 1960. For half this $36 billion, 80 million acres could have been purchased by the government at $225 per acre to bring production into line. While this control approach would have greatly reduced government cost, it has the same disadvantages as the Conservation Reserve Program and in addition is in disfavor by farmers.

Crop easements and related devices have been suggested to reduce crop production. One approach is for the government to grant farmers a sizable noninterest loan in return for cropping rights on a farm. The land could be grazed, and cropping rights could be regained by repaying the loan. In many instances the land would be permanently placed in grass, and the loan would never be repaid. An advantage of this method is that the loan would compensate the landowner for the lower land price that would attend removal of cropping rights. This would cushion the impact on landowners of removing production controls on land where prices had been inflated by previous farm programs.

Mandatory Controls · Mandatory programs have been used extensively for wheat and tobacco, but efforts to move in that direction for more of agriculture were rebuffed by Congress and wheat growers in the early 1960's.[1] The restrictions on acreage, production, or sales become mandatorily binding on all producers only after approval in a referendum by a substantial majority, usually two-thirds of all growers.

The big advantage of mandatory programs is that they reduce production and raise farm income at a minimum taxpayer cost. Unfortunately, the decrease in taxpayer cost is offset by higher costs of food to consumers. Mandatory programs also restrict the freedom of farmers in production and marketing decisions and tend to "freeze" production patterns that are sometimes inefficient. This criticism has been partially overcome by making allotments negotiable and transferable among areas as has been done with cotton and tobacco.

Demand Expansion · Raising farm income through demand expansion is the solution perhaps most widely accepted by laymen to the problem of low farm income. Three areas of possible

1. A survey of 500 wheat growers in Oklahoma and Kansas indicates that farmers rejected the "mandatory wheat program" in the 1963 referendum, not because it was mandatory and restricted their decision making, but because they were protesting the way the wheat program had been administered in the past.

demand expansion include (a) domestic expansion through food stamp plans, advertising, school lunch, etc., (b) finding new uses for farm products through research, and (c) expansion of export market for U.S. farm commodities. While (a) and (b) may have some success in the long run, they do not now offer reasonable hope for closing the gap in farm demand.

Food aid is one form of commodity program to support farm income. Farm production can be removed from the market by paying farmers not to produce or by using the commodity as foreign aid. Government foreign aid can be given in food or other forms. Much food aid has been predicated on the assumption that the presence of excess capacity in agriculture means that our food has no cost to the U.S. Government. Another assumption is that a dollar (market value) of food aid is equal to a dollar of aid in any other form. These assumptions are not valid, and a mechanism is badly needed to allocate optimally the combination of (a) food versus nonfood foreign aid, and (b) food aid versus domestic production control as a means to handle excess capacity in U.S. agriculture. A simple augmented market mechanism can do this. The proposal is that all foreign aid be given in unspecified (cash or credit) form, or at least in a form that would give recipient nations considerable choice among several goods and services that would be consistent with economic development. A discount would be given on cash aid used by recipient countries to purchase excess U.S. commodities. The discount per dollar (market value) on our food would be equal to the cost to the USDA of inducing our farmers not to produce a dollar of output.

Further clarification roughly in line with recent conditions follows. If U.S. stocks are at desired levels and production capacity is in excess so that an acreage diversion program is used that removes 50 million acres and costs $40 per acre, and the program removes $2 of production per dollar of U.S. Treasury outlay, then each dollar spent on food aid needs to return benefits equal to $.50 in cash equivalent aid, or cash aid is cheaper. It then costs the U.S. Government an equivalent amount either (a) to control production and to give cash aid, or (b) to allow the commodity to be produced and to export the commodity as foreign aid. The benefit to the aid recipient is equivalent under (a) or (b). Assuming $100 additional of treasury outlay, $50 can be used to control production and $50 given as foreign aid, or the $100 can be used to purchase farm output and export the surplus as foreign aid. The farmer also receives an equivalent "profit" if his variable production cost is $50 to produce $100 of output. He can produce and profit $50, or he can be paid $50 not to produce and thereby also receive a "profit" of $50. Existence of these considerations would imply an equilibrium situation from the standpoint of the United States Government, U.S. farmers, and countries receiving foreign aid.

The above estimates are approximately in line with current conditions in the U.S. based on estimates of the average value of food aid to recipient countries and USDA calculations of the average cost of acreage diversion. The interesting implication is that food aid in recent years appears to have been at an "average" equilibrium level between food aid and domestic production control. Substantial divergencies from equilibrium existed at the margin, however, and the proportion of food and nonfood aid is likely to have been severely out of balance.

Miscellaneous Programs · In addition to those listed above, numerous approaches to farm income and adjustment problem are possible. A solution that has had some success since the 1930's is self-help programs—using marketing orders and agreements, cooperatives, and other organizations of farmers. This approach has been most successful for dairy and specialty crop marketing. Many such efforts of farmers to band together for "orderly" pricing and marketing of major commodities except dairy have failed. Nevertheless, the rapidly declining numbers of farmers enhances the future feasibility of such approaches.

Another method is to support farm income on an actuarial basis. With a plan patterned somewhat after the insurance concept of Social Security, farmers would pay into a fund in favorable financial years and draw out of it in years of depressed earnings. The government might match the input of farmer dollars into the fund in order to induce more farmers to participate.

Many contend that more direct policies are necessary to encourage and to smooth farm adjustment. Examples are government subsidized programs of vocational training and general education to equip farm youth for alternative employment. Another possibility would be government grants to help farmers pay moving expenses and settle in new employment.

Proposals have been made to reduce farm output and hence to raise farm income by slowing the rate of technological advance in agriculture. These proposals, such as curtailing scientific effort or placing a tax or limit on fertilizer use, have received little support, perhaps because of the high social cost of reduced farming efficiency.

In conclusion, I emphasize that there is no one program that satisfies all participants in the farm policy milieu. No program at the same time gives farmers high income and complete freedom, gives consumers plentiful food at low prices, and gives the government food reserves for emergencies, low administrative burden and low tax burden. We must recognize that farm policy is made out of compromise and hard choices.

In Search of Principles
of Farm Policy

GEORGE E. BRANDOW

*In his 1961 presidential address to the American Farm Economic
Association, Professor Brandow, a distinguished student of agricultural policy, distilled his views on the basic economic and
social objectives against which U.S. farm policy should be
judged. This article, based on that address, appeared in the*
Journal of Farm Economics. *December 1962. Professor Brandow
is a member of the Department of Agricultural Economics and
Rural Sociology at the Pennsylvania State University.*

THE CONTRIBUTION of agriculture to the development of the
American economy has been enormous. Much of this has been
an achievement of the human mind—the discovery of new knowledge, its dissemination through various forms of education, and
its application through the skills of farmers. As we have made
great progress in solving production problems, others have arisen:
how to adjust our resources to new modes of production, how to
share the fruits of great productivity equitably, how to modify
our economic institutions as our increasing power over nature
creates new difficulties and greater opportunities.

Laissez-faire was the dominant policy for agriculture up to the
early 1930's. It served the nation well in a time of great geographic expansion, rapid population growth, and rising per capita
demand for food. The economic collapse of the 1930's brought in
government programs on a large scale. Following World War II,
rapid technological advance became the principal source of farm
price and income difficulties, and government programs were
broadened in scope. After about thirty years, however, we are
still hotly contesting whether agriculture should return to laissez-
faire, still debating what other policy might be better, and still
vaguely hoping that a stroke of genius or good luck will solve our
farm problems. We find ourselves, not with a decrepit agriculture

after 30 years of departure from laissez-faire, but with so productive an agriculture that we scarcely know how to deal with it.

In discussing principles of farm policy, I shall try to bring together general ideas about the ends and means of economic activity, the farm setting in which the generalizations are to be applied, and certain guidelines applicable to farm programs. However, I shall offer no specific blueprint for policy for the next ten years. This country is still seeking a consensus on a general approach to farm policy, and we can well devote our time to the broader aspects of policy issues.

OBJECTIVES OF FARM POLICY

Principles of farm policy deal with how society can best achieve its objectives in the agricultural sector of the economy. Value judgments are involved, of course, in deciding what should be the goals of any kind of human activity. So far as possible, this paper is oriented toward what I believe to be the goals and values that dominate American social thought and behavior. In the language of one school of welfare economics, I try to judge what the community welfare function is like. Within this context, four objectives for farm policy stand out.

The first of these is *productive use of farm resources*. Though seldom so expressed, this is in a sense an equity objective, for it deals with the obligation of a particular sector to organize its activities so as to contribute to the well-being of the rest of society. If society is to function effectively, such an objective must be a dominant one, relaxed when conflicting objectives must be compromised but eventually reasserted.

The second objective is *equitable income* for persons engaged in agriculture. It is the reciprocal of the first for it expresses the obligation of society to have due regard for the well-being of groups within it. In general, it is a weaker objective, and moderate concessions are commonly tolerated to achieve other purposes—mobility of resources, for example. But equity does require that no group be too badly off, and the requirement is stronger when the group contributes to a gain in the general welfare.

The third objective is *consistency with other economic policy*. Foreign trade and fiscal policy are two areas especially important here. The fourth objective is *freedom of individual thought and action*. Complete freedom is impossible, of course, when even as few as two persons associate with each other. But reasonable freedom of economic action is an important part of freedom in general and is a valued end in itself.

This list does not include a group of closely related goals such as preserving the family farm or maintaining the number of farmers. Agricultural fundamentalism is now being transmuted into beliefs and values common to all our people. The case for public concern about the farm problem rests mainly on economic justice, reflected in the income objective, rather than on any special worthiness of farmers. The family farm, so far as it is an efficient way to produce, comes under the resource productivity goal. The influence of sentiments transcending these objectives has not died out, but their hold has weakened greatly.

The objectives conflict in the sense that there is no way of fully satisfying them simultaneously. Any sector required to shrink its labor force over a long period is in serious economic trouble, especially if it dominates large geographic areas as agriculture does. It is the beginning of wisdom in farm policy to recognize that no perfect solution exists. Here as on most economic and social issues, successful policy making takes the form of replacing one set of problems with another set easier to live with. There will always be something for critics to criticize, always something to spur efforts to try to do better.

APPRAISING ECONOMIC PERFORMANCE

We evaluate economic policy by judging how closely the actual performance of the economy approaches the objectives we have for it. Consider the resource productivity objective. It has two aspects, static and dynamic. The static aspect concerns the efficient allocation of resources to satisfy demands under a given set of technological and institutional conditions. The dynamic aspect, as I shall use the term, deals with improvement in the means of transforming inputs into outputs—new technology, greater human skills, more effective economic institutions.

Dynamic forces, especially technology, play a thrusting, originating, and upsetting role in economic life. Better ways of transforming inputs into outputs call for reorganizing economic activity. Reallocation of resources toward static equilibrium under the new methods follows and plays a passive role. Frequently, however, the gains in total welfare made possible by technology are realized only partially if at all when technology is first introduced; the chief gains are made as reallocation occurs, reemploying released resources and producing a preferred output mix. Usually the process is not a step-by-step affair but a continuous, churning movement in which the targets of resource reallocation keep changing and static equilibrium is seldom attained.

Though this is what a progressive economy is like, much of conventional economic theory is discouragingly static in spirit; and if noneconomists do have a little economic training, the static part usually is what they have. Great attention is given to equilibrium conditions for consumers, firms, resources, and the economy as a whole under given technology and tastes. Change is analyzed by contrasting two equilibrium positions, implying that equilibrium is the normal state of affairs and suppressing consideration of lags and frictions of adjustment. Actual supply and demand elasticities for products and factors are of little importance in this setting, for the consequences of departures from equilibrium are given scant attention.

Actually, however, the income consequences of being out of equilibrium pose some of the most important economic problems we have, and the vastly complicated process of adjusting resources, especially labor, is vitally important to the effectiveness of the economy. We should not judge the performance of the farm economy by seeing whether marginal conditions for static equilibrium are fulfilled; farm policy will be a failure if agriculture ever becomes as stagnant as that. The appropriate test is whether adjustments are proceeding in desirable directions and as rapidly as is feasible. This is a much looser criterion than the conceptually neat marginal conditions, but it is the realistic one.

A related point affecting the appraisal of policy concerns price. It is too readily assumed in farm policy discussions that free prices and good resource allocation are virtually equivalent. Price supports are sometimes blamed for holding labor in subsistence agriculture, although labor earnings have been so low there for so long that other reasons must be far more important. The same comment applies, though with less force, to labor in commercial agriculture. Excess supplies of products or labor are not necessarily evidence that prices are too high or that the appropriate policy is to reduce prices.

A great deal of resource allocation in desirable directions can and does take place when prices are administered. We observe this constantly outside of agriculture, where market structures often result in highly inflexible prices. It is entirely conceivable that a manufacturing industry might double or halve its resource use over a decade—depending on whether the market for its product expanded or contracted—while prices of inputs and outputs were constant. Much of the allocation of industrial labor takes place by workers' going where jobs are available rather than in response to varying relative wages. If a farm price program involves restrictions on output or inputs, the restrictions can have far more influence than price in allocating resources; and if the restrictions are well-chosen, the shifts in resource use can be in desirable directions. We cannot judge economic performance by looking only at price; we must look at the real economic phenomena themselves and at the circumstances surrounding price determination.

I feel somewhat apologetic about these remarks, for the full range of economic thought includes all I ask for here and covers it much better than I could do. In recent years, economists have given much attention to economic growth, stability conditions, the role of education, and other matters that certainly are not static economics. Yet, the views to which I object greatly influence policy predictions and prescriptions, especially among men of practical affairs, and the views originate in economics. Perhaps we can take the well-known Keynesian dictum to mean that the economists in question are all defunct. If so, today's economists, looking at today's world in light of present human aspirations, at least have a formidable task of education before them.

Laissez-Faire as a Means of Achieving Farm Policy Objectives · The free market has great merit in many ways. It is an unexcelled, decentralized, decision-making device for coordinating complex operations like producing cattle on the western range, moving them to feedlots, and distributing beef products of many kinds and grades to nearly 200 million people over half a continent. It encourages individual initiative and permits a maximum of economic freedom. The free market allocates resources most readily when alternatives are close and when any change directly affects only a minor part of an interrelated system.

The impact of rapid technological advance upon agriculture as an aggregate puts demands of an entirely different order on laissez-faire. Output-increasing practices are adopted by farmers with no regard for effects on prices. Because farm-level demand elasticities are typically low, incomes and labor earnings are depressed. The principal way by which output can be restrained and incomes restored is to reduce capacity by moving out resources, especially labor. Since most technology is labor-saving, output is not very responsive to changes in the labor force in this dynamic situation.

Two critical matters are involved in the adjustment process. One is the practicable mobility of farm labor. The age of many farmers, their lack of skills for other work, substantial unemployment in industry, and other practical obstacles limit the rate at which labor can move out of agriculture into more productive and better-paying employment elsewhere. Given the nature of the obstacles to mobility, one may doubt that an extreme income disadvantage for farm people results in much more mobility of a useful kind than does a moderate disadvantage. A basic question here is the elasticity of the supply function for farm labor, a matter on which our information is not very good.[1]

The second critical matter is agriculture's inability under laissez-faire to hold excess production capacity idle, as the market structure of industry frequently permits it to do. Commonly, industrial producers can feed output into the market at prices bearing some relation to cost and can hold in reserve new capacity constructed in anticipation of future market growth or old capacity rendered by new methods. Up to a point, such control over market supply is desirable, even essential, in a progressive

1. Estimates by G. E. Schuh ("An Econometric Investigation of the Market for Hired Labor in Agriculture," *J. Farm. Econ.*, 44:2, pp. 316–17, Model I, at means) imply that a one percent reduction in farm prices would in the long run reduce the hired farm labor force by .34 percent. The effect on family labor, which comprises about three-fourths of the farm labor force, presumably would be less.

industrial economy.

If industrial labor requirements are reduced, workers are laid off. Often substantial gains from technology are retained by the capital and labor remaining in the particular branch of industry. Labor sloughed off in the process and not re-hired elsewhere loses its identity in the anonymous ranks of the unemployed. The costs of unemployment insurance and relief are borne, directly or indirectly, by the public, and unemployment is regarded as a national problem.

In contrast, agriculture tends to hold labor, even at very low returns, until it can find other employment. Agricultural economic difficulties are viewed as distinctively a farm problem, and any assistance to farmers is regarded as a special concession to a favored group. Agriculture, operating close to capacity, often is considered greatly overextended, even when manufacturing is operating from 15 to 24 percent below its plant capacity, as it has been doing over the past 5 years.[2] But the farm problem differs from some of the basic problems of our economy more in external appearance than in substance. We do not regard unemployment and depressed industrial areas as matters of no public concern. Neither should we so regard the farm problem—and we do not.

The technological revolution now going on in agriculture, which is immensely significant for the welfare of ourselves and for all of mankind, puts a heavy burden on the free price system. Many persons, farmers included, might prefer laissez-faire and the farm incomes that would go with it to any government program for agriculture. Neither they nor I can really know unless wholly free markets are actually experienced. My judgment is that most farmers and most informed members of the nonfarm public would find laissez-faire so unsatisfactory that another policy would be tried.

POLICY NEEDS AND GUIDELINES

Acceptable alternatives to laissez-faire for agriculture will not fundamentally change the farm economy from its private enter-

2. Federal Reserve estimates, from *Measures of Productive Capacity*, 87th Congress 2d Session, Joint Economic Committee print, 1962, p. 16. Estimates from some other sources differ in concept from the one used here.

prise form, and prices will continue to coordinate much economic behavior even under far-reaching farm programs. Let us assume a laissez-faire, free price economy and consider in what ways it needs to be supplemented or modified for a closer approach to farm policy objectives.

Innovation and Adjustment · One broad class of supplementary measures does not affect markets for farm products directly. One such measure is public support for agricultural research and extension. Though not a cause for concern now or in the near future, agricultural productivity will need to advance further to satisfy long-run food requirements and to contribute to productivity in the economy at large. We can be reasonably sure of technological progress if applied and basic research continue. The latter is especially a public responsibility. The benefits may be multiplied many times as results are put to use abroad as well as at home. We must have success along these lines, but we should be prepared to deal with problems success creates.

Facilitating labor mobility is extremely important to both the resource productivity and the equitable income objectives. A satisfactory income situation cannot exist in agriculture in the long run if many more persons are seeking farm employment than there are productive opportunities available. Labor mobility is the only thoroughly satisfactory answer to the tendency of added income to be capitalized in land values, though I do not think the effects of capitalization fully cancel out the benefits of income gains.

The most satisfactory way to make large adjustments in the labor force is to enable young people to enter those occupations where their opportunities are greatest. Education is the obvious means of doing this, and federal aid could stimulate and strengthen the whole effort. Retraining adults, improving the Employment Service, and similar programs should be pushed, but their results may be modest without a broader educational base.

A high level of nonfarm employment is essential for rapid adjustment of the labor force. The attractiveness of off-farm jobs will be greatly increased if they can be made available in rural areas. I am not sure that we know how to maintain full employment or that such knowledge as we have will be put fully to use. In any event, employment and education policy are both much broader than farm policy and are not likely to be much influenced by farm needs.

It may be argued, as the recent CED report[3] does, that such aids to labor mobility, together with the prospect of lower farm prices and incomes in the near future, would shrink the farm labor force sufficiently in a few years to make price programs unnecessary. I doubt it for reasons already given. But the day may come when cumulative adjustments and internal changes in agriculture will eliminate the major needs for price programs. The dominant problems of agriculture will not always be what they are today. I hope that our profession does not become so committed to any one interpretation of the farm situation that we fail to discern basic changes when they first appear.

One final comment about education, aids to labor mobility, and creation of nonfarm job opportunities in rural areas: slow to operate though they are, these are the principal means of solving the subsistence farm problem. Price policy for commercial agriculture—farmers having annual sales exceeding $2,500—will have little effect on subsistence farming.

Price and Related Programs · The function of price programs is to afford some income protection for farmers without unacceptably impairing other farm policy objectives. Though past farm programs have had serious faults, experience with them suggests that this is a practicable aim. If we had had no price programs over the past thirty years, would agriculture be more technically advanced than it is? Would the reduction in the farm labor force have been much faster—especially, would more farm-reared people now be productivly employed elsewhere? Would the size of farm have increased more rapidly? I think not, or at least not much. Resource productivity has not been materially impaired in its most essential aspects.

I think, however, that average family incomes are higher than they otherwise would be—perhaps as much as one-fourth higher. Whether this has been imputed to labor or to land is important

3. Committee for Economic Development, *An Adaptive Program for Agriculture*, 1962.

but less important than whether family welfare has been increased. Farm policy is one but not the only cause of why foreign trade and fiscal policies are in a less tidy state than we would like. Farmers' freedom of decision has been little infringed and only as substantial majorities have approved it; improvements upon past programs should at least produce a better policy than complete laissez-faire.

Income goals: A question so far treated very loosely is the standard to apply in seeking equitable income for agriculture. Two criteria seem to me to establish limits within which choices about farm programs might be made. One limit represents minimum welfare. The incomes of the mass of farm people should permit them to stay financially solvent, to educate their children, to take care of essential living needs, and to enjoy such amenities as have become thoroughly incorporated into the American way of life outside of agriculture. This level of living is judged, for the purposes of price programs, by looking at average family incomes of commercial farmers from all sources. I do not know exactly what the minimum should be, but I do not think actual income has fallen to the minimum in the postwar period. The minimum leaves sufficient income incentive, especially in respect to the less well-off farm people, to provide a strong motivation for labor mobility.

The other income criterion is rates of earnings on labor and investment on efficient farms comparable with rates earned in similar situations outside of agriculture. This criterion is suggested by equilibrium conditions under perfect competition. No injustice is done nonfarmers if farm incomes are this high. I would take a crude but operational definition of efficient farms for the purpose—say, the largest farms producing 80 percent of all farm products sold. With this inclusive definition of efficient farms, the comparable earnings criterion represents a substantially higher family income than the minimum limit proposed above. The average commercial farm family has a large investment and apparently supplies more man-hours of labor than the average nonfarm family. Family income would average higher in commercial agriculture than among nonfarmers if the comparable earnings criterion were fulfilled.

There are, of course, formidable difficulties in arriving at an operational definition reflecting the intent of the comparable earnings criterion. Here as for other criteria, working definitions may have obvious theoretical shortcomings but still serve their purposes fairly well.

Choice of programs: Strong efforts are justified to hold farm income up to the proposed minimum even if significant impairment of other objectives must be accepted. If no labor moves out of agriculture when farm income is at the minimum, something will be seriously wrong with the labor market. Limited direct payments, voluntary land retirement coupled with modest price supports, and disposal of farm products outside of commercial markets at home and abroad are among the programs suited to achieving the minimum income goal. The Treasury cost of programs is an important consideration, for heavy taxation has a number of undesirable effects, and the government must perform several functions that cannot be paid for in any other way.

At the other income extreme, comparable earnings, the public's obligation to farmers is much weaker. Price incentives for resource allocation will be lacking, and the public should insist that programs provide other means of doing the job. Thus, programs aimed at the maximum income objective should hold production in line with utilization justified at full market prices; the location of production should be shifted toward the most efficient areas; and no obstacles should be raised to enlargement of farms to the most efficient size. Some supply management proposals contain these features. Where such programs are feasible, they will sharply restrict farmers' freedom of decision and will contain other provisions not liked by farmers.

The minimum-income and comparable-earnings programs are the suggested limits for choice. For some commodities, feasibility restricts programs to a particular kind or even to none at all. Farmers' preferences for income or freedom from restrictions are crucial when feasible alternatives are available.

Among the least acceptable of all programs by these criteria is the production of goods for no use except stock accumulation beyond any reasonable need. Variable inputs used in production and resources used for storage are wasted, and the stocks add to the difficulty of devising other programs later on. Though by no means all of present Commodity Credit Corporation stocks are useless, this has been an outstanding defect of past policy.

Some portions of agriculture are especially strategic in an effort to stabilize and protect farm income. Though there is no time to justify this conclusion, I think factor earnings would be reduced more sharply in the production of the major field crops than in any other part of agriculture if farmers were to return to laissez-faire. As a minimum, programs to support agriculture should be directed to these crops. A more ambitious policy would strengthen programs for them and would extend to other products as means were available and as producers endorsed the means.

Foreign trade: One of the most difficult areas to weave into a consistent farm policy is commercial foreign trade. Other countries are no more prepared than we are to engage in free trade for most farm products, and it is by no means self-evident that this position is wrong. We shall have to seek the principal gains of comparative advantage by means of a conscious trade policy rather than expecting comparative advantage to reveal itself under laissez-faire. Despite all sorts of interference in the past, our present commercial trade seems roughly consistent with comparative advantage, except for rice, sugar, and wool. International commodity agreements may become a stronger and widely used means of regularizing trade in farm products.

The burden on the political process: Congress has not been able to act on farm policy with the rationality and decisiveness I have implied to be necessary. Making economic decisions of any kind through the political process places a heavy burden on the system, a burden for which it was not originally designed and one to which our political attitudes and institutions have been slow to adjust. This is a strong if not decisive argument for laissez-faire for agriculture. I think that experience with the farm problem and even the declining importance of the farm vote may enable Congress to lay down a more consistent and enduring agricultural policy, but this is in the class of poorly informed guesses.

In a much fundamental sense, however, we cannot resign our selves to inability to make economic decisions through the political process. We now have a mixed economy in which policy for economic growth and stability are highly important. Consider, also, the problems and opportunities presented to us by the onrush of science and the rise of human aspirations throughout the world. About twenty years ago the phrase "one-world" seemed visionary; now it seems too narrowly confined. In coming decades we shall have to make and execute positive economic policies of enormous complexity and importance. We simply must be able to do this if our free society is to rise above its challenges rather than be submerged by them. Economists cannot afford to accept as a restriction on their analysis the assumption of a permanently inept political performance.

I wish I could end this paper on a high note of optimism and with the assurance that a way lies open to solve the farm problem once and for all. But as applies to many another economic or social problem, we shall have to work our way out of this one gradually over a long period of years. We can, however, alleviate the problem. We can hope to retain a highly productive agriculture, to continue to adjust the farm labor force, and to hold family incomes in commercial agriculture at socially acceptable if not high levels. This will require farm programs, largely combinations of ones with which we already are familiar. One of the last articles John D. Black[4] wrote was on the topic of the extremes of farm policy proposals. If factions at the extremes can give up hopes of miracles that cannot happen under either laissez-faire or government programs, we can have a more settled and consistent farm policy than in the past.

4. Black, John D., "The Extremities of Current Agricultural Policy Proposals," *Quarterly Journal of Economics,* 72:3, August 1958, pp. 307–26.

How Much Should Government Do?

KERMIT GORDON

*As Director of the U.S. Bureau of the Budget in the 1963–65
period, Dr. Gordon gained a unique perspective on the conflicting
and often inconsistent objectives of the nation's agricultural programs. This article, published in the* Saturday Review, *January
1965, pinpoints some of the conflicts which emerge as supporters
of individual programs vie for continued public support.*

IN A COMMUNITY where I onced lived, there was a civic association dedicated to the economical conduct of the local government.
Since I shared this interest, I undertook to look into the policies
of the association in order to decide whether or not I should join.

I never did become a member, for I discovered that the association had a view of the meaning of economy that I could not
accept. The association had a simple, one-plank program—
opposition to any proposals for *new* programs that cost money.
I found no evidence that the group had any interest in looking
critically at the usefulness of ongoing programs, or weighing the
prospective benefits of new proposals against the realized benefits
of old programs, or searching for ways to cut the costs of governmental activities without reducing their benefits. Just a single
objective—oppose anything new.

I remember thinking at the time how great a distortion of the
meaning of economy this view conveyed. But I later discovered
that Edmund Burke fretted about the same question two centuries ago. "Economy," said Burke, "is a distributive virtue, and
consists not in saving but in selection . . . Parsimony requires
no providence, no sagacity, no powers of combination, no comparison, no judgment."

My friends in the civic association were practicing parsimony
under the guise of economy. If there is a common conservative
error in the way the citizen looks at public budgeting, this is
probably it. For parsimony is not only distinguishable from

129

economy—it is often the enemy of economy. To accept the status quo of government programs while opposing innovation is to run the risk of spending money on objects of lesser urgency while denying recognition to more compelling needs. And this, of course, is the very opposite of economy. It is waste.

The path of parsimony often leads to a narrow preoccupation with a single measure of the soundness of government finance— the total size of the public budget. If the budget does not increase over the previous year, it is thought on that ground alone to be a good budget. But this is clearly an imperfect test. A budget unchanged in total size from the year before may constitute simply a timid extension of established programs, however questionable some of them may be, or it may reflect a searching effort to expand here and contract there in order to increase the benefits flowing from a given amount of expenditure.

This is what President Johnson had in mind when he said in his budget message last January:

> An austere budget need not be and should not be a standstill budget. When budgetary restraint leads the government to turn its back on new needs and new problems, economy becomes but another word for stagnation. But when vigorous pruning of old programs and procedures releases the funds to meet new challenges and opportunities, economy becomes the companion of progress.

If the confusion of parsimony with economy is the error that often entraps conservatives in their thinking about public budgets, there is a closely symmetrical error that often appears on the liberal side. This is the confusion of profligacy with progress—the disposition to look with favor on an increase in total public spending just because it is an increase. This preference for rising expenditures rests on two convictions—the conviction that rising expenditures are needed to stimulate the economy and promote economic growth, and the conviction that the public sector of the economy is too small relative to the private sector.

But as to the first of these, it is clear that a need for fiscal stimulus is not in itself sufficient to justify higher public expenditure, for any stimulus that can be provided through increased expenditures can also be provided through reduced tax rates.

As to the second of these, the proponents of public-sector

expansion soon make clear that they are talking not about expansion of our programs for defense, space, veterans, agriculture, or interest on the public debt—which together constitute more than 80 percent of the administrative budget—but rather about our programs in health, education, welfare, housing and urban renewal, mass transportation, air and water pollution, area development, and related fields.

Certainly, then, however convincing the argument for increased spending in this limited sector, it is hardly logical basis for favoring increased *total* spending on principle. The case for an increase in total spending must rest on judgments concerning all major programs in the budget, not merely on judgments concerning one sector.

Parsimony and profligacy are false guides to policy for exactly the same reason: both deny the necessity for choice. Neither, in Burke's words, requires providence, sagacity, combination, comparison, or judgment. Neither faces up to the budgetary challenge of the 1960s.

The necessity for choice—for a reexamination of the premises of existing programs, for a weighing of alternatives—is always an imperative of responsible budget-making. But we live in a time when this imperative has taken on a special urgency.

New claims on the federal budget, many of them bearing credentials of the highest merit, press in on every side. We need more education and better education, from the primary grades through the graduate and professional schools. We should expand our job training and retraining programs, both for the unskilled and for those whose skills are obsolete. We must intensify the war on poverty. We need improved outdoor recreation facilities, efficient urban mass transportation, and better mental health facilities. We need to bring the benefits of medical research discoveries to more people more quickly. We should step up our attack on air and water pollution.

These and other demands—new, compelling, and costly—make it doubly necessary that we look carefully at the programs that have already found a place in the federal budget. They are not suspect simply because they are there; but neither does their long tenure exempt them from periodic scrutiny to determine whether their shape and size are appropriate.

The problems of adapting public programs to social change are difficult even in the most favorable circumstances. But when social change proceeds as rapidly as it has in recent years, the difficulties are compounded. Let me try to illustrate the problems of adaptation by drawing on two cases of unusual difficulty—farm policy and water resources policy. These are simply illustrative; others could readily be cited.

We are currently spending between $3.5 billion and $4 billion for farm commodity programs. The rationale for these farm income supports has changed drastically over the years. In the 1930s, farm income supports were basically a relief measure designed to prevent the literal collapse of the farm economy. During the Second World War, and to a lesser extent during the Korean War, income supports were a stimulus for needed production increases. Since then, supports have been used primarily to counteract the price- and income-depressing effects of the increase in farm productivity.

The revolution of the past several decades in farm technology has been accompanied by a revolution in the social and economic structure of the farming industry. In 1963 there were 3.5 million farms. The 1 million farms with cash receipts of over $10,000 accounted for only 27 percent of the number of farms but for almost 80 percent of the sales of farm products. These 1 million farmers could produce all of the nation's farm needs, including our large commercial exports. Taking into account earnings from off-farm work, the 1963 average income of these 1 million relatively successful farmers was over $9,500, up 13 percent from four years ago. These 1 million farmers earn average rates of return on their capital investments and labor almost equal to the corresponding averages in the nonfarm economy.

Our farm income supports basically operate through the price support technique—although in recent years some direct income payments have crept into the system. This implies that the distribution of the direct and indirect assistance provided by the federal government is roughly the same as the distribution of cash receipts. On this basis, about 80 percent of our assistance goes to the 1 million farmers whose average income exceeds $9,500. The other 20 percent of assistance is spread thinly among the remaining 2.5 million farmers.

These figures highlight the dramatic impact of changing farm technology on government farm programs. The farms that produce most of the nation's food and fiber no longer fall into the lowest one-third of the nation's income distribution. Most are successful business firms. Their continued success is of course not independent of government commodity programs, whose elimination would cause a sharp fall in the income of all farmers. But these programs are no longer a means of distributing income to the neediest groups in our population; they are *not* welfare programs. From a welfare standpoint, the chief claimants to assistance are the 2.5 million farmers who do not now and cannot in the future be expected to operate successful commercial farms. Yet their needs cannot be met through farm commodity programs. Rather, they require assistance in the painful transition to non-farm jobs, to which most of them or their children will certainly have to move.

This is an area in which our current programs and attitudes are, at least in part, based upon conditions that no longer exist. In the interest of both the farmer and the nation at large, we need to reexamine the hidden premises of our current policies and shape them anew, in closer correspondence to the facts of today's world.

Federal expenditures on water resources and related activities, for example, currently amount to about $1.5 billion per year and are rising at some 3 to 4 percent annually. These projects serve five major purposes: irrigation, flood control, navigation, hydro-electric power, and recreation—and in many cases one project serves two or more of these purposes.

These outlays constitute national investment in productive facilities. They have played a major role in our national growth, and many regions of the country owe much of their current prosperity to past national investment in water resources. Here, too, however, our current policies and practices are partly based upon objectives and concepts that have been overrun by events. This does not mean, necessarily, that we are spending too much in this area, but we may well be spending too much on some aspects of water resource development and too little on others. Let me illustrate with a few examples.

The nation's reclamation program dates from the Reclamation Act of 1902. Since then the total value of projects authorized has been $9.8 billion. Of this amount, about $5 billion has been spent; annual expenditures are now running at about $325 million.

Reclamation investment is principally irrigation investment. Of the $9.8 billion authorized for the program to date, some $5.7 billion has been or will be allocated to irrigation. Under the reclamation program the prices charged for irrigation water are heavily subsidized. The $5.7 billion cost bears no interest, and of this $5.7 billion only $3 billion will be repaid by irrigation water users. For projects that Congress is likely to be considering next year, the typical investment costs for irrigation will range between $500 and $1,500 an acre, most of which will not be recovered in the price of irrigated water.

Reclamation law was designed primarily to help develop the West by irrigating arid lands. The program was initiated at a time when the nation sought to encourage family farm settlement on public lands in the West. Over one-fourth of the irrigated lands in the West was developed under this program, and about 5 percent of total U.S. agricultural production takes place on reclamation-irrigated land.

Two major and closely related kinds of economic change have occurred during recent decades to raise the problem of how best to adapt the reclamation program to new needs. The first, and most obvious, is the problem of surplus agricultural production. Our farm commodity programs, through acreage controls, marketing quotas, and diversion payments, seek to limit agricultural production. But subsidized irrigation tends to increase production. In most cases, but not all, the crops irrigated are not the same crops as those subject to production limitations. But through the complex chain of market and producer substitution, increased production of one crop tends to aggravate the surplus situation of other crops.

These facts do not imply that irrigation investment is *per se* undesirable. Though we are limiting total agricultural production, there is still room for a shift, within the total, from less efficient to more efficient areas of production. Nevertheless, it is clear that irrigation policy must be based upon an integrated approach that looks at the most desirable locational pattern of agricultural production.

A second major set of economic changes arises out of the

growing need for water for municipal and industrial uses. The urbanization and industrialization of America—in the new West as well as in the older Eastern Seaboard and Middle West—has dramatically increased the demand for urban water.

In many parts of the nation—particularly the Southwest— water has become an increasingly scarce resource. Now, if there is any one principle of economics that economists of every persuasion would accept, it is that the price system is an exceptionally useful mechanism both for conserving a scarce resource and for allocating it to uses with the greatest value. But we rely too little on this mechanism in considering the water problems of the nation. Additional agricultural surpluses have little value. Yet irrigation water for agricultural purposes is priced far below cost. Added water for municipal and industrial uses makes a major contribution to the burgeoning urban economies of the West. But projects designed to add to municipal and industrial water often receive less attention and, unlike those for irrigation water, are priced to recover full costs. The city of Los Angeles currently pays $20 per acre-foot for water from Boulder Dam and will soon be paying $63 an acre-foot for water brought down from Northern California. Many Southern California irrigators pay $2.25 per acre-foot for water from Boulder Dam, and for new federal irrigation water will be paying perhaps $10 per acre-foot.

The need is clear, I believe, to think through the implications of a rapidly changing economy for the composition and structure of our water resources program. The solutions will not be easy. We cannot and should not ignore the plight of the commercial farmer whose livelihood depends upon irrigated water and whose water table is falling year by year. We have an obligation to those agricultural communities whose heavy investment in the land was based upon continued availability of water supplies. Nevertheless, having said this, I believe we must take steps gradually to adapt this program, designed to meet the problems of agricultural settlement, to the needs of the rapidly growing urban communities of our nation.

The pursuit of the goals of the Great Society requires that we give equal attention to the need for innovation and the need for reform. The Great Society must be an efficient society. The responsibility of the federal government to heed the new needs of an evolving society is no greater than our responsibility to assure that the old programs are using the right number of dollars.

The task of modernizing the federal budget will not be accomplished in one year or four. It is a continuing struggle, for the barriers are formidable and the pitfalls many. But it is an effort that should command the support and assistance of all who choose economy over both parsimony and profligacy.

Food and Fiber for the Future

NATIONAL ADVISORY COMMISSION ON
FOOD AND FIBER

*This succinct summary of the Commission's report appeared in
the* Coop Grain Quarterly, Summer 1967. *The work of this 29-
member panel, appointed in 1965 by President Johnson and
chaired by Dean Sherwood O. Berg of the University of Minnesota, is the most recent milestone in the continuing debate on
farm policy. The views of both the majority and the minority are
presented.*

MAJORITY POSITION: AN OVERHAUL IS NEEDED

Economic events of the 1960's have both signaled the need and
created the opportunity for revising farm policy.

1. The burdensome surpluses of grains over and above safe
reserves have vanished, as a consequence of both massive exports
for commercial sale and food aid to other countries and limitation
of output under the wheat and feed grain programs.

2. Foreign demand for food is growing, and long-range prospects for U.S. commercial exports of grains and soybeans are
favorable.

3. Agricultural technology is advancing so rapidly that the
consequent and necessary changes in farm size, location of crop
production, and agricultural employment are lagging.

Freely functioning private markets are the best mechanism for
guiding the changes in agricultural production and marketing
that will be required in the future. Government policies should
be designed to minimize interference with markets.

*We recommend that the United States adapt its policies to
accomplish a market-oriented agriculture.*

The term "market-oriented agriculture" means taking fuller
advantage of the market's ability to allocate resources and distribute incomes, in the interest of making the best employment of
our land, labor, and capital. It means greater reliance on the

137

market as a reference in both private and public economic decision making. In this concept there is room for programs, private and public, that improve the operation of markets.

When markets do not function effectively because of either private or governmental actions, they do not serve the purpose of guiding production and marketing according to consumer wants and needs. Therefore, government policy ought to try to improve the functioning of imperfect markets. This could involve many things:

1. Increasing the number of sales opportunities open to farmers where the numbers of buyers in a market is limited,

2. Increasing the bargaining power of farm groups where their market power is weak,

3. Assisting farmers to manage supplies and market their produce in an orderly manner where they are plagued by overproduction and surpluses, and

4. Refraining from using price support programs in ways that interfere with the effective functioning of markets.

In a market-oriented agriculture the Government would not intervene directly to set prices or regulate production once the excess capacity of the farming industry was eliminated.

A market-oriented agricultural policy would aim at improving the farmer's income in the long run by reducing the overcapacity of the industry. Positive steps would be taken by Government to encourage adjustment of cropland and to help the people who are leaving agriculture anyway, under any policy, to make better incomes in nonfarm occupations.

Under the policies we recommend, the reduction in excess productive capacity would be speeded up. *If*, ultimately, the excess capacity were eliminated, agriculture would employ only those people, acres, and dollars that could earn a return comparable to what they would earn in other industries. At that time, there would be no need for Government programs for income support or supply adjustment.

Until then, however, standby programs providing for price supports at or near world price levels, supply adjustment mechanisms, and income deficiency payments should be provided. Such standby programs when applied should not block long-range adjustments of agriculture.

The United States is in an excellent position now to reshape its commercial policy for agriculture.

The 1965 Farm Act gives the Secretary of Agriculture considerable discretion in applying the provisions of the law on price supports, diversion payments, and other incentives for participation in acreage adjustment programs and income-deficiency payments.

Under this legislation, it is possible to maintain free market prices for the biggest segment of American agriculture—grain and livestock farming. With prices of grains at approximately world levels, there is little prospect for gain to American producers through production reduction—except for those commodities where the United States is such a dominant influence in world markets as to set the world price.

Price supports should be set 5 to 10 percent below a moving average of world prices. This would permit markets to operate effectively. Although commodity loan rates for feed grains, wheat, soybeans, and upland cotton are competitive in world markets, price supports for some other commodities are set above the world levels. These supports should be reduced so that prices can move to market-clearing levels.

In case of a clear national need to increase the output of a particular farm commodity, incentives to farmers might be increased above the normal market incentives for a time. This could be done by price-deficiency payments or by higher commodity loans or by price supports. At other times, however, we believe it is better to allow the market to guide production.

Under present conditions of surplus productive capacity, it is clear that most farmers cannot earn parity incomes through the market alone. And even if much of the excess capacity were eliminated, there still would remain a serious problem of farm income instability because of unpredictable changes in output due to weather, and because of sudden shifts in demand, especially export demand.

We recommend, therefore, that direct commodity payments be made to farm producers to enable efficient commercial farmers to receive parity incomes, when returns from the market do not provide such incomes.

Direct payments can be made to farmers as a means of protecting their income with less interference to the market than by the use of high price supports, export subsidies, and import quotas. Consideration should be given to the limitation of payments for the largest farm businesses.

We recommend that the Department of Agriculture study the possibility of varying payments partly on the basis of level of individual farm income—to accomplish the purposes of voluntary supply adjustment programs at minimum cost and without undue subsidy to large farm business.

As now operated, however, the commodity programs may offer farmers an incentive to increase production, thus tending to defeat the purpose of reducing surpluses. For instance, the wheat program offers farmers a payment per bushel for 45 percent of the normal production, calculated as the acreage allotment times the "projected yield base." This projected yield base is computed on a moving average of yields adjusted for trend. Wheat growers naturally will try to increase yields in order to enlarge their yield bases. The same principles apply in the current cotton and feed grain programs.

We recommend that payments be made in such a manner as not to encourage additional production.

We believe that some forms of Government assistance to farmers in adjusting production and maintaining their incomes will be needed so long as excess production capacity exists.

Programs designed to convert excess crop acres to grass, forestry, and recreational uses should be redesigned and expanded. Such programs should be aimed at retiring crop acreage with the least comparative advantage for crops and the highest risk of wind or water erosion. Whole farm units—and perhaps some whole areas of marginal cropland with severe slope and of land in the high, dry plains—should be converted permanently from crops to grass cover or forestry. Such changes would contribute positively to the goal of reducing the overproduction capacity of agriculture. However, farm families and rural communities in marginal crop areas would face substantial adjustment costs.

To provide the incentive for land use shifts, and to indemnify the affected persons, communities, and regions for their losses, we recommend a program patterned after the present limited

Great Plains Conservation Program and the Cropland Adjustment Program. This program should be expanded to cover all marginal cropland areas of the country.

To cope with the problem of overproduction in the years ahead, supply adjustment programs may be necessary for some commodities.

We recommend that supply management programs be voluntary. In order to facilitate crop-acreage changes to meet market demands of the future and to encourage the growing of crops in the most efficient areas for those crops, we recommend that acreage allotments and marketing quotas be made negotiable or transferable. In the case of voluntary programs, the historical bases could be made transferable.

Acreage allotment programs for supply management tend to be self-defeating, as we have mentioned above, so long as they contain incentives for farmers to increase yields. Setting the bases for payments once and for all would help counteract this tendency. Production quotas in quantity (bushels or pounds) also would make the programs more effective. Whenever production restraints are needed, quantity quotas ought to be applied wherever possible in the interest of efficient management.

Reclamation and land development projects paid for by public investment have significantly increased farm production in the past three decades, during which agriculture was plagued with overproduction and surpluses. By 1961, Bureau of Reclamation projects had brought into production about seven million high-yielding acres. These acres were growing about $1.1 billion worth of crops—which just about offset the reduction which had been achieved at that time through the Conservation Reserve.

Clearly it is unsound policy to invest public funds in new farm capacity at a time when the overriding problem is too much capacity. Public funds for agricultural reclamation, irrigation, drainage, and development projects should be justified on the basis of whether they represent the cheapest means of getting additional farm production—if needed.

We recommend that public subsidy for capacity-increasing farm practices be discontinued. We recommend further that the funds now used in the ACP program for capacity-increasing practices be redirected to projects for improving the conditions of rural life.

Commodity loans and purchase agreements have greatly contributed to price stability and orderly marketing of nonperishable crops. They should be continued—modified when necessary as to support price levels to harmonize with the objectives of market-oriented commodity programs.

We believe that there is a need for stability mechanisms which compensate in part for unavoidable and unpredictable variations in weather and natural factors affecting farm output.

The most appropriate mechanism would be a storage program to lessen marketings in bumper years and increase market supplies in poor crop years. The purpose of such a storage program would be to stabilize supplies through the operation of an "ever-normal granary."

We recommend a program for adjusting carryover stocks of major storable farm commodities to maintain reasonable stability of available supplies of those commodities.

The Government should first establish the size of the normal carryover needed for protection in each commodity based on the variability of supply and demand for that commodity.

Definite rules for management of stocks would be established to guard against excess acquisition because of political pressure or excessive stock dispositions to hold consumer prices in check.

Once the total capacity of agriculture is in balance with long-run demand, there should be little or no need for annual acreage adjustment. But a well-managed inventory program would still be necessary and would make important contribution to maintaining a reasonable degree of price stability in a market-oriented agriculture.

In addition to carryover stocks for stabilizing market supplies, the nation needs reserve stocks of the major annual crops to assure adequate supplies to meet unpredictable or emergency needs for foreign aid and for national security.

We recommend that a national security or strategic reserve including emergency stocks for food aid, be established. This reserve should be isolated from the market except as offsetting sales and purchases are required to maintain the quality of the reserve stocks.

On the basis of past variations in production and demand,

reasonable total carryover objectives would be: 550 to 650 million bushels of wheat, 35 to 45 million tons of feed grains, 10 to 12 million hundredweight of rice and 5 to 6 million bales of cotton.

U.S. agriculture should take advantage of the rising demand for agricultural products around the world and exploit its comparative advantages in production. This is one of the prime reasons why we recommend a market-oriented agricultural policy.

In addition to adjusting price supports to world levels, this country ought to eliminate or reduce its export subsidies and eliminate or loosen its import quotas. These quotas and subsidies are inconsistent with a market-oriented agriculture. Such restrictions and incentives provide little long-run benefit to producers.

U.S. agriculture as a whole has a great deal to gain from liberalizing world trade in farm commodities. We are confident that if the industrial countries should reduce their barriers against farm product imports, the United States would enlarge its exports substantially. But to gain such concessions, this country must be ready to reduce its own trade barriers for both industrial and agricultural products.

We recommend that new legislation be enacted to replace the expiring Trade Expansion Act, to permit further reciprocal trade negotiations with other countries, and that strong efforts be made by the Administration to achieve further positive results in enlarging world trade.

In future trade negotiations, particular attention should be given to reducing trade barriers for products that farmers buy from the rest of the economy.

If American agriculture is to compete fully in world markets, it must be able to buy its inputs at prices no higher than the same inputs available to farmers in other countries.

The United States will need to increase its imports of products which are competitive with or identical to products produced in this country. These include a small number of farm products which this country raises at high cost compared with foreign producers, and which are now protected by import quotas.

We recommend that in a new round of trade negotiations, the United States be prepared to remove these quotas and replace them with adequate tariffs as direct protection for the commodity producers affected. Specific plans should be made in advance for

*meeting the adjustment problems of farmers who could not com-
pete effectively with the tariff protection provided.*

The United States is the world leader in efforts to achieve trade
liberalization and expansion. An important inconsistency between
our general trade policy and our agricultural commodity programs has been the paying of subsidies to maintain or expand
exports while keeping domestic prices above world levels. The
nation now pays export subsidies for tobacco, wheat and flour,
rice, certain dairy products, flaxseed, and peanuts.

*We recommend that the United States, as the world's leading
trading nation, gradually reduce and eliminate the use of export
subsidies and substitute other methods for meeting the income
needs of American farmers.*

Trade in agricultural products has been expanding recently
between the Communist countries and the Western democracies.
Because of special U.S. restrictions on trade with the Communist
countries, U.S. farmers have been able to participate in this growing market only to a small degree.

There are three important barriers to expansion of trade in
farm products with the Soviet Union and Eastern Europe. One
is the requirement of export licenses on all nonstrategic goods
destined for the Soviet Union, Albania, Bulgaria, Czechoslovakia,
East Germany, and Hungary.

A second is the administrative requirement that 50 percent of
wheat shipments to Eastern Europe and 50 percent of all grain
shipments to the Soviet Union must be shipped in U.S.-flag
vessels. Since the cost of shipping in American-flag vessels is much
higher than in foreign ships, U.S. exporters are at a serious disadvantage in competition with exporters in Canada, France, or
Australia where no restriction is imposed.

Feed grain exports to Eastern Europe are also limited by shipping restrictions. In issuing export licenses, the U.S. Department
of Commerce requires that a part of any cargo that includes feed
grains for an East European country must be delivered to a buyer
in Western Europe. This increases the cost of shipping by a significant margin in a field as competitive as the world feed grain
market.

A third barrier to expanding trade with the Soviet Union and
Eastern Europe is that imports to the United States from these

countries are not accorded most-favored-nation status. They must pay the higher tariff duties of the Tariff Act of 1930, instead of lower rates negotiated since under the reciprocal trade agreements laws. As a result, they do not find it advantageous to export to us, and this adversely affects their buying of U.S. farm products.

We recommend that commercial trade with the Soviet Union and Eastern Europe in nonstrategic goods, including food and fiber products, be placed under the same rules which apply to the rest of the world. The United States should negotiate with these countries, as a part of general settlement of political and economic problems, for an expansion of trade and should offer most-favored-nation status and the elimination of licensing, in return for appropriate assurances from them of fair treatment of our export trade.

We recommend that steps be taken to permit U.S. shipping firms to operate at rates competitive with those offered by foreign fleets.

MINORITY POSITION: A REPETITION WITH DIFFERENCES OF DEGREE

American agriculture is perhaps the world's most efficient producer of food and fiber. This reflects a highly successful U.S. development program for agriculture that combines market orientation, individual initiative, and public policies.

Ability to produce food has grown rapidly. Its real cost has gone down steadily. Resources have been saved or freed from farming for growth in other sectors of the economy.

The problem of equity in distributing the gains of progress will continue for some time. Capital and technology will continue to flow into U.S. agriculture, displacing both labor and land. Without some kinds of programs to supplement farm incomes, the burden of this progress will continue to fall on agriculture and rural communities.

Since technological progress is in the national interest—and, indeed, is supported partly by Government funds—it is also in the national interest to help agriculture make the necessary adjustments. However, neither the nation nor the farm sector gains if the national policies help farmers avoid adjusting and maintain a historical structure that is no longer the most effective for our growing needs.

Programs for the future must be focused more sharply on helping agriculture adapt itself quickly and fairly to the ever-increasing pace of agricultural and industrial change. The programs should focus most heavily on the people suffering the most from agricultural progress—persons displaced from farming with inadequate skills for nonfarm employment and the low-income farmers, who cannot be helped with price support and land diversion programs.

With the continuing technological revolution and scientific transformation of farming, the ability to produce food and fiber will continue large, relative to domestic and commercial export demand, for at least a decade and a half. Workers will continue to be displaced and an increasing number of farm youths must look to other sectors for employment. Commercial farms will become larger and more specialized. Their use of capital and advanced technology will further productivity and the cost advantages associated with large volume.

The nation needs to strengthen those parts of our national farm programs which extend national economic growth, efficiently and equitably compensate farmers for their contribution to this growth, and add to economic stability and other goals of the national society. It needs to modify other programs, such as those relating to conservation and natural resources, which are only partially oriented to the purposes for which they were created and recognize the new conservation needs that have developed. It needs to add programs which better bring economic opportunity to many people who are now bypassed on farms and in rural communities.

We have come to these conclusions:

1. Technology will continue to increase the productivity of resources in agriculture, but these increases are firmly in the national interest as well as the interest of a hungry world and should be encouraged.

2. The so-called "excess capacity" problem in agriculture is a problem of excess resources released by the march of research and technology.

3. The important excess resources, from the standpoint of both compassion and national interest, are the human resources.

4. Present national farm policy, oriented largely around price and property, can do, and does, very little for those who are really bearing the cost of technological progress.

5. By providing only modest opportunities for manpower adjustment while contributing to rising land values, these programs may have aggravated the problems of the small- and medium-sized operator rather than helping in their solution.

6. These programs, tied to land and prices and with the objective of re-establishing historic relationships (for example, parity price concepts), result in the production of items that consumers do not want and the use of resources that could be better employed elsewhere.

7. These programs, being scarcity-oriented, are inadequate for the times and will become increasingly inadequate in the future.

8. Agriculture needs to become more responsive and more productive to meet the food and fiber needs of the future.

9. Agricultural production needs to become more closely oriented to consumer wants and expanding export opportunities.

10. Consumer wants and expanding export opportunities are best expressed through market prices and production costs.

11. Agriculture has become more and more commercial in recent years and more responsive to changes in prices and costs.

12. The more productive segment of agriculture can operate in a market-oriented economy with adequate returns to efficient farm operators.

13. It would be the better policy to address the problems of others in agriculture by direct means—direct income assistance and by providing nonfarm employment opportunities—rather than to interfere with prices and resource use in agriculture.

14. Unless logically sequenced positive steps are taken to modify farm policies toward these ends, the food and fiber industry will likely fail to fulfill its emerging role in history, both at home and abroad.

We recommended that the United States adapt its policies to accomplish a market-oriented agriculture.

The alternative to market orientation and resource adjustment is a higher cost agriculture—an agriculture which retains inefficient producers and production patterns. This high-cost agriculture would, of course, be dependent on income transfers from the rest of the public, and would have to be protected from the competition of more efficient producers in other countries.

"Market-oriented policy" does not mean that agriculture should be abandoned completely by public policy. It means, rather, that Government assistance would be provided in ways that would least interfere with the market's allocation of resources and distribution of returns.

In a market-oriented agriculture, market-clearing prices would be used to guide production, and distribute the returns to producers for their labor and investment.

Farmers would be guided by profits in producing the various commodities. They would be under no restraints except their own managerial ability, technical capacity, and the availability of resources.

The Government would not intervene, either directly or indirectly, to set acreage allotments, prices, marketing quotas, marketing orders, or create other barriers to production and trade. Resources would be free to move to the most profitable uses and the most advantageous production regions.

Farmers' incomes would be, in general, determined by market prices and production.

Rising world demand for agricultural products offers an opportunity to free U.S. farming and the U.S. consumers and taxpayers from the costly programs which have become institutionalized over the years. The shift to a market-oriented agriculture would entail several fairly far-reaching consequences.

First, the market would place a greater premium on efficient operations, and particularly on economies of scale. This would obviously be favorable for the large, commercial farmer who has the advantage of numerous resources and a lower cost structure. It would also be favorable for consumers, since more economical production would likely mean lower actual food costs, and certainly lower food prices than would otherwise prevail. Finally, some modest gains may be forthcoming from the output of the released resources.

On the unfavorable side, it would surely mean increasing competitive pressure on the less successful farmers. It would mean an intensification of the current trend toward fewer and larger farms—with the successful operators buying out the less successful and combining their resources into more efficient productive units.

The establishment of a market economy does not mean that agriculture would be abandoned to its own devices to suffer through all emergencies by itself.

Income protection in agriculture as in other sectors of our society, should be extended to the individual rather than property. Toward this end, the concept of "temporary income supplements" is proposed.

The term "temporary income supplements," as used in this report, means payments made directly to farm operators to offset a temporary net income deficiency. Need for such temporary income transfers could rest on net income history, current net income, and socially accepted minimum family income levels.

Temporary income supplements are fundamentally different from the direct payments used under present programs to encourage acreage diversion or to offset low commodity prices.

The direct income transfers would go directly to the individuals who were bearing the brunt of the adjustment problem. Direct income transfers must not be tied to future production, so they will neither encourage greater production nor raise U.S. domestic prices above the world level.

Temporary income supplements would be similar in concept to the unemployment compensation offered to nonfarm workers. These direct transfers would be designed to protect individual farmers with a history of sound management from sudden steep drops in income. The benefits would be tied to each farmer's income history, but not tied to future production.

In the long run, agricultural commodity price supports cannot be reconciled with a market-oriented farm economy and a liberal trade policy. In the event of an unforeseen world market glut of a U.S. price-supported commodity, the United States would be obliged to support the entire world market if it used non-recourse loans without quantitative restrictions on imports.

While quantitative import restrictions should be avoided, it nevertheless may be desirable to provide U.S. farmers a moderate level of protection on "basic" commodities over time. This could be accomplished by the Federal Government guaranteeing to farmers a modest proportion of the five-year moving average of world prices (perhaps 80 percent), made good by price deficiency payments from the Federal Treasury. Such price deficiency payments would be the difference between what the farmer realized in the market and the guarantee of the Government. Payments could be made upon presentation of the farmer's sales receipts to the Department of Agriculture, showing the unit price received and the quantity sold.

Since North America is perhaps the only major area in the world with a substantial reserve of agricultural productive capacity, it seems only reasonable that the United States should establish and maintain food reserves in the interest of national security and the furtherance of U.S. foreign policy.

The Government should first establish the size of reserve that is needed for protection in each commodity—based on the variability of supply and demand for that crop. It could never exceed that total.

The Government should then purchase this reserve stock in the open market.

Also consistent with the use of open market prices to measure demand and supply, the stocks should be released on the basis of price.

It must be forbidden, however, to ever have more than the authorized amount in reserve stocks. In this way, the reserve policy is for the most part removed from being used as a commodity support program.

Government could extend food aid to developing countries without having to have either price supports or large Government-owned inventories. Using wheat as an example, announcement would have to be made on July 1 of a given year as to how much wheat was to be programmed for food aid for the following calendar year. This would become part of the estimated demand function for wheat to which farmers would respond at planting time.

The adjustment problem that faces U.S. agriculture is clear. Too many resources are available for farm production—which results in agriculture's capacity to over-supply its markets at prices which cover costs and return profits to many producers.

U.S. farm policy should be directed toward establishing a fully market-oriented agricultural economy as quickly as possible without imposing undue hardship on the agricultural sector.

The present agricultural commodity programs should be modified and administered to encourage the major adjustments which will lead to a market-oriented agriculture and thereby ease the adjustment.

Price support and loans should be systematically reduced and production restraints removed over a specified period of years. All interim programs should further the interregional and intercommodity shifts in poduction and resource use needed to reduce excess capacity.

Future farm policy must also put much greater emphasis on the welfare of those whose economic opportunities in agriculture are narrowing.

Farmers' incomes should be maintained at adequate and stable levels during the transition to market orientation.

During the transition period, the income support needed for efficient commercial farmers should be provided to the extent possible through direct payments. These payments can, and should, be graduated downward over time in order to achieve their eventual elimination.

U.S. farm production should take full advantage of the rising demand for food and fiber around the world, and exploit the comparative advantages in the production of food and fiber commodities.

Maintaining U.S. prices at world market levels is most important in the long-run expansion of exports.

Since this country has much more to gain than lose, it should take the leadership in working toward a gradual reciprocal lowering of the barriers to increased world trade in farm products.

Export subsidies and import quotas give little benefit to U.S. producers in the long run. In the long run, the United States should concentrate its agricultural export efforts and production resources on the commodities for which we have a comparative advantage.

Export subsidies should be eliminated. During the transition period, producers who had been receiving export subsidies should receive loans at less than world market prices and deficiency payments at appropriate levels.

As pointed out elsewhere, price deficiency payments should gradually and systematically be scaled down over time until the commodities are fully oriented to the market.

Consistent with the national security requirements of the United States as strictly interpreted by the National Security Council, we recommend that the United States take the leadership in abolishing import quotas as rapidly as practicable and as rapidly as reciprocal actions on the part of U.S. customers warrant.

If some form of protection is required, this should be in the form of appropriate import duties.

We believe, as does the majority, that economic and political reforms now occurring in East Europe make this a propitious time to eliminate many of the barriers to trade.

We believe, as does the mapority, that economic and political *trade with the Soviet Union and Eastern Europe in nonstrategic goods, including food and fiber products, be placed under the same set of rules which apply to the rest of the world. The United States should negotiate with these countries, as a part of general settlement of political and economic problems, for an expansion of trade and should offer most-favored-nation status and the elimination of licensing, in return for appropriate assurances from them of fair treatment of U.S. export trade. We urge the elimination of the 50-percent U.S.-flag vessel and part-cargo requirements as applied to commercial trade. We concur in the recommendation that steps be taken to permit U.S. shipping firms to operate at rates competitive with those offered by foreign companies.*

To achieve a market-oriented U.S. farm policy consistent with liberal international trade and an efficient allocation of U.S. agricultural resources, commodity prices should not be supported above 90 percent of the 5-year moving average of world market prices. The supports for commodities currently priced above world market levels should be moved to these levels. During the transition period, producers' incomes should be supplemented, when necessary, by price-deficiency payments.

Price support loans should move as soon as practicable toward recourse loans rather than nonrecourse loans.

Direct price deficiency payments are currently provided for wheat, feed grains, upland cotton, and wool. Direct payments are a better way of supporting producer incomes during the transition period than are high price supports and export subsidies because they can be made without influencing production. However, these are inconsistent with market orientation and should be gradually and consistently scaled downward until they are eliminated.

Direct payments should not encourage additional production. This can best be avoided by setting the bases for these payments for the duration of the program.

In order to facilitate the interregional and intercommodity shifts needed to eliminate excess cropland capacity, meet the market demands of the future, and increase agricultural efficiency, current acreage allotments and marketing quotas should be made negotiable or transferable across State lines as well as within States.

The objective of allotment transferability is to enable U.S. commodity production to flow to the areas of greatest comparative advantage at competitive market prices with the unneeded marginal crop acreage shifted to less intensive uses.

A proportion of the allotments could be made eligible for transfer each year, so that the entire national allotment would come up for possible transfer within the lifespan of the program. A fixed proportion of the allotment in each county and state might be made eligible for sale to farmers in other areas on a first-come, first-served basis.

Programs designed to convert excess crop-acres to grass, forestry, and recreational uses should be redeveloped and expanded. Such programs should use such incentives as are needed to secure early and substantial results, and should concentrate on the crop-acreage with the least comparative advantage for crop cultivation and the highest risk of wind or water erosion.

As a part of the transition program to provide incentive to make the land use shifts that are needed, and to indemnify the affected individuals and regions for their losses, we recommend a program patterned after the present limited Great Plains Conservation Program and the recent Cropland Adjustment Program.

Public funds for agricultural reclamation, drainage, and development projects should be justified on the basis of whether they represent the cheapest means of getting needed additional farm production.

Public subsidy of capacity-increasing practices on farms should be discontinued and such programs under ACP and SCS reoriented to accomplish the necessary land use adjustments.

If farm policies are modified to pursue real and lasting agricultural adjustment, we believe that the nation can expect to realize a prosperous market-oriented agriculture by the end of the next decade.

Part Three   Food Marketing Policy

The Food Commission: Its Product and Its Role

GEORGE E. BRANDOW

George E. Brandow is Professor of Agricultural Economics, Pennsylvania State University. He was Executive Director of the National Commission on Food Marketing during 1965 and 1966. In the following article, presented to the Annual Meeting of the American Farm Economic Association, in August 1965, he discusses the work of the Commission.

I. THE COMMISSION'S WORK AS AN ECONOMIC STUDY

The law establishing the National Commission on Food Marketing assigned it some elusive and controversial questions. The Commission was to study and appraise the changes taking place in the "marketing structure" of the food industry and where they might lead; efficiency; services to consumers; market power; regulatory activities; services such as market news; and the effects of imports. The legislative history of the law showed strong interest in farm-retail price spreads and the position of producers. The central question was the nature of competition in the food industry and how well it comported with goals of efficiency, equity, and diffusion of power.

Developments in the Industry: Its Market Orientation · In much of the food industry, selling—as contrasted with production and physical distribution—is becoming increasingly decisive in business success. The industry and the agriculture that supplies it are highly productive; differences in operating efficiency do not sharply distinguish the principal competitors. High consumer

155

incomes, wives' desire to spend less time in the kitchen, and other attributes of our affluent society create a market in which ability to make effective nonprice appeals and to influence consumer preferences is a potent way to get and hold markets.

Thus, emphasis on product differentiation by creating new products, by brand advertising, and by other forms of promotion plays a steadily larger role. Retailers similarly seek to differentiate their services by store improvement, trading stamps, supermarket bingo games, and other attractions. The public is benefited by useful new products and better stores; it pays for much promotion and trivial product proliferation without receiving corresponding value. Inefficient methods of distribution to stores are retained in part because manufacturers seek to influence store display of their products. Advantages of large size in selling may overshadow economies of scale in production as a determinant of firm size, and access to consumers is a leading source of market power.

Market Structure · The top 20 to 50 firms are acquiring a larger share of the business in most fields of the food industry, while small firms—which operate under several handicaps—are generally declining in number. The share of business controlled by the top four firms is rising in some fields and declining in others; antitrust action has held down four-firm concentration in some cases. One of the strongest and most important trends toward concentration is in purchasing by chain retailers and group wholesalers. This is constricting alternatives available to suppliers and tends to beget concentration on their part.

In no important part of the food industry do economies of scale in processing and distribution require firms to become so large that there is room in the national market for only a few. But neither do diseconomies of scale restrict expansion motivated by other reasons. The potential public benefit from horizontal mergers on the part of the largest firms in already-concentrated fields is virtually nil, while the erosion of conditions necessary for effective competition and a diffusion of power is a significant loss. Since much of the food industry is not yet highly concentrated, prevention of such mergers—one of the mildest of antitrust restraints—can be an effective if not wholly sufficient policy.[1]

Vertical integration has attracted wide attention in food and agriculture. Frequently it has meant economies that are ultimately reflected, at least in part, to consumers. Costs of selling, procurement, and physical distribution may be reduced, operating efficiency may be increased, quality control may be improved, or the adoption of new technology may be hastened. Vertical integration often upsets the previous power balance in the industry. Integration by retail chains, or the threat of it, has at times forced processors to yield to chain demands for private-label goods with no advertising costs or excess profits loaded into prices, or to adopt more efficient distribution methods. Apparently the same power has been used at times to exact less justified concessions from suppliers. Vertical integration both backward and forward—and by retailers, manufacturers, or farmers through cooperatives— opens up new business strategies that may violate the canons of fair competition.

The market-oriented food industry, engaged as it is in mass merchandising, contains numerous incentives for vertical coordination of one kind or another. Integration through ownership will selectively increase in the food industry; less formal coordination through contracts and standing business arrangements will become more pervasive. The gains and losses from vertical integration are complex, and the Commission found no general basis for opposing it.

High diversification, especially among manufacturers, is becoming more widespread in foods. The reasons are numerous: desire to move into the most rapidly growing parts of the industry, aversion to present fields if price competition is keen, efforts to put highly developed selling skills to wider use, reduction of business risks, and fear of antitrust action if market shares in the principal fields of operations are increased. The conglomerate giant has great resources and an opportunity to use a wide range of competitive practices, some of them potentially pernicious. But no clear, general case either for or against conglomerates has yet

1. Some of the Commission's critics have argued that antimerger policy is not warranted until high concentration demonstrably impairs performance —that is, lock the stable after the horse has been stolen.

been made, and they will become more important in the food industry. The growth of these firms is a reason why concentration in the food industry as a whole is increasing, although trends at the four-firm level vary among particular fields.

Market Power · Two groups in the food industry have substantial market power—retailers and large manufacturers, usually diversified, with strong brands. Market power is, of course, affected by the firm's own size and structure and by the structure of the market in which it operates. Increasing concentration of retailers' purchases has been a plus factor in retailers' position. The large, diversified manufacturers in the dry grocery field derive power from the high concentration in the various subfields in which they sell.

Yet market structure alone does not fully explain relative bargaining strength when buyers and sellers meet. Access to consumers in the market-oriented food industry is highly important: retailers operate the stores in which consumers shop; strong manufacturers' brands are created mainly by intensive promotion. In the national market for dressed meat, the selling side is more concentrated than the buying side, and in local markets for fluid milk the same situation usually exists; yet buyers commonly are in the stronger bargaining position. Nor is product differentiation solely or always mainly the result of a tendency for oligopolists to forbear from price competition; the nature of the consumer market makes it an attractive strategy in many other cases.

Aspects of Performance · The Commission found the food industry generally efficient and progressive. Of the specific inefficiencies noted, most involved distribution from manufacturers' plants; and as has already been indicated, manufacturers' desire to influence store display usually was a factor in holding to costly methods. Advertising and sales promotion were considered valuable for information purposes, especially in introducing new products; but little or no public value was credited to the substantial though immeasurable costs incurred to persuade consumers to select rival goods or services when in the absence of promotion one would be as satisfying as another.

Profit levels in food retailing, comparatively high in the late

1950's, were more nearly in line with other branches of retail trade in 1965. In some branches of food manufacturing, high profits attested to substantial ability to administer prices, but earnings on net worth were modest in several important fields— meat packing, canning, freezing, dairy products, bread baking, flour milling, and others.

The Commission found that "Lower farm–retail price spreads would be possible (though means of doing this might be very difficult) without reducing services to consumers or unreasonably lowering earnings of the food industry. This is particularly true of a few products for which specific inefficiencies or unusually high selling costs have been noted. But farm–retail price spreads would remain high because processing and distribution are costly even when efficiently performed."

In this connection, regularly published farm–retail price-spread data for meats and poultry were found far from satisfactory. Data collected by the Bureau of Labor Statistics and used for price-spread calculations by the Department of Agriculture overstate retail prices and tend to understate short-term price changes because price "specials" are not adequately taken into account. The overstatement of the retail price of beef was almost 10 percent in 1964. Apparently, retailers' gross margins on beef widened considerably less during the price decline of 1963 and 1964 than the published price spreads showed.

The food industry appears to have its share, but perhaps no more, of unfair trade practices, power plays by the strong against the weak, discriminations, and other forms of commercial sin (if I have the right term). A persistent problem appears to be price discrimination induced by buyers, although only proscriptions against sellers have much effectiveness. This remains a major weakness of the Robinson-Patman Act. The Act is distinguished by being poorly conceived in many details and yet having a generally constructive effect on competition in the food industry.

Postion of Consumer · The finding that the industry is generally efficient and progressive and that profit levels are about in line with other parts of the economy means that consumers are, on the whole, well served. Instances of inefficient distribution, excessive promotion, and unnecessarily high profits, however, detract from the job that ideally might be done.

Consumer sovereignty is an essential organizing principle, but a major requirement is to enable consumers to have the unbiased information they need to play the role effectively. Standards of comparison become elusive when prepared and semiprepared foods begin to replace staples, when sizes and shapes of packages proliferate, when strong impressions of differences among brands are created, and when retail prices are constantly juggled as a merchandising device. The finding that retail prices of advertised brands of common foods averaged about 20 percent higher than prices of comparable private-label products is impressive evidence that better-informed buying could save consumers money. And it would compel a generally better performance throughout the industry through greater emphasis on price competition.

Position of Producers · Numerous developments in the food industry are increasing the pressure on farmers to tailor production to markets, as to both quantity and quality. The traditional price system is less workable: increasingly inelastic demand at the farm level is forcing the major burden for clearing markets on adjustments in production, but the necessary time lag is satisfactory neither to the food industry nor to farmers. A market-oriented industry tends to specify the raw materials it wants rather than making do with whatever farmers produce. Distribution efficiencies and other reasons lead to bypassing central markets; the closer relation between particular buyers and sellers encourages farm production for specific outlets.

Adaptation of farming to this changing environment is taking several forms. Cooperative marketing, vertical integration both backward and forward, contract farming, marketing orders, and government farm programs are all responses of a sort. Fewer and larger farms are conducive to most of these changes, and a few parts of agriculture are moving out of a purely competitive environment.

The Commission was specifically instructed in its statute to report findings and conclusions on, among other things, "changes in statutes or public policy . . . appropriate to achieve a desired distribution of power as well as desired levels of efficiency," and "the effectiveness . . . of regulatory activities of the Federal Government. . . ." The conclusions are conservative in the true sense of the word, for they seek to assure the effectiveness of the competitive system under changing conditions and to retain it as the means for organizing the nation's economic activities in the food sector.

Industry Structure and Trade Practice · The central conclusion regarding market structure was that horizontal mergers by the largest firms in already concentrated fields should not be permitted under the Clayton Act. The Department of Justice and Federal Trade Commission were urged to develop guidelines as to circumstances under which mergers would be opposed. Standards paralleling those in selling should be applied to purchasing. Corporations intending to merge should give advance notice, and the regulatory agencies should have power to issue temporary cease and desist orders to defer questionable mergers or trade practices.

Believing that public disclosure alone has salutary effects, the Commission suggested that large conglomerate and integrated firms should report operating results by major fields as well as for the total company. In order to avoid continued hit-or-miss attention to the food industry, the FTC should be charged with making a continuing review of market structure and competition in the industry, and to report annually thereon to the Congress.

In the Commission's view, the Department of Agriculture should exercise more initiative in administering the Packers and Stockyards Act and the Perishable Agricultural Commodities Act, and eggs should be added to its jurisdiction. Responsibility for dressed meat and poultry, however, should be exercised only by Justice and the FTC. The Commission urged that the regulatory work of USDA should be administratively separated from other functions. Recognizing that terminal livestock markets now have strong competition from rival marketing methods, the Commission proposed relaxation of some stockyards regulation.

Consumers and Producers · The Commission's conclusions gave heavy weight to measures to improve consumer information. These included compulsory consumer grading of well-established, nonperishable foods wherever feasible, the establishment of more standards of identity, and more informative packaging and labeling. A consumer agency in the executive branch of the government was proposed. The Commission put forward no measures to restrict advertising and sales promotion other than to give consumers better independent sources of information.

On the subject of farmer bargaining power, three measures representing ascending degrees of effective collective action of producers were suggested. The first was more emphasis on cooperative marketing; this was supplemented by a proposal for legislation protecting farmers' right to form cooperative and bargaining associations. The second was extending eligibility for federal marketing orders to all regionally produced farm products. The third, a more nearly new idea, was essentially an extension of marketing orders to include production and marketing control and to negotiate prices and other terms of trade. These instruments were called agricultural marketing boards and were to be brought into being and operated somewhat like marketing orders. A board, however, was to include representatives of handlers and the public.

The Commission pointed out that, historically, American policy has sought an equitable and workable distribution of power by restraining concentrations of great strength and by lending support to the weak. In this same tradition, it favored both antimerger policy and bargaining power for farmers. In recognizing the need for stronger group action by farmers, however, the Commission turned to a terminable government instrument under which the public interest might be protected rather than proposing blanket exemption for producer cooperatives from the antitrust laws.

Other Subjects · The Commission emphasized the importance of better data about markets in several respects. It suggested that USDA be authorized to require submission of price, volume, and related information needed for its market news work. It urged the Bureau of Labor Statistics to review its methods of collecting retail food prices and the USDA to improve the accuracy of its price-spread data. Other comments were made on other subjects but are omitted here for brevity.

II. THE COMMISSION AS A POLICY INSTRUMENT

In principle, the idea of a commission was excellent. In light of the importance of the industry and the extensiveness of public policy affecting it, an independent review of where we are, probable future trends, and the appropriateness of current policy makes a good deal of sense.

But how best to do the job remains an open question. The Food Commission model does not seem to be the correct one. Members of Congress are overworked and far too busy to give such an assignment the attention it should have. Furthermore, most of them—perhaps not all—are ideologically and politically committed in ways that make a fresh, independent approach to the subject next to impossible. Only in exceptional circumstances can one expect to assemble a committee that is at once informed, uncommitted, free to work on the problem, and influential in putting conclusions or recommendations into effect. Since the ideal is seldom practicable, the most valuable product would seem likely to come from a largely professional group of economists and lawyers charged with making comprehensive analyses and with presenting as wide a range of ideas and proposals as the group thought merited public discussion.

The Food Commission's report came at a time when Vietnam was pushing all other matters into the background, when higher incomes were making farmers more content with the status quo than they had been for a long time, and when general prosperity was intensifying the usual public apathy about antitrust issues. A modest wave of concern about consumer protection was the only currently popular topic to which the Commission report had much relation. The report itself was moderate and low-key; intended to be a responsible report, it was not a sensational one.

The treatment accorded even so restrained a report by the industry and some members of the Commission itself is instructive about the politics of an effort such as this. Early drafts of the report were "leaked," some trade association officials issued statements of shock and bewilderment, the trade press heavily emphasized and often editorially castigated those parts of the report critical of the industry, advertising media protested, and letters of outrage went to the Commission and members of Congress. Rank and file members of the food industry—and, to the extent possible, the general public—were given a distorted and probably lasting impression of the report before it was issued.

In the immediate future, the report may well help to bring about several changes in government activities that can be made administratively. The possibilities include reorganization of USDA regulatory activities, some changes in procedures in regulating stockyards and the Perishable Agricultural Commodities Act, revision of the methods by which the Bureau of Labor Statistics collect retail food prices, revision of some USDA price-spread data, and perhaps more specific attention to the food industry by the FTC. Immediate legislation seems less likely, although the report may have some influence on such current legislative proposals as the Bandstra bill on packer feeding of cattle and the "truth in packaging" bill.

But the Commission's assignment was properly conceived in long-run terms, and evaluators will have to wait five to ten years to know whether it was worth the effort. Both the Commission's report and information contained in the ten technical studies may have widely diffused but nonetheless significant effects. If the Commission's work leads to more accurate appraisals of the numerous specific issues which legislators, administrators, businessmen, and farmers will face in the next decade, the most important potential result of the Commission's work will have been achieved.

Why the Growing Farm-Retail Price Spread?

JEROME W. HAMMOND, WILLIS E. ANTHONY,
and MARTIN K. CHRISTIANSEN

Jerome W. Hammond and Willis E. Anthony are Assistant Professors and Martin K. Christiansen is an Associate Professor in the Department of Agricultural Economics, University of Minnesota. In this article, published in the Minnesota Farm Business Notes, *they critically examine the findings and conclusions of the report of the National Commission on Food Marketing.*

IN 1964, the National Commission on Food Marketing (NCFM) was established to investigate widening farm-retail price spreads. Research by the Commission took many pertinent issues into consideration, though part of the information was blurred by the political controversy surrounding the Commission's proposals. The following article is based chiefly on information developed by the Commission. The purpose is to consider the more important factors that have an impact on the farm-retail price spread.

Let's first examine how price spread data are compiled. The farm-retail price spread is calculated from the "market basket" data of the U.S. Department of Agriculture. The market basket is a per family measure of total value of a fixed quantity of food purchases. It includes 62 farm-produced foods.

Obviously, physical characteristics of farm products change through processing. For example, it takes 2.25 pounds of live beef to produce 1 pound of retail beef cuts. To obtain a price spread, it is therefore necessary to calculate the farm equivalent quantity of retail foods. The farm equivalent quantity of the retail quantity then is valued at the farm level price. So the farmer's share of the retail market basket is the farm equivalent value as a percent of the retail value. The remaining percentage (the difference between the retail and the farm value of the market basket) is the *farm-retail price spread.*

FIG. 1. *Farmer's Share and Marketing Margin as Percent of Retail Value of Market Basket, 1947–65, U.S.*

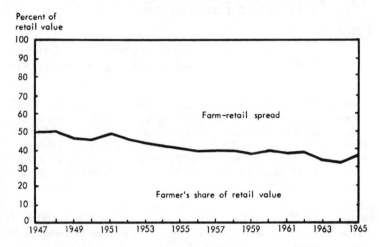

SOURCE: NCFM Technical Study No. 9, June 1966, p. 2.

FIG. 2.   *Market Basket Data, 1947–65, U.S.*

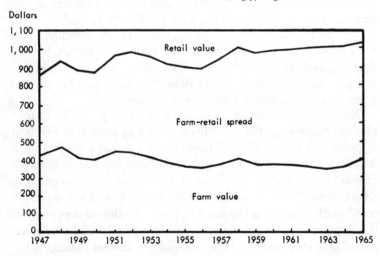

SOURCE: NCFM Technical Study No. 9, June 1966, p. 2.

Yearly percentage figures for the farmer's share and the farm-retail spread provide a basis for comparison (Figure 1). In 1947, the farmer's share of the market basket was 51 percent. By 1963 and 1964, it was 37 percent.

Farm-retail spreads vary considerably among commodities. For example, in 1964, the farmer obtained 71 percent of the consumer's dollar for the butterfat used in butter, resulting in a farm-retail spread of 29 percent. But, at the same time, the value of corn in corn-flakes returned only 9 percent of the retail value to the farmer and wheat in bread returned only 19 percent.

The farm-retail price spread for the market basket has increased since 1947. This increase has been reflected in both declining farm prices and rising retail food prices (Figure 2). Therefore, rising marketing costs have resulted in only moderately rising food prices. Four sets of factors associated with changing price spreads are explored below. They are: marketing input prices, increased food processing, the merchandising mix, and technology.

MARKETING INPUT PRICES

Wage Rates · Labor prices in all industries increased substantially during the period studied by the Commission. Indices of hourly wage rates for several types of workers in food marketing industries are presented in Table 1. All show a consistent upward trend. In fact, the minimum increase for 1958–64 was 20 percent. Increases in wage rates for most other types of workers probably would be similar.

Since labor is the most important item in the marketing bill (42 percent in 1965), the wage increase undoubtedly has been a significant factor in increasing the marketing margin. However, this situation has been moderated to some extent by the substitution of laborsaving equipment and methods.

Advertising Rates · Advertising prices have undergone considerable change. Table 2 shows the Commission's reported indices of costs for exposing a commercial message to 1,000 persons or families. The largest price increase, 45 percent from 1956 to 1964, was for prime time network television advertising. Spot radio, which accounts for a small proportion of total advertising ex-

TABLE 1. *Indices of Hourly Wage Rates for Workers in Selected Industries* (1958 = 100)

Type of labor	1950	1958	1959	1960	1961	1962	1963	1964
Nonsupervisory food store employees		100	101	106	111	115	119	124
Wholesale trade	68	100	104	107	111	113	117	120
Biscuit, crackers, and cookies (production workers)		100					124	
Cereal preparations (production workers)		100					124	
Bakers		100	105	109	115	118	118	122
Wrappers in bakeries		100	105	109	115	120	119	123
Hourly labor cost for marketing all farm food products (1957–59 = 100)*	69	100	103	108	112	117	121	126
Manufacturing of nondurable goods	70	100	104	107	110	117	116	120

* *Marketing and Transportation Situation*, ERS, USDA, August 1966, p 15.
SOURCE: Calculated from data in NCFM Technical Studies No. 5, 6, and 7.

TABLE 2. *Index of Costs per Thousand, Selected Advertising Media, 1956–64* (1956 = 100)

Year	Prime time network television	Fringe time spot television	Spot radio	Maga-zines, four-color pages	Maga-zines, black and white pages	Sunday supple-ments, four-color pages	Sunday supple-ments, black and white	Daily news-paper
1956	100	100	100	100	100	100	100	100
1957	106	98	100	104	104	103	103	103
1958	111	101	101	113	112	113	110	104
1959	117	104	102	113	113	119	116	110
1960	122	108	102	116	117	119	116	110
1961	127	111	102	121	124	121	118	114
1962	134	114	103	123	127	123	119	117
1963	140	121	103	123	126	124	120	111
1964	145	122	105	124	127	123	119	123

SOURCE: NCFM Technical Study No. 6, June 1966.

penditure, had the smallest price increase—5 percent from 1956 to 1964.

Price increases for television advertising have had a large impact on firms marketing national brand foods such as breakfast cereals, crackers, and cookies. Breakfast cereal companies spent 43.9 percent of their advertising expenditures on network television and 38.3 percent on spot television for a total of 82.2 percent in 1964.[1] And the cracker and cookie industry spent 52.4 percent of its total advertising expenditures on network television and 10.5 percent on spot television for a total of 62.9 percent.[2] While other food industries may spend less on TV advertising, unit advertising costs have increased for all.

Building and Equipment Costs · The Commission's food retailing study provided data on cost and investment per square foot of store area (Table 3). These per unit costs have increased moderately since 1955, although year-to-year changes have been erratic. The erratic cost patterns may be attributed to changes in construction and building materials, since construction costs have increased continually.

TABLE 3. *Indices of Supermarket Building Costs and Overall Investment per Square Foot of Store Area, 1955–64*
(1955=100)

Year	Building cost	Overall investment
1955	100.0	100.0
1956	113.3	100.0
1957	118.3	107.9
1958	116.5	113.1
1959	115.1	109.5
1960	119.8	118.4
1961	115.3	118.8
1962	112.5	110.0
1963	112.1	128.7
1964	115.9	114.8

TABLE 4. *Indices of Natural Gas and Electric Rates, 1950–64*
(1950=100)

Year	Natural gas	Electricity
1950	100	100
1955	134	92
1960	173	93
1961	182	93
1962	185	93
1963		91
1964		89

SOURCE: NCFM Technical Study No. 7, p. 266.

1. NCFM Technical Study No. 6, p. 148.
2. Ibid., p. 149.

Power Rates · Natural gas rates almost doubled between 1950–64 (Table 4). Consequently, agricultural processing firms that use this power source have had increased processing costs. Firms that use electricity have been in a more favorable cost position, since electricity rates dropped 11 percent between 1950–64.

Profits · The Commission compiled profit rates as a percent of net worth for several food industries. There was no apparent pattern of increase or decrease (Table 5). Profits in food industries generally were lower than those in nonfood industries.

INCREASED FOOD PROCESSING

Another reason for the expanding farm-retail price spread is the cost of increased food processing. The confluence of several factors make the trend appear reasonable.

A crucial factor is consumer willingness to buy food processing services, both in restaurant and home-consumed foods. Such willingness is associated with rising incomes, coupled with increasing competition among demands for time and changing preferences for leisure use. Data in Table 6 support the proposition that more services are associated with food. Total unit marketing services increased by 23 percent from 1940 through 1963.

Increased U.S. urbanization has led to some additional processes in food marketing. As more consumers mass in metropolitan areas, there must be more transportation and food handling. And more food must be shipped greater distances from farmers to processors to consumers, requiring more refrigeration, freezing, and canning. Further, increased handling calls for more health and sanitation safeguards.

Technological development also has played an important role in expanding food processing. There has been substantial invention and innovation in packaging, freezing, curing, canning, cooking, portion control, dehydrating, etc. The competitive strategy of product differentiation also fosters more processing, since it is easier to differentiate a highly processed product than a raw one.

These factors have led to inclusion of many new items in the food bill. Some are difficult to distinguish. For example, parking

TABLE 5. *Profits as Percent of Net Worth for Selected Food Industries, 1950–64*

Profits as percent of net worth

Year	7 baking companies	61 fruit and vegetable canning firms	Meat packing industry	Large food retailing corporation	Bakery products	Dairy products	Sugar refining	Retail food corporation
1950	15.8	NA*	7.3	NA	NA	NA	NA	11.2
1951	NA	NA	6.5	NA	NA	NA	NA	7.5
1952	12.4	NA	4.1	NA	NA	NA	NA	NA
1953	NA	NA	6.6	NA	NA	NA	NA	8.8
1954	11.9	NA	3.7	9.5	11.9	9.5	.7	9.3
1955	NA	NA	7.8	NA	NA	NA	NA	9.4
1956	12.2	NA	7.9	NA	NA	NA	NA	9.6
1957	NA	NA	5.4	NA	NA	NA	NA	9.5
1958	11.7	NA	5.1	11.9	10.2	8.8	.9	10.2
1959	NA	NA	8.4	9.6	11.4	9.1	2.5	8.6
1960	11.7	NA	6.6	11.0	12.1	9.3	—.7	8.8
1961	NA	NA	5.0	9.9	10.8	9.2	4.4	7.7
1962	9.8	NA	6.6	NA	NA	NA	NA	NA
1963	NA	7.3	6.9	NA	NA	NA	NA	NA
1964	11.4	6.7	9.2	NA	NA	NA	NA	NA

---

* NA = not available.

SOURCE: NCFM Technical Studies No. 1 (p. 66), 4 (p. 212), 5 (p. 108), 7 (pp. 284–5), and 8 (p. 211).

TABLE 6. *Index of Food Marketing Services, 1940–63*

Marketing Services

Year	Total	Unit	Volume
1940	100	100	100
1945	133	126	126
1950	145	118	123
1955	167	118	142
1960	190	123	154
1963	201	123	164

SOURCE: Trelogan, H. C., and N. Townshend-Zellner, "The Nature of New and Different Processing Differs Among Product Groups," *J. Farm. Econ.*, 47:1, Feb. 1965, p. 45.

172   J. W. HAMMOND, W. E. ANTHONY, AND M. K. CHRISTIANSEN

lots are a part of every new supermarket. Their cost enters into store overhead and, therefore, into every grocery bill.

Fruits and Vegetables · A significant portion of the rising marketing costs of fruits and vegetables can be explained in terms of consumption patterns. Between 1947–63, per capita consumption of fresh fruits and vegetables declined from 330 to 219 pounds, while per capita processed fruit and vegetable consumption increased from 83 to 103 pounds. Utilization of processed fruit increased from 47 percent of the total market in 1945 to 62 percent in 1962. Utilization of processed vegetables increased from 37 to 48 percent of total production.

Sweet peas and sweet corn are two vegetables in which Minnesota farmers have a sizable stake. The NCFM did a survey of canning and freezing costs which is summarized in Table 7. Although the data do not show a time trend for costs, they do show the cost structure incurred as consumption shifted from fresh to processed products.

The data also show the modest role that the raw product prices play in the total processing cost. Raw product costs of both corn and peas represent a higher proportion of total costs in the freezing than in the canning industry. This fact reflects the higher raw product quality requirements of freezers.

TABLE 7. *Proportions of Processing Cost Allocated to Selected Items for Canned and Frozen Corn and Peas, 1964 (percent)*

Cost Item	Canned		Frozen	
	Corn	Peas	Corn	Peas
Raw product cost	15.5	23.6	32.5	42.7
Labor	10.2	6.1	12.2	5.7
Supplies	40.9	32.1	17.5	17.5
Fuel, power, and water	1.8	1.2	6.5	5.7
Selling and distribution	6.5	6.4	10.2	9.7
Overhead	25.1	30.6	21.1	18.7
Total	100	100	100	100

SOURCE: Calculated from data in NCFM Technical Study No. 4, June 1966, pp. 200–1, 239–40.

Food Grains · In most instances, grain processing obliterates the characteristics of the farm product before it reaches the consumer. Some processes are being added to the basic grain commodity. Frozen baked goods and sugar-coated breakfast cereals are obvious examples.

Wheat products, including flour and breakfast cereals, account for approximately three-fourths of domestic food grain consumption. Hence, costs of milling, baking, and cereal manufacturing account for a substantial part of the farm-retail margin in food grains.

A major change has been the shift from flour manufacturing to more profitable convenience products for consumers. In 1965, three of the four largest milling companies received less than one-third of their total volume from flour and mill feed. Prior to 1950, all four had received more than 80 percent from flour and mill feed. According to the Commission, this trend will accelerate as millers produce more flour mixes, refrigerated doughs, frozen baked goods, and pet foods. Consequently, manufacturing and packaging costs most likely will rise.

All costs except ingredients have increased markedly for bread and bakery products since 1956 (Table 8). Data for the sample firms show that manufacturing costs have increased by 17 percent Some of this cost increase is due to higher wage rates, but part is due to expanded manufacturing services.

Selling and delivery costs increased by 32.5 percent during 1956–65. The Commission found a glaring inefficiency in this area.

TABLE 8. *Changes in Bakery Costs, 1956–65*

Item	1956	1965	Percentage change, 1956–65
Net sales	15.82	17.93	13.3
Ingredient cost	5.56	5.56	0
Manufacturing	3.86	4.50	16.6
Administrative	0.84	1.04	23.8
Selling and delivery	4.74	6.28	32.5
Net profit before income tax	0.82	0.55	−32.9
Loss on damaged and stale returns	0.91	1.19	30.8

SOURCE: NCFM Technical Study No. 5, p. 106.

Delivering and selling baked goods now cost almost as much as it costs to grow the wheat, mill the flour, and bake the bread. About 42 percent of distribution cost is for the driver-salesman. The vehicle cost has declined from one-fourth to one-fifth. But "other expenses" increased to nearly 40 percent during 1955-65. These other expenses include discounts and allowances, sales supervision, shipping clerks, advertising, insurance, and bad accounts—all costs of servicing distribution. The "stale returns" deduction from gross sales also may appropriately be added to distribution costs, since it reflects overstocking by baking companies intent on maintaining their share of the grocer's shelf.

Relative manufacturing costs have declined for breakfast cereals (Table 9). Both ingredient and packaging costs have declined, while selling and merchandising expenses have increased. These facts suggest that there has not been a substantial increase in processing service costs for breakfast cereals.

Ingredient costs for manufacturing crackers and cookies have declined, while packaging and material costs have increased.

TABLE 9. *Sales, Cost, and Profit Data Comparisons between NCFM Survey Data (1964) and Federal Trade Commission Data (1940)*

Items	Breakfast cereals		Crackers and cookies	
	1964	1940	1964	1940
Total net sales	100.0	100.0	100.0	100.0
Materials and supplies	35.1	47.7	43.6	34.6
Manufacturing payroll	10.8	6.1	15.2	13.0
Other manufacturing costs	6.8	10.3	4.2	8.8
Total manufacturing costs	52.7	64.1	63.0	56.4
Selling expenses	9.2	5.8	20.5	23.2
Advertising	15.2	13.1	1.7	2.6
Administrative and general expenses	4.3	3.3	4.8	4.7
Other expenses	4.5	1.3	2.0	1.7
Total selling, general, and administrative expenses	33.2	23.5	29.0	32.2
Total manufacturing, selling, general, and administrative expenses	85.9	87.6	92.0	88.6
Net profit before federal income taxes and additions	14.1	12.4	8.0	11.4

SOURCE: NCFM Technical Study No. 6, pp. 206–7, 210–11.

While there have been few physical changes in the basic products, there have been developments and additions in packaging services. Selling expenses for crackers and cookies have declined slightly.

Poultry and Eggs · The NCFM found that since World War II, two major changes have occurred in the form in which poultry meat is sold. In 1947, 80 percent of the chickens and 75 percent of the turkeys sold were New York dressed (only the blood and feathers removed). By 1963, about 11 percent of chickens and 5 percent of turkeys were marketed that way.

New technology, as well as shifting consumer tastes played a role in this development. Location of eviscerating plants in producing areas and a shift to large-scale poultry production on a commercial scale led to virtually complete market dominance by ready-to-cook birds. Thus another set of service costs to be borne by the farm-retail price spread was added to marketing.

These costs are reflected in data in Table 10. In 1947, the farm-retail price spread for chickens was 16.7 cents per pound—3.1 cents in the farm-wholesale and 13.6 cents in the wholesale-retail functions. By 1965, the farm-retail spread had grown by 3 cents; the retail spread had *declined* 3 cents, but the wholesale spread had increased 6 cents. The Commission also developed turkey price spread data, but no discernible trends appeared.

Eggs have been marketed in almost the same manner for decades. Nevertheless, while the retail price has declined, both the farm-wholesale and wholesale-retail spreads have remained at about the same level (Table 11). Hence, the farmer's share of the retail egg dollar has declined.

Labor costs account for less than one-third of the egg margin. Containers, transportation, and building costs for moving and storing eggs account for a higher proportion of the price spread than for other poultry products.

Livestock and Meat · Marketing and processing services in livestock are complex. A meatpacker takes a complicated raw material—the live animal—and disassembles the carcass into parts. While most of the parts become meat products, byproducts also are involved. In recent years, byproducts have accounted

TABLE 10. *Fry Chicken Prices, Price Spreads, and Farmer's Share of Retail Price, 1947–65*

Year	Retail price to con- sumer	Farm value	Farm- retail spread	Farm- er's share
	cents per pound			per- cent
1947	54.8	38.1	16.7	70
1950	54.8	37.4	17.4	68
1955	52.9	34.6	18.3	65
1956	46.3	26.9	19.4	58
1957	45.2	25.8	19.4	57
1958	44.7	25.4	19.3	57
1959	40.7	22.0	18.7	54
1960	41.4	23.1	18.3	56
1961	37.3	19.2	18.1	52
1962	39.4	20.9	18.5	53
1963	38.8	19.9	18.9	51
1964	37.8	19.5	18.3	52
1965	39.8	20.3	19.5	51

SOURCE: NCFM Technical Study No. 2, p. 69.

TABLE 11. *Grade A Large Egg Prices Per Dozen, Price Spread, and Farmer's Share, 1947–65*

Year	Retail price to con- sumer	Farm value	Farm- retail spread	Farm- er's share
	cents per dozen			per- cent
1947	67.1	47.8	19.3	71
1950	58.2	38.0	20.2	65
1955	59.8	40.1	19.7	67
1956	59.4	39.8	19.6	67
1957	56.6	37.4	19.2	66
1958	59.6	39.5	20.1	66
1959	52.3	31.4	20.9	60
1960	56.6	37.1	19.5	66
1961	56.6	35.9	20.7	63
1962	53.3	32.2	21.1	60
1963	54.4	33.4	21.0	61
1964	53.9	32.9	21.0	61
1965	53.8	30.1	23.2	57

SOURCE: NCFM Technical Study No. 2, p. 74.

for 10–15 percent of farm livestock value.

Few additional services have been added to red meat sold in retail stores in the past few years. Efforts to establish a wide market for prepackaged, frozen cuts have not been successful. Some additional services have appeared with processed meats. Sliced and packaged bacon, sausage, and luncheon meats now are common, though freeze-dried and dehydrated meats remain specialties. Though many precooked and ready-to-eat meats are available, their appearance on the dinner table is only slightly more common than it was a decade ago. For these reasons, factors other than additional processing explain the expanding farm-retail price spread for meat, particularly for fresh meat.

Less than half the margin for meat goes to the packing plant. Labor accounts for more than half the farm-retail spread at all levels. Rising labor costs reflect both rising wages and additional meat trimming and cutting.

There has been an increasing proportion of meat slaughtered and processed under federal inspection, a requirement for interstate shipment. Since federal standards for health, sanitation, and plant construction are more stringent than most state standards, the added costs of meeting them may account for a small part of the increasing margin.

Dairy Products · In 1965, almost half the dairy production was fluid milk, nearly one-fourth was butter, and more than 10 percent was cheese. Processing services added in marketing vary widely among these products. The margin for each group of products has changed, and the total margin has changed as the product mix has shifted.

In 1965, retail milk prices had increased 22 percent from 1947–49, while the farm value remained unchanged. Thus, the price increase was due to an increase in the price spread, which occurred chiefly in the 1950's (Table 12). Although no specific data show components of the increasing margin, it is in part due to added services, such as disposable containers and dealer servicing of retail shelves, as well as to added labor costs and other marketing inputs. In 1964, labor accounted for about one-third of the margin.

About 53 percent of the farm milk produced in 1965 was used

TABLE 12. *Fresh Milk Retail Price, Farm Value, and Farm-retail Spread, 1947–49 to 1965 (cost per ½ gallon)*

Year	Retail price	Farm value	Farm retail spread
1947–49	38.7	21.7	17.0
1950	37.8	20.0	17.8
1955	42.9	20.9	22.0
1957–59	46.6	21.9	24.7
1960	48.3	22.1	26.2
1961	48.2	22.1	26.1
1962	47.8	21.7	26.1
1963	27.6	21.5	26.1
1964	47.7	21.7	26.0
1965	47.3	21.8	25.5
Percentage change:			
1947–49 to 1965	+22.2	+.05	+50.0
1957–59 to 1965	+1.5	−0.5	+3.2

in manufacturing dairy products. Due chiefly to the decline of butter consumption, the proportion of milk going into manufactured products has declined. Had costs of producing manufactured products and fluid milk remained stable, this situation could imply a declining price spread rather than an increasing one.

The dairy industry has experienced a large shift among manufactured products. During 1935-65, cheese production more than doubled, and frozen product production increased nearly fivefold. These products are undergoing more processing, e.g., preslicing of cheese and more and improved packaging.

With manufactured products, at least two additional services appear. Dairy manufacturers now provide more services to retail stores and wholesale accounts, and there is greater emphasis on containers and packaging.

THE MERCHANDISING MIX

The NCFM reports indicate a shift in industry emphasis from production and distribution to merchandising—product and packaging innovation, advertising and promotion, and the addition of convenience and service to food products. The shift is largely a reflection of the changing consumer market. Food manufacturing and marketing firms have recognized these changes and altered their marketing techniques in an effort to maintain or increase sales. Factors associated with the changes in the consumer market include the shift to an urban society, rising levels of education, increased affluence and leisure, a shift to more highly skilled occupations, the increase in the number of working women, and the greater mobility and independence of the family.

Food Retailing · One NCFM report states that "in the early days of chain store development (1910–30), the basic competitive strategy was to sell for less." But, "Price competition in food retailing has been declining during the past 10 to 15 years." The report suggests three groups of factors influencing the change. "First, the cost advantage of the early chains which had supported aggressive price competition was, for the most part eroded away. The independent suppliers copied chain methods, and discriminatory price concessions to chains were made less common by antitrust enforcement. Second, consumers became increasingly affluent and less sensitive to price. Third, changes in retail service changed the competitive forces from the item to the retail store as a whole."[3] The essential point is that the competitive emphasis among food retailers has shifted toward advertising, promotion, and services.

Once services have been offered, they cannot be easily withdrawn. Parking lots and air conditioning are built into a store. Similarly, though trading stamps may give a store a competitive edge for a time, competing stores usually adopt the device also. Then, when giving stamps has lost its effectiveness, discontinuing the practice may put the store at a competitive disadvantage.

Trading stamps were the fourth largest category of retailing costs in 1964, accounting for 7 percent of expenses and representing 1.3 percent of sales. Since this average included stores that did not offer stamps, it underestimates the cost to stores that did. Advertising and promotion (excluding trading stamps) accounted for 6 percent of expenses and amounted to 1.1 percent of sales in the same year. Therefore, the combined expense of advertising, promotion, and trading stamps ranked second only to store labor.

When compared on a percentage point basis, advertising and promotion expense, including trading stamps, has increased more rapidly than any other major expense item. A Harvard-Cornell data series of operating results of food chains indicated that between 1955–60, advertising expense, including trading stamps, increased 1.99 percentage points, which is equivalent to about 37 percent of the total percentage point increases in all expenses during the period. Between 1961 and 1964–65, the expense of promotional giveaways rose .24 percentage points—equal to 32.4 percent of the percentage point increase in total expenses for the period.

The Harvard-Cornell series and the Super Market Institute surveys both indicate that occupancy expense expressed as a percent of sales increased about 40 percent between 1954–64. This increase was equivalent to 15–16 percent of the percentage point increase in all expenses. For the most part, the rise in occu-

3. NCFM Technical Study No. 7, p. 167.

pancy expense was caused by a combination of high real estate and construction costs and the opening of large stores with large parking lots. Improved and more attractive facilities also were factors. The opening of large stores has resulted in a declining utilization rate of physical facilities. The Super Market Institute reported that weekly supermarket sales per square foot of selling area were lower during 1961–64 than during 1954–60.

Increases in the number, size, and operation hours of supermarkets have increased physical facility costs. Between 1954 and 1964, the population density per supermarket declined from 11,770 to 6,260. At the same time, average supermarket size increased. Those opened in 1964 averaged 20,000 square feet of store area; those opened in 1954 averaged 15,000.

Increased services offered by food retailers include carryout, check cashing, utility bill payment, and money order service, and services including special equipment such as air conditioning, music, and vending machines. Although their precise individual effects have not been isolated, all these factors have contributed to the gradually rising cost of food retailing since the early 1950's.

Food Manufacturing · Food manufacturers are among the largest users of advertising (Figure 3). In 1961, advertising expenditures by manufacturers of food and kindred products amounted to $1,181 million. Data from the Internal Revenue Service indicate that food manufacturers accounted for 12 percent of all corporation advertising in 1962. However, this fact may significantly underestimate total advertising and promotion expenditures, since the figure apparently includes only direct advertising expenditures.

Advertising expenditures of food maufacturers have increased at a rapid rate. Between 1947–54, they nearly doubled, increasing from $362 million to $713 million. By 1961, the expenditure level was over three times that of 1947. Compared to sales, advertising expenditures of all food and kindred product manufacturers increased from 1.1 to 2.1 percent during the same period (Table 13).

The heaviest users of advertising relative to sales are soft drink, confectionery product, and miscellaneous food product manufacturers. Advertising costs for soft drink and miscellaneous food

FIG. 3. *Total Advertising Expenditures of Selected Industries, 1961.*

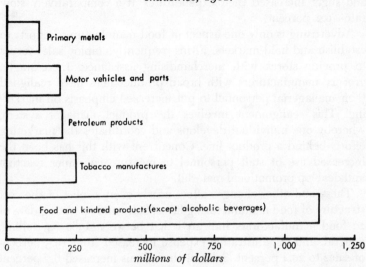

SOURCE: *Statistics of Income, Corporation Income Tax Returns,* U.S. Treasury, Internal Revenue Service, 1961–62.

TABLE 13. *Advertising Expenditures as a Percent of Sales for Manufacturers of Food and Kindred Products, 1947, 1954, and 1961*

Products	1947	1954	1961
Food and kindred products (excluding alcoholic beverages)	1.1	1.8	2.1
Meat products	.3	.5	.5
Dairy products	1.2	1.9	1.6
Canning and preserving products	1.8	3.9	2.5
Grain and cereal products	1.2	2.0	2.9
Bakery products	1.6	2.3	2.8
Sugar	.1	.2	.3
Confectionery products	2.6	2.8	4.2
Soft drinks	3.5	5.0	6.2
Edible oils	1.4	2.3	2.9
Miscellaneous food products	3.3	6.2	8.0

SOURCE: NCFM Technical Study No. 8, pp. 285–6.

products manufacturers increased by 2.7 and 4.7 percent, respectively, between 1947 and 1961. Manufacturers of meat products and sugar increased their expenditures at a comparatively slow rate—0.2 percent.

Advertising is only one aspect of food manufacturers' efforts to establish and hold markets. Firms frequently employ sales forces to provide stores with merchandising assistance. Increasingly, grocery manufacturers with broad product lines have realigned their managerial personnel to put increased emphasis on marketing. This realignment involves the product manager system, whereby one individual develops and coordinates the marketing efforts behind a product line. Concurrent with this has been the increased use of staff personnel to measure consumer reaction and develop promotional material.

These and other changes affect nearly every aspect of the cost structure of food manufacturing firms. Sales and operating data of 22 food manufacturers indicated that between 1960–64, selling, general, and administrative expense increased from 19.5 percent of sales to 20.4 percent. Sales of these firms increased 6.7 percent annually, while selling, general, and administrative expense expanded at an even faster rate —an average of 7.8 percent per year. The NCFM estimates that between 70 and 80 percent of these expenses were for marketing purposes.

TECHNOLOGY AND FACTOR PRODUCTIVITY

Technological developments have increased factor productivity, thereby offsetting some farm-retail margin increases which otherwise would have occurred. In all industries, automation has reduced labor requirements and speeded the production process. Regarding warehousing and delivery, the Commission stated, "Deliveries have been speeded by use of pallets in shipping, clamp trucks, and dataphone systems whereby buyers directly transmit orders to computers located in manufacturers' plants and/or warehouses."[4] Major developments in the dairy industry have included clean-in-place equipment and bulk assembly equipment. The use of continuous dough machines and bulk handling of

4. NCFM Technical Study No. 6.

ingredients have been major baking industry advances.

Although many technological developments have occurred in food processing industries, aggregate measures of their impact on input-output relations are difficult to obtain. The most common indication of changes in productivity is that of output per worker or output per man hour. This measure provides some clue to productivity, although capital usually is substituted for labor, so the increases in output per worker or per man hour are likely to overstate the total changes in input-output relations.

Labor productivity measures in selected food industries are presented in Table 14. Average sales per worker in constant dollars in food retailing increased from $9,373 in 1929 to $44,259 in 1963—more than a 300-percent increase. Value added per production worker in the biscuit, cracker, and cookie industries more than doubled—from $7,061 to $18,842 between 1947–63. Indices of production per man hour in the dairy industries indicate changes from 21 to 47 percent from 1954 to 1964. The increase was 22 percent for all food industries.

Another measure of increased productive efficiency in agricultural marketing is the number of persons served by the food marketing worker. Such data show that the number of persons supported by the marketing worker increased from 32.7 to 36.3 between 1940–63.[5] The increase is not large, but any increase is significant in view of marketing service increases.

SUMMARY AND IMPLICATIONS

Prices of nonfarm inputs in marketing have risen relative to farm prices. Wage rates have shown some of the largest increases, and advertising media prices also have increased substantially.

Additional food processing accounts for additional food marketing costs. Large proportions of our fruits and vegetables now are consumed in processed rather than in fresh forms. Poultry products undergo more processing now than in the 1940's. The livestock and red meat industries probably have shown the fewest increases in processing. The dairy industry has seen more and improved packaging.

5. Trelogan, H. C., and N. Townshend-Zellner, "On Agricultural Marketing Research," *J. Farm. Econ.*, 47:1, Feb. 1965, p. 45.

TABLE 14. *Labor Productivity Measures in
Selected Food Industries, Selected Years, 1929–64*

Item	1929	1947	1948	1954	1960	1963	1964
Sales per worker in grocery stores	$9,373		$22,223	$31,179		$44,259	
Value added per production worker, biscuit, cracker, and cookie industries (dollars)		$7,061				$18,842	
Tons handled per manhour, retail chain warehouses		1.85		2.02	2.11	2.11	2.26
Index of output per manhour, all food industries (1958 = 100)				100	108	118	121
Index of output per manhour, fluid milk industry (1958 = 100)				100	107	125	136
Index of ouptut per manhour, ice cream industry (1958 = 100)				100	104	117	122
Index of output per manhour, all dairy industries less fluid milk (1958 = 100)				100	109	137	147

SOURCE: NCFM Technical Studies No. 3 (p. 258), 6 (p. 116), and 7 (pp. 15 and 229).

Increased emphasis on merchandising (advertising, promotion, and trading stamps) by both retailers and food manufacturers appears to have increased the farm-retail price spread.

Though the structure of the food industry may influence the farm-retail price spread and though structural changes have occurred, the NCFM did not find substantial supporting evidence.

The major moderating force on the widening farm-retail spread has been technology. Productivity indices illustrate large gains in factor productivity. Without these gains, marketing spreads would be much larger.

Several conclusions for marketing policy follow from this evaluation:

1. Performance of the food marketing industry is good in terms of technological development. Furthermore, excessive profits are not widespread nor are they a major problem.

2. More stringent restrictions (anti-monopoly and antimerger) on structural change in the food marketing industries would have had little or no impact on the farm-retail price spread.

3. A study with a different emphasis than that of the NCFM would be necessary to more precisely define and measure those factors that have affected the farm-retail price spread.

Public Policy Toward Mergers in Food Retailing

WILLARD F. MUELLER

Willard F. Mueller is Director of the Bureau of Economics, Federal Trade Commission. In this paper, which appeared in the Agricultural Policy Review, *he discusses the public policy implications of the findings of the National Commission on Food Marketing*

ALTHOUGH MANY Americans speak glibly about the competitive process and the free enterprise system as things to be cherished and maintained at nearly any price, most are silent about what they would do to preserve them.

There are no "natural" forces built into our economic system which guarantee the preservation of competition if business firms are left entirely alone to set their own rules, or worse still, to change them at will. Therefore, we have antitrust laws to establish guidelines to guarantee the maintenance of the competitive process.

The relevant framework for interpreting the legality of mergers is to be found in the Celler-Kefauver Act of 1950 which amended the Clayton Act (1914). This amendment is designed to strike at monopoly in its incipiency, not in its full blown form.

Since the competitive impact of a merger must necessarily be analyzed within its industrial context, especially its effect on market structure, let us review briefly structural developments occurring in food retailing in recent years.

STRUCTURAL CHANGES IN FOOD RETAILING

Prior to World War II, the number of food and grocery stores increased as population expanded. However, in the postwar years, this trend has been reversed—not only has the per capita growth in food retail outlets been brought to a halt, but the actual number of outlets has declined.

This drop in the number of retail outlets can be attributed mainly to a decrease in the number of single store operators, which may have come about partly because of upward migration; i.e., single store operators becoming affiliated with chains. However, this alone does not explain the great shift from single to multiunit grocery store companies, nor is it the cause of the sharp increase in concentration in both local and national markets.

There is no longer any doubt that market concentration in food retailing has reached record levels in many metropolitan areas. Between 1954 and 1963 there was a steady upward trend in local market concentration as sales have become increasingly concentrated among relatively few firms operating a number of stores.

Whereas local metropolitan areas are appropriate for measuring concentration in the sale of grocery products, the level of buyer concentration must be measured in broader geographic areas depending upon the products purchased.

Growing concentration at the national level has resulted both from the increasing share of business done by large retail chain organizations and the increasing affiliation of independent retailers with voluntary and cooperative buying groups. Between 1948 and 1963 the 40 largest corporate chains expanded their share of food store sales by 50 percent, while the 30 largest cooperative and voluntary wholesalers doubled their share.

Another interesting development in the food store sector is the rapid expansion into the other areas of food distribution by the largest chains. Especially important in this category were their sales in supermarkets located within discount houses, sales to independent retailers with whom they had become affiliated, sales to other food wholesalers and retailers, and nonstore food sales.

Concentration in Distribution · Although it is impossible to measure precisely the level of buyer concentration in food distribution, it is clear that it has risen appreciably in recent years. While there were still 218,615 retail grocery store companies in 1963, most grocery store products purchased in essentially national markets were bought by fewer than 100 corporate chains or buying groups. Buyer concentration is very high even for some products sold in essentially national markets: e.g., frozen fruits and vegetables. The level of concentration is even greater for grocery products which are purchased in local or regional markets (e.g., fluid milk).

COMMISSION CONCLUSIONS

All of these developments and the economic factors underlying them led the National Commission on Food Marketing to reach conclusions which have important implications for public policy.

The Commission concluded that "concentration in retail buying and selling seems destined to increase. Rapid growth of local firms and increasing concentration in local markets can be expected to affect national concentration. Most important, the active use of merger by large firms as a means of growth presages increased concentration. The continuing growth of wholesalers and buying organizations shows no tendency to stop and, when considered in conjunction with the growth of retailers, can only result in increased concentration of purchases."

It was further concluded that the increasing concentration of purchasing power restricts alternatives open to suppliers, stimulates compensating concentration on their part and weakens the effectiveness of competition as a self-regulating device throughout the industry. *The principal danger of impairment of competition appears to be merger and acquisition by dominant firms.*

Mergers and Increased Concentration · Mergers have been a major source of increased concentration in the retail distribution of food and grocery products both on a national and a local level. Two time periods of increased merger activity stand out, the 1920's and the post-1948 period. Beginning in 1955, acquisitions among retail grocery organizations increased to between $400 and $500 million a year— 82 percent of them being by the nation's 20 largest chains.

Mergers of large grocery chain organizations clearly have had a major impact on national concentration. An FTC Staff Study shows that practically all of the increase between 1948 and 1963 in the top 20 chains' share of food store sales was the result either directly or indirectly of acquisitions. The report estimates that had these chains made no acquisitions, their share of the U.S. grocery store sales would have increased by less than one percent.

Competitive Significance of Mergers · Mergers may affect competition in various ways. The most obvious are those effects flowing from the merger of direct competitors in the same retail market. The precise competitive impact of such mergers depends on the relative size and financial success of the merging firms, the structure of the market, and the probable future structure of the industry.

Consider the merger in 1960 between Von's Grocery Company and Shopping Bag Stores in Los Angeles. Both companies were viable competitors ranking third and sixth, respectively, in the Los Angeles market. The merger made it the second largest chain in the market.

Concentration in this market was increasing quite apart from this merger, and the future of competition in this market was already in doubt. This, then, raises the question of how the merger act should be applied in this setting. Quite clearly the Los Angeles market was not yet sufficiently concentrated to warrant an inference of monopoly, so the problem facing enforcement agencies and the courts was to decide just where the line should be drawn.

After careful evaluation of the situation, the Supreme Court concluded this merger fell within the incipiency range as defined by the Celler-Kefauver Act. Some economists are very critical of the decision and argue that economic science is not exact enough to tell us the precise point at which a merger crosses the borderline of incipient monopoly. Our competitive system could become irreversibly concentrated while economists continue to debate the issue!

The Von's decision, of course, covers only horizontal mergers in the sales of grocery products. Most mergers in food retailing involve companies operating in different metropolitan areas. These so-called *market extension* mergers may affect competition not only in the sale of grocery products, but in their purchase as well. All such mergers contribute to increased concentration in the purchase of grocery products which grocery manufacturers sell in essentially national markets. On the other hand, some market extension mergers may have only a miniscule effect on concentration.

This then raises the question of where the line should be drawn between legal and illegal market extension mergers.

FTC ENFORCEMENT POLICY

The Federal Trade Commission recently spelled out the criteria which it used in identifying mergers in the food distribution industries which pose a threat to competition. It decided that in the future, it would focus particular attention on mergers of companies with sales in excess of $100 million. Also, future mergers by food retailers or wholesalers with combined annual food store sales in excess of $500 million would raise a sufficient question as to their legal status to warrant attention and consideration.

The FTC concluded that market extension mergers by retailers with combined annual sales of less than $500 million do not pose a serious threat to competition except when they involve some competition overlap. The Commission indicated, however, that it would investigate all but very small mergers by such companies.

The Commission will require every food retailer and wholesaler with annual sales in excess of $100 million to notify the FTC at least 60 days prior to the consummation of any merger, acquisition or consolidation involving any food retailer or wholesaler.

What are the implications of this enforcement policy? (1) It spells out those mergers which, in the Commission's view, pose the most serious threat to competition and those which do not. (2) It identifies particularly mergers (of all types) made by the country's largest food chains and wholesalers. (3) It clarifies the legal status of market extension mergers among retailers with combined sales of less than $500 million.

In conclusion, then, it would seem that current and future enforcement policy toward mergers is designed to channel merger activity away from the very largest food retailers and wholesalers. Not only will this policy contribute to the maintenance of competition in the food retailing industry, particularly in the purchase of grocery products sold in national markets, but its net impact should also be to promote economic efficiency by channeling mergers toward those companies which do not yet enjoy all the economies of large scale procurement and distribution.

PART FOUR Bargaining Power for Farmers and Farm Workers

Agricultural Cooperatives and the Antitrust Laws

Donald F. Turner was Assistant Attorney General of the Antitrust Division in the U.S. Department of Justice when he presented this address to the National Conference of Fruit and Vegetables Bargaining Cooperatives in 1966. He provides an outline of the special status of Cooperatives under the antitrust laws.

THE PROBLEM of how the antitrust laws should deal with farmers wishing to form cooperatives to sell their products is not an easy one. Congressional consideration of this problem led to the enactment of Section 6 of the Clayton Act and of the Capper-Volstead Act, both giving some exemption from the antitrust laws to agricultural cooperatives.

I should first like to discuss the nature and the extent of the exemption given to agricultural cooperatives by Congress. This exemption is embodied in two statutes. Section 6 of the Clayton Act, enacted in 1914, provides that "nothing . . . in the antitrust laws shall . . . forbid the existence and operation of . . . agricultural or horticultural organizations . . . not having capital stock . . . or to forbid or restrain individual members of such organizations from lawfully carrying out the legitimate objects thereof."

As time went on, Congress deemed this exemption too narrow. The Section's limitation to organizations "not having capital stock" and its failure to sanction expressly certain cooperative marketing activities inspired the Capper-Volstead Act of 1922. Section 1 of that Act provides that producers may "act together in associations, cooperative or otherwise, with or without capital stock" for the purpose of "collectively processing . . . , handling and marketing [their] products. . . . Such associations may have marketing agencies in common and . . . may make the necessary contracts and agreements to effect such purposes." Section 2 of the Act provides that the Secretary of Agriculture may restrain any cooperative from monopolizing or restraining trade "to such an extent that the price of any agricultural product is unduly enhanced."

Were I forced to summarize, and thus probably oversimplify, the effect of these and related statutes upon the exemption for agricultural cooperatives, I should say that they have led to the formulation of two general rules. First, farmers and producers may form cooperatives without violating the antitrust laws, but once formed, cooperatives should by and large be treated like other businesses under the antitrust laws. Second, membership in cooperatives must remain voluntary.

The fact that cooperatives, as a general rule, are to be treated like other businesses is shown by the history of the Clayton and Capper-Volstead Acts and by the decisions of the courts interpreting the cooperative exemption. Before the enactment of Clayton Act Section 6, some courts had held that organizations of producers such as farmers that determined the price at which their joint product would be sold were combinations in restraint of trade. Under these decisions, if a group of farmers simply made an agreement to market their wheat together and to set a single price, they automatically violated the antitrust laws. The history of Section 6 shows that that section was inserted in the Clayton Act to bar this type of prosecution by the federal government. The legislative history of the Capper-Volstead Act also shows that the Act was intended to give farmers acting together through agricultural cooperatives the same unified competitive advantage and responsibility available to businessmen acting through corporations. The House Report on the Capper-Volstead Act said: "*Instead of granting a class privilege* [the bill] . . . aims to *equalize* existing privileges by changing the law applicable to ordinary business corporations so that farmers can take advantage of it." (Emphasis added)

Moreover, the courts' decisions show that while farmers cannot be prosecuted for joining together to form cooperatives, these cooperatives will be treated essentially like other businesses. In *United States* v. *Borden Co.*[1] a milk producers' cooperative allegedly conspired with a milk drivers' union and a group of milk distributors in order to fix prices. The Court held that the Sherman Act would forbid such a conspiracy because the agricultural cooperative exemption does not allow agreements in restraint of trade made between cooperatives and non-cooperatives. In *Maryland & Virginia Milk Producers Assn.* v. *U.S.*[2] the Court held that Section 2 of the Sherman Act and Section 7 of the Clayton Act applied to agricultural cooperatives. In particular, the Court held that a cooperative violates the antitrust laws when it engages in predatory conduct, or when it makes an acquisition which may substantially lessen competition. Many lower court decisions reflect the same tendency to view the agricultural cooperative exemption as one designed primarily to allow farmers to form cooperatives but intended to treat cooperatives, once formed, like any other business.

There may be some exceptions to the general rule that cooperatives should be treated like other businesses. First, the very fact that farmers are allowed voluntarily to form a cooperative association suggests that they may lawfully obtain by the cooperative device a degree of market power which individual businessmen could not obtain by a similar combination.

Similarly, the Capper-Volstead Act specifically states that cooperatives may have marketing agencies in common. Presumably, therefore, two or more cooperatives in a particular area would not be precluded from joining together to create a single marketing agency merely by the fact that they had marketed or could market in competition with each other. In contrast, the formation of a common marketing agency by a competing group of, say, steel manufacturers would almost certainly be illegal.

While the cooperative exemptions may indeed permit the acquisition of some degree of market power, it remains at least doubtful—as my predecessor Judge Barnes suggested in an

1. 308 U.S. 188
2. 362 U.S. 458

address twelve years ago—that an agricultural cooperative may obtain a monopoly or near-monopoly of the marketing of any commodity free of Sherman Act prohibitions. Of course, the Capper-Volstead Act itself applies to a cooperative which monopolizes. In Section 2 it provides that if the Secretary of Agriculture, after a hearing, finds that a cooperative association monopolizes or restrains trade "to such an extent that the price of any agricultural product is unduly enhanced thereby," he shall issue an order directing the association to cease its unlawful activities. But it is by no means clear that this remedy is exclusive.

I have been speaking of exceptions to the general rule that a cooperative, once formed, is as subject to antitrust law as are other businesses. It can be argued that agricultural cooperatives are given greater freedom than other businesses by the Capper-Volstead Act provision that cooperatives "may make the necessary contracts and agreements to effect the collective processing, preparing for market, handling and marketing of products." I do not agree. The provision certainly does not mean that cooperatives may engage in any activity, however anticompetitive, so long as they are securing greater profits for their members. I believe this provision simply was intended to make clear that the protection afforded cooperatives is extended to reasonably ancillary contracts or agreements which would otherwise, by narrow construction of the exemption, be held unlawful. I also believe that the statutory reference in Section 6 of the Clayton Act to "legitimate objects" has a similar limited purpose. This view was reflected in *U.S.* v. *King*,[3] decided some 40 years ago. There a cooperative handling a substantial share of the Maine potato crop circulated among members and nonmembers a blacklist that urged a boycott of potato dealers delinquent in payment for their purchases from the cooperative. Despite Section 6's exemption for operations of producer associations, the court sustained an indictment under the Sherman Act, for it did "not think that the coercion of outsiders by secondary boycott . . . can be held to be a lawful carrying out of the legitimate objects of such an association. The Clayton Act means," the court went on, "that organizations such as it describes are not to be broken

3. 229 Fed. 275, 250 Fed. 908.

up and dissolved as illegal nor held to be combinations or conspiracies in restraint of trade but they are not privileged to adopt methods of carrying on their business which are not permitted to other lawful associations." This principle was reaffirmed by the Supreme Court a few years ago in *Maryland & Virginia Milk Producers* v. *U.S.*

This general discussion has specific application to the lawfulness of mergers involving cooperatives. It suggests that while mergers between cooperative and noncooperative organizations are fully subject to the antitrust laws, somewhat different standards may be used in judging mergers between cooperatives. In particular, as a cooperative appears to be entitled to acquire some degree of market power simply by enrolling new members in its organization, it should have the right to acquire this same power through horizontal merger when the merger is identical for all practical purposes to an increase in the size of one of the cooperatives through the voluntary accession of new members. Thus, if at the time a merger between cooperatives is to take place each member of the cooperative is free to withdraw and to be reimbursed the value of his share in the organization, the merger seems equivalent to the voluntary enrollment of new members into the organization and as such no more subject to attack under the antitrust laws than that organization would be if it had enlisted the same members originally.

On the other hand, when cooperatives make other kinds of acquisitions, it seems reasonably clear that the applicable legal standards are substantially those governing mergers generally. This lesson, too, I draw from the *Maryland & Virginia Milk Producers* case, invalidating defendant's acquisition of a significant competing distributor.

I have been discussing the first general rule applicable to the behavior of agricultural cooperatives. A second important rule is that membership in such cooperatives must remain voluntary. This rule has been applied by the courts in cases dealing with the Fishermens Cooperative Marketing Act, an act creating an exemption for fishermen very similar to that created for farmers. In *Hinton* v. *Columbia River Packers*[4] the Court held that a

4. 315 U.S. 143

fishermens' association could not require the canners with whom it dealt to promise to buy fish from association members only—a requirement that would have forced nonmembers to join or lose their source of livelihood. Other cases make clear that the exemption granted fishermen does not allow a cooperative to attempt to force other fishermen to join the association.

To summarize once again my view of the current state of the law: I believe 1) that while farmers may form agricultural cooperatives with comparative immunity and make all agreements reasonably ancillary to their proper business, such cooperatives, with few exceptions, must conform to the same antitrust rules that govern other business; and 2) that membership in cooperatives must be uncoerced.

I should like now to turn to the question of whether or not the current legislative exemption from the antitrust laws for agricultural cooperatives should be expanded. My present conclusion is that a case for expanding the exemption has not been made out.

To the extent that the cooperative exemption permits farmers, by combination, to obtain some degree of market power, the exemption seems to me to be justifiable only by relying upon what has been called a theory of "countervailing" power, namely a claimed need to offset undue bargaining power on one side of the market by a comparable bargaining power on the other. In some, perhaps many, markets for agricultural produce, farmers may face a limited number of buyers who are able to depress the price for farm produce below the price that would obtain under competitive conditions. In the absence of any direct way of dealing with such power on the buying side, permitting combination among farmers on the selling side is a vehicle for avoiding exploitation.

The ability to form cooperatives allows the farmers to overcome the power of the large buyer in two ways. First, to the extent the cooperative gains some control over the supply of a product, it can bargain with the buyer in order to achieve a somewhat higher price than the buyer would have to pay individual farmers selling separately. Second, farmers may form their own cooperative marketing agencies, thus bypassing the powerful marketer who would otherwise be able to achieve an unduly high profit at the expense of the farmer.

It is important to note that this justification for the agricultural cooperative exemption is to allow the farmers to overcome exploitation and earn a reasonably competitive profit. Its purpose is not to allow a monopoly profit.

This also explains why it is important that membership in cooperatives be voluntary, that cooperatives not be permitted to coerce outsiders by shutting off their access to markets. This requirement not only protects the farmers' basic interest in freedom of association, but it also increases the likelihood that cooperatives will be able to earn competitive profits but unable to achieve monopoly profits. When the profit that an individual farmer can make is too low because he is faced with a buyer possessing monopoly power, he will wish to join a cooperative association, for by joining the cooperative he will be able to sell all he produces at a price that is certainly no lower and is probably higher than the one he could obtain on his own. On the other hand, when the price obtained by the cooperative association is greater than the price that would be set through competition, demand will be short of what farmers would wish to produce and sell at such a favorable price. At this point the cooperative must impose some sort of quota system upon its members. Otherwise surpluses will be produced that will lower the market price. At this point an individual farmer may believe with good reason that he can make more money by quitting the cooperative, by producing all he desires and by selling his product at a price just slightly below that charged by the cooperative. The fact that such farmers are free to leave the association will thus tend to drive the price of the product down towards the competitive level.

There are, therefore, good reasons for insisting that membership in a cooperative remain voluntary, and for refusing to let a cooperative coerce outsiders by depriving them of access to markets. The same reasons make it inappropriate to permit the cooperative to become in effect the sole bargaining agent for members and nonmembers by entering into agreements with buyers setting the price those buyers must pay to anyone from whom they buy. Whatever one may say as to whether membership in labor unions should be voluntary, it seems clear to me that the issue of "majority rule" is much different when we consider the marketing of farm produce or any other commodities than when we discuss collective bargaining in labor relations. In labor relations, collective bargaining involves matters vastly more complex than bargaining over the sale of goods. Not only is the collective bargaining agreement complex, but the terms applicable to the various individual workers are inextricably interrelated. For example, it would be literally impossible to have individual independent bargaining with an employer over such matters as seniority. Moreover, to permit the employer to bargain individually with workers would create an attractive avenue for subverting the union by paying individual employees higher wages than those in the union agreement, in hopes that eventually, by destroying the group, the wages can again be lowered. To be sure, it is conceivable that monopolistic buyers could similarly endeavor to subvert a cooperative by bribing members away. But this seems much less likely, to say the least, because a cooperative can quickly re-form and thus deprive the buyer of his expected gains, whereas reconstituting a union is typically a long and painful process.

In explaining my belief that the exemption for cooperatives should not be expanded beyond the dimensions of present law, I have been assuming, as I have said, that the fundamental purpose of permitting cooperatives to obtain some degree of market power is simply to end exploitation and obtain for the farmer fair competitive prices. I suppose it could be argued that an antitrust exemption should be broadened for the conscious purpose of enabling the farmers via the cooperative device to obtain higher than competitive profits and in this way a larger share of the national income. If farmers as a group are not obtaining what might be thought to be a fair share of the national income—an issue on which I render no opinion—surely there are better ways than monopoly for redressing the balance. For monopoly means inefficiency and waste in the allocation of our nation's resources, and we can ill afford any conscious policy of adding to the waste and inefficiency that existing monopoly has produced.

Before concluding, I should note that there is little or no reason to believe that exposure to the antitrust laws has unduly hampered the expansion of the agricultural cooperative movement. The growth of cooperatives during the last 50 years has been remarkable and prodigious. At the turn of the century agricultural cooperatives were of negligible importance to the economy. Yet by 1963 there were more than 8,900 marketing, purchasing and related service cooperatives doing $18.3 billion worth of business. More than 7 million farmers were members. The volume of business done by cooperatives has increased more than 70 percent over the past decade, and in the decade prior to that the volume of business handled by these cooperatives tripled. There is little reason to believe that the antitrust laws will stand in the way of continued desirable expansion and growth.

I do not wish to imply by anything I have said that the present development of agricultural cooperatives has reached the point where monopoly has become a serious problem. There is no evidence I know of suggesting any such dire assessment. There is no reason I know of to depart from our long-standing policy of encouraging cooperative growth. It is clear, however, that agricultural cooperatives are no longer a negligible factor in our nation's economic life. And as cooperatives grow in size and importance, as they assume more and more of the characteristics of large corporate businesses, it becomes even more important that the essentials of our competitive policy be applied to private businesses and to cooperative businesses without discrimination.

Proposed and Existing Organizational
Efforts for Farmers

DON PAARLBERG

*Don Paarlberg is Hillenbrand Professor of Agricultural Economics
at Purdue University. His evaluation of the alternative approaches
by farmers to achieve bargaining power in the market place was
published in the* Agricultural Policy Review *in 1967.*

LABOR HAS bargaining power through its unions and negotiates
wages by collective bargaining. Industry limits output and
thereby attains its price objective. Of the major economic groups,
only farmers passively accept for their products whatever the
market will bring. This is galling and humiliating, especially if
prices are weak. Farmers make economic decisions individually
and face in the market the concentrated economic power of
labor and industry. Farmers have reasoned that if they could
somehow organize and combine as labor does and as they suspect
industry does, they could exercise market power, name the price
for what they sell, and improve their economic position.

A number of efforts have been made to exercise this kind of
market power. Years ago a high price for tobacco was sought by
holding the product off the market; "night riders" burned the
barns of those farmers who refused to cooperate. In the early
1920's, a lawyer named Aaron Sapiro went up and down the
farm country preaching the message of cooperation, greater
bargaining power, and supply control. Innumerable cooperatives
were set up, with ambitious price objectives. Though a few of
these survived, most collapsed. During the 1930's, the Farmers'
Holiday Movement used coercion as a means of supply control
in an unsuccessful effort to force prices up by keeping farm
products from the market.

These efforts failed because farmers, acting privately, were
unwilling or unable to exercise the degree of supply control
necessary to attain their price objectives. To gain really strong

bargaining power, really strong control of supply was essential, and the only way that could be effected, if at all, was with the police power of the state.

Consequently, government programs were adopted for a number of farm commodities, through which farmers could be subjected to a degree of discipline greater than they would impose upon themselves. For three decades after the launching of large-scale government programs, relatively little was heard about the private exercise of farm bargaining power.

Recently renewed interest in private farm bargaining power has become evident for several reasons.

The 90th Congress will have fewer than 50 representatives from farm districts as compared to 250 members 40 years ago. Declining farm population and reapportionment have chipped away at agriculture's political base. If a vocational group is to continue receiving a large share of its income from the federal government, it will have to do so by the exercise of political power or by a good public image. For agriculture, both of these resources are being eroded. Consequently, farmers wish to develop market power of their own, less vulnerable to political fortune. Besides, there is displeasure with the manner in which government programs are operated, with their uneven impact on various commodities, and with the onus of being dependent upon them.

THREAT TO FARMER DECISION-MAKING

We are in the midst of an agricultural revolution which is cumulative and irreversible, and greatly changes farmers' decision-making function. These changes have led to the development of the new and potent idea of splitting up the factors of production and reassembling them in optimum form. The economic efficiency latent in this organizational change is, in certain cases, very great indeed. Managerial ability can be recruited, trained and given responsibility not just for a small unit, but for a large one. Capital can be brought in from the outside in aggregations suited to the new managerial concept. Farms can be consolidated or operated as associated units, making maximum use of new mechanical equipment and new managerial techniques. Farm labor can be hired and given specific, well-defined tasks to perform, as is factory labor. This system is capable of standard-ized quality, close scheduling of output, and considerable gains in overall efficiency.

Who is going to capture control of this new juggernaut? Will it be the processors or the chain stores, integrating toward their source of supply? Will it be those who supply the factors of production such as feed, seeking assured outlets for their wares? Will it be the financial community, through the power latent in the extension of credit? Will it be labor, through control of this strategic service? Or government, as has been the case for a number of commodities? The farmer sees in the new agri-business complex a threat to one of his most precious possessions, his decision-making role, and he is determined to prevent this from happening if he possibly can.

Toward Building Private Market Power · There are several moves farmers are making toward building up private market power so as to retain their long-cherished decision-making role.

First is a move based on the naive notion held by the National Farmers Organization that market power can be achieved simply by forming an association and demanding higher prices. With this assumption, the sole function of price is to determine the real incomes of farmers and consumers. Farmers are considered the more deserving of the two and the price should therefore be high. The wiser heads within the organization know that something positive must be provided to warrant a higher price: better quality, a standardized product, scheduled deliveries or supply control. The NFO has made a maximum and unsuccessful effort to achieve favorable contracts through withholding actions. It must now redefine its goals or gradually fade away.

A second related movement is the much more modest Agricul-tural Marketing Associations of the American Farm Bureau Federation. These associations are intended, at least in their present stage, to give farmers a greater role in negotiating terms of sale for commodities produced and sold under contract. Whether more far-reaching goals would be developed in the event that present objectives were achieved is a matter not now clear. The approach is neither sufficiently promising to farmers nor threatening to processors to generate anything like the interest which has characterized the NFO efforts. Actual results to date have been relatively modest.

Another effort, as yet embryonic, is the proposed adoption of some enabling legislation that would give farm people broad authority to organize, with the help of government, to exercise market power. By vote, farmers could designate an organization as their sole bargaining agent, with which processors would be forced to deal. Farmers would acquire production rights which would be so used as to induce a high price for their product. In short, government would delegate cartel rights to agriculture and would protect these rights. Something like this was proposed in Congress five or six years ago and was defeated. But the idea is by no means dead.

Another effort, a much more modest proposal, was embodied in Senate Bill 109, considered and pigeon-holed by the 89th Congress. This bill was intended to prevent discrimination on the part of the food trade against members of farm bargaining associations. The bill has been resubmitted to the 90th Congress. In support of it are most of the farm organizations—opposed to it are a number of food processors and their trade organizations.

Finally, and perhaps most important, there is renewed interest in farmer cooperatives as a means of increasing farm bargaining power. The record is uneven and gains have been small, but cooperatives are a way of retaining the decision-making function for farm people and providing a limited degree of market power, privately exercised.

SUMMARY

Real gains in market power will be achieved privately by organized effort and will generally be small. The chief reason is that many people are willing to offer their labor and management in agriculture for a relatively low wage. The country has not been willing to limit access to agriculture on any large scale, either publicly or privately. Entry into agriculture is essentially free. Private bargaining groups, if anything, are less capable of restricting entry than is government. It follows that gains from bargaining power will accrue mainly to those few groups and commodities which can restrict entry, and will be modest rather than dramatic.

Second, if higher prices are to be achieved through bargaining power, additional services such as better quality, scheduling of deliveries or standardization will generally have to be provided. Price enhancement is likely to be approximately proportional to the costs of added services supplied, and will represent an earned return rather than a gain achieved by the mere existence of a bargaining organization.

The real issue at stake in the bargaining power controversy is whether the buyers of farm products are to be divested of the initiative and status associated with being price-namers, and whether farmers are to advance from their low status as price-takers. The farm bargaining-power movement, if it were to develop constructively, would mediate this issue by converting both parties into price-negotiators. If this comes about, the contract, negotiated in advance of delivery, would gradually replace the old-style central market system of selling. This change is already under way.

Considerations of equity argue for some equivalence of bargaining power on both sides. Some argue for equating power at a high level, so that industry, labor and agriculture can arbitrate from positions of great strength on approximately even terms. It is this idea that led to our present labor legislation and is behind the proposal for an agricultural equivalent of the Wagner Act.

The rival group favors equating market power at a low level so that farmers can deal with labor and industry on more-or-less even terms. This would require more bargaining power than farmers now have. By this view, monopoly power in industry, labor and agriculture are all bad, whether achieved by government legislation or by the private flexing of muscles.

If bargaining powers were to be equated at a low level, certain policies would be appropriate. In industry: strong enforcement of anti-trust legislation. For labor: enactment of legislation that would curb the abuse of power. In agriculture: the development of bargaining groups that permit farmers to participate in the determination of contract terms.

Thus, many arguments about farm bargaining power in their outward forms are economic, but in their inward forms are largely psychological and political. For this reason, the topic is a difficult one for economists to handle and decisive considerations lie, in large part, outside their discipline.

Bargaining in Agriculture and Industry: Comparisons and Contrasts

VARDEN FULLER

Varden Fuller is Professor of Agricultural Economics at the University of California at Berkeley and Editor of the American Journal of Agricultural Economics. *In the following article from the December 1963 issue of the* Journal of Farm Economics *he contrasts the problems of achieving effective bargaining power in agriculture and industry.*

ACCORDING TO a line of thought that has had considerable persistence but not much popularity, the sellers of labor and the sellers of farm commodities have similarity of problems or even common cause. When the extreme of this idea has been tried in practice—in political alliance or in other mutual assistance attempts—the supposed commonality of interest has proved to be quite illusory. There remains, nevertheless, in both labor and farm circles a thread of belief that collective bargaining is as appropriate for farmers as for labor, and that counterpart approaches could be as effective in agriculture as industry. The validity of this belief is, I assume, the central question at hand.

Comparing farmer with labor union bargaining—as presently practiced in both instances—produces more contrasts than similarities. The market structures in which farm products and labor services are sold have certain similarities. These include homogeneity of undifferentiated products or services and fewness of buyers as against numerousness of sellers. But in bargaining tactics, which now are highly standardized and broadly used by labor and occur variously here and there in farming, the foreground picture is heavily colored by contrasts. Even sharper contrasts appear in the background of legislative protections and restraints and in the organizational structures and postures through which collective bargaining has been sought.

BARGAINING AGENCY AND PROCEDURE

If workers organize but are refused recognition as bargaining agent, they may appeal to the National Labor Relations Board for a representation election. If a majority vote is obtained, the union is certified as bargaining agent. Employers must recognize a certified union and must bargain in good faith with certified and also with voluntarily recognized unions.[1] Many additional provisions which protect the right and process of organization as well as the continued existence of the union and the collective bargaining relation are incorporated in the same laws. These particularly are the Wagner Act of 1935 and the Taft-Hartley Act of 1948. The nearest to a parallel for farmers that I know of is a comparatively weak provision in California law enacted in 1961 which declares: "It is the public policy of the State of California to establish and support the right of any farmer to join voluntarily and belong to cooperative bargaining associations."[2] This provision undertakes only to prohibit various possible types of interference or discrimination that might be practiced by processors or handlers by reason of a producer's membership in or association with bargaining organizations.

A labor union which is certified or voluntarily recognized becomes the exclusive bargaining agent, having both the authority and the responsibility to represent all workers in the bargaining unit. Short of dissolution of the firm or the union, it is a relation that may exist for a reasonable number of years though not necessarily in perpetuity. Minority voters in the original election as well as new employees entering the bargaining unit subsequent to recognition are required by union shop or other provisions of enforceable contract to become and remain members of the union and to pay dues.

Although the original bargaining unit may have been much smaller, the trend of labor union bargaining has been toward

1. This protection is not available to workers employed outside the broadly interpreted interstate commerce clause unless they are situated in one of the few states which have "Little Wagner" laws.

2. Agricultural Code, State of California, 1961, Chapter 4a, Sections 1223–1229.

master or standardized agreements covering large areas or major portions of industries. The national union has become dominant over the local; either with or without formal associations of firms the industry has become dominant over the firm. Bargaining is conducted in an increasingly larger and more centralized arena with the results subject only to minor adaptations in local situations. Within their chosen arenas the parties on each side may elect whether to confront each other on a multi-union, multi-employer, or even multi-industry basis. The range of issues that may be considered is restricted only by general statutory constraints. Under law, the parties must negotiate though they need not accept any particular proposal or even consider a proposal on a matter that is not commonly regarded as a negotiable item.

Whether the confrontation of the parties is restrictedly bilateral or comprehensively multilateral, the pros and cons of a wide range of topics can be argued for and against. Trading and log-rolling can occur. Package proposals are pulled apart and reassembled. Numerous and extended meetings may be required. Although it is not the usual way, either or both parties may conduct part of their negotiation campaign through pubilc propaganda. In any event, persuasiveness on either side lies implicitly beyond recognizing meritorious arguments and in the ultimate possibility of strike or lockout.

Finally, it is to be noted that union collective bargaining agreements increasingly are long term, up to five years or so, but with provision for within-term adjustments on specified provisions.

Contrast this bargaining with that which is characteristic of bargaining on some processed fruits and vegetables in California, which in form and content is perhaps not fully typical of all farmer bargaining but is a pattern of considerable stability and longevity. It begins with a cooperative in which membership is "open door" and voluntary, and which is subjected to and protected by state and federal legislation governing agricultural cooperation. The first step is a contract between the cooperative and each of its members which grants authority to the association to act on the member's behalf in the sale of his crop. With sufficient membership to hope to be impressive, the bargaining cooperative asserts itself to the processors and requests recognition of its right to represent its members in collective bargaining. The processor may recognize or not, as he chooses. If recognition is given, a contract is written which acknowledges the fact of bargaining recognition and specifies whatever nonprice terms are agreed to but leaves the price settlement open for annual determination in accordance with a prescribed procedure. If the processor refuses to recognize the cooperative as bargaining agent, there is little that the would-be bargaining group can do other than to bring pressure by threats or actual attempts to withhold supplies of the commodity in question.

Whether the approach to the processor is the initial one of recognition or a subsequent one of actual bargaining, the association, under constraint of law, has to deal with each processing firm separately. The equivalents of a master agreement are obtained only through standardized proposals and by "most favored nation" types of clauses.

If recognition is given and bargaining commences, the determination of annual price proceeds in approximately this way: A month or so before harvest, the association arranges to meet with each individual processing firm. The purpose of this series of meetings is to discuss the industry situation and outlook. Following these, a unilaterally determined price proposal is made by the farmers' association simultaneously to each processor. In accordance with the provisions of their agreement the processor has a specified time in which to accept or reject. Moreover, the agreement is likely to specify that timely acceptance by a sufficient number of processors will make the offer binding upon all firms with whom the association has bargaining contracts, but such a provision also voids the association's price proposal if the minimum required acceptances are not forthcoming. Thereupon another round of proposal-acceptance or rejection will occur. Ultimately, if the harvest commences without a price determination having been made, it is agreed that a "reasonable" price will be paid and if necessary will be determined in accordance with procedures and concepts contained in the California Agricultural Code, with the possibility of final resort to the courts. But such a last resort is not favorably regarded by either party and is more a spur to settlement than a method.

CAN FARMER BARGAINING BECOME A COUNTERPART
OF LABOR BARGAINING?

The foregoing limited and sketchy comparisons are only a fraction of what might be made but are enough to imply the greater bargaining power of labor. Some of labor's power lies within the structural and internal governmental characteristics of its forms of organization; the remainder lies in the statutes which the labor movement has obtained through militant and aggressive effort. Conceptually, it seems reasonable to say that farmers could obtain a parallel set of legislative protections to collective bargaining and likewise remodel their organizations toward greater effectiveness in bargaining. Can they really do it and are they likely to make the attempt?

First to be considered are some important aspects of market structure, then some of organizational philosophy and political posture.

Disposal of Unmarketed Supply? · If a bargaining organization exists and has any effect, its first and principal interest is higher price. Raising the price of almost any good or service under usual circumstances means less quantity demanded. While labor unions are apparently not interested in minimizing their membership, it is quite clear from their behavior that they are usually willing to sacrifice employment and membership to price. Absorption of any consequent diversion of supply is left to individual initiative and the operation of the labor market. There is no leftover surplus of physical commodity to plague the union bargainers or the industry. In contrast, there is no apparent possibility that surplus tomatoes or peaches would come to be seen as a general social problem as are surplus coal miners. The farmer bargaining association can limit itself to trying to get the best deal it can for the supply available each year but if it attempts to obtain and maintain prices higher than will clear the market, diversion or controlled production is required.

In regard to diversion of present supply and also future supply response, the full range of formidable complications so familiar to agricultural economists is in prospect. In contrast, under labor union bargaining, the potential supply of labor at the contract wage may continuously exceed the volume of employment. Complications similar to those of agriculture would not likely appear in most industries. Excluded automobile workers are not likely to open new automobile plants, nor excluded coal miners new mines. However, under sufficient wage pressure, nonagricultural managements may consider alternatives such as subcontracting, disintegration, or plant relocation. But there are few direct parallels of the opportunity open to canners who, under price pressure, may consider whether to produce a considerable part of their own raw product requirements or to enter into contractual arrangements with growers wherein title to the crop is always held by the processor.

All the possible complications of agricultural supply under vigorous bargaining apply even more intensely if strike is being considered or attempted. If there are supply control measures available to farmers that are the counterparts of or substitutes for the diversion, rationing, and entry control mechanisms of labor unions, they are not apparent to me.

Exclusive Representation and Compulsory Bargaining? · A voluntary membership organization that deals only for its members is never likely to obtain better prices or conditions than will be given to nonmembers. Appeals to solidarity and mutuality are not likely ever to give such a bargaining unit power equal to the compulsory membership-exclusive agency arrangements which labor unions have. But the tradition of farm organizations is voluntary membership. Farmers' associations have aligned themselves with open-shop "right to work" laws. It would be a considerable breach of tradition and precedent for farmers to seek legislative and privately negotiated provisions to compel total adherence of all producers within the relevant group. Nevertheless, farmers presumably could seek federal or state legislation to adapt the referendum arrangements now used in marketing orders to the election and certification of an exclusive bargaining organization, which the minority would be compelled by law to support. Such a proposal could also include a compulsory fair bargaining requirement. Are farmers likely to seek such a legislative package? The antidemocratic implications would be a force against it. There are two other opposing considerations: The farmer typically has less specialized interests than the worker; whereas the worker's occupational interest can be served by one bargaining agent, the farmer may need two, three, or more. Potential conflict of interest could militate against both the formation of a political front necessary for obtaining legislation and the winning of a bargaining election if legislation were obtained. A related factor that historically has been essential to labor union solidarity is a basically antagonistic attitude toward employers as a class. Farmers in some instances in the past may have had the essential posture of solidarity against their buyers, but with the current propensity to regard agriculture as an integrated whole, inclusive of processing and handling, it is doubtful that the essential feeling of militancy and solidarity exists.

Suppose that somehow the concepts and attitudes of farmers were to be revised, conflicts resolved, and unity achieved to a point that permitted effective exercise of legislative pressure to obtain laws that would encourage and enable farmer collective bargaining. What are the chances of success? Not strong, I would say, because the legislative climate presently and for the prospective future is less favorable than that of the 1930's when labor, agriculture, and other major interest groups got their principal dispensations from government. Now, quests by organized labor or organized agriculture to use the power and authority of national or state government toward the achievement of private group objectives are not likely to evoke much support in the legislative bodies.

COLLECTIVE BARGAINING SUCCESS

Having made these comparisons of collective bargaining strength, I don't want to leave the impression that I believe labor union bargaining has been an overwhelming success. Labor unions do have power but they are confronted by power. Whether it is a matter of countervailing or original power and how much of each on either side is an interesting question but one not to be taken on now. Increments of power have been countered in both private and public spheres. Greater industry centralization and cohesion have matched the growth in the power of national unions. The power granted unions in the Wagner Act of 1935 was redressed substantially by the Taft-Hartley Act of 1948. Collective bargaining is all too much like cigarette advertising. Efforts to improve relative position are countered; efforts to withdraw or retrench are unlikely to be reciprocated. So the race becomes more one of trying to stay in position than actually getting ahead.

Labor economists have troubled themselves mightily over union maximization objectives and whether they have been achieved. The results are inconclusive. As is true of any organization in momentum, organizational goals and behavior patterns become a mix of the wants of the individual members and the needs of the organization itself to survive and prosper. Economists are prone to reject survival as the test of success. They would apparently feel more comfortable if evidence could be adduced that the gains of bargaining were at least equal to the costs, but who has the model and the method to do any such thing?

While doubt must prevail as to whether unions have had a substantial influence on real earnings per member, there is less doubt of their influence on reducing hours of work and on the significant enlargement of fringe benefits. Moreover, the union has a significant role in the administration of various fringe benefit plans—health, welfare, vacation, retirement. These peripheral activities probably do more to give the member a sense of identification with his union and a feeling of its power and achievement than does the negotiation of recurrent money wage increases. When one adds such additional matters as protection of seniority rights and protection against arbitrary termination he begins to understand that unions are not really forced to the test of whether they have produced a significant increase in real dollar earnings.

I want to conclude on an affirmative but not unqualifiedly optimistic note regarding the prospects of farmer bargaining. Attaining power in bargaining need not depend entirely on legislative protections; reciprocally, legislation does not guarantee that power will come into being. Nor are measurable tangible gains an absolute essential. Moreover, organizations whose respective interests within their industry are partially in conflict can and do coexist and with a measure of benefit to each other. Although it is difficult in their formative years, organizations in their maturity can contribute to standards of product quality, ethical practices, discipline, morale, communication and information. Many labor unions have emphasized these aspects even as they have bargained aggressively on wages and fringes.

Achievements in the collateral nonprice areas share along with possession of bargaining power in determining the respect and esteem that the organization has in the industry and community. Moreover, labor union experience strongly suggests that bargaining activity and activity in the complex of collateral functions are complementary to each other, in terms both of membership adherence and accomplishments vis-à-vis bargaining adversaries.

Farmer bargaining has tended to center heavily upon price. Farmers' bargaining organizations tend to specialize in this function, on a single commodity basis. It may be difficult or perhaps impossible for farmers' bargaining associations to build a complex of fringe benefits and collateral activities. But given the weaknesses they face in the lack of protective legislation and in the adverse characteristics of their economic environment, it seems to me important that they should make considerable efforts in this direction if they place much value on the bargaining objective. Lacking the power to compel membership, the bargaining association needs all the persuasive inducements it can muster. In the lack of power to compel bargaining, the association needs more than a membership and the desire to bargain. To move effectively into the bargaining orbit, farmers need both a manageable vehicle and a launching pad. A price target alone will likely not suffice for either. A broad foundation of interest and service for members may offer the prospect of assembling the organizational vehicle. A tactical program incorporating substantial elements of *quid pro quo* for bargaining partners may be the means of getting the vehicle off the ground.

Hired Farm Labor

NATIONAL ADVISORY COMMISSION ON
FOOD AND FIBER FOR THE FUTURE

This selection from the 1967 report of the National Advisory Commission on Food and Fiber proposes that labor legislation affecting farm workers be modernized to conform with labor legislation protecting workers in other sectors of the economy.

FARM WAGE WORK is highly seasonal. The annual average number of hired workers in 1965 was about 1.5 million—but over 3 million people did some farmwork for wages in the year (Figure 1). A large proportion of these workers did only a few days of work, mainly in the summer and fall. Over half lived or worked in the South, and most worked on large farms.

FIG. 1. *Hired Farm Workers Employed Monthly*
BY CHIEF ACTIVITY DURING YEAR

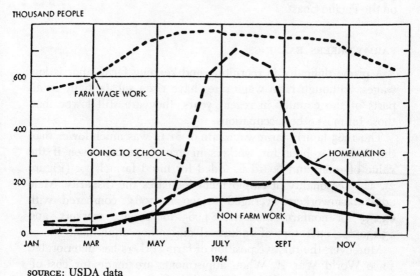

THOUSAND PEOPLE

FARM WAGE WORK

GOING TO SCHOOL

HOMEMAKING

NON FARM WORK

| 600 |
| 400 |
| 200 |
| 0 |

JAN   MAR   MAY   JULY   SEPT   NOV

1964

SOURCE: USDA data

215

In 1964, about 650,000 farmworkers were year-round employees who spent most of their time in farmwork (150 days or more). Another 1.3 million persons worked 25 to 149 days on farms. Some 1.4 million casual workers worked less than 25 days. The short-time workers were mainly housewives, students, and others who were not in the labor force except for very short periods. The casual and seasonal workers were, however, vitally important to farmers, since they worked at those crucial periods of peak labor demand which can mean success or failure for the farm operation.

This seasonality causes problems for the farmer. He must recruit workers for peak seasons, but cannot offer them work during the rest of the year. It also causes problems for the seasonal employee, who must either find other seasonal farmwork or a seasonal off-farm job.

United States Department of Agriculture studies made in 1966 (See Table 1) showed a tightening of the farm labor market— primarily due to the apparently permanent migration of workers from areas offering casual and seasonal farm employment to expanding industrial and commercial areas. A portion of this migration was associated with defense industries, particularly on the Pacific Coast.

FARMWORKERS' EARNINGS

A prime difficulty in recruiting and keeping farm labor is low wages. Although farm wage rates have risen substantially in all parts of the country in recent years, they are still lower than those for most other occupations.

The 1965 hourly farm wage rate of $1.14 was much lower than the $2.61 per hour for workers in manufacturing, even if the value of room and board is added for hired farm labor (Figure 2). The seasonality of employment increases the disparity. Male adult farmworkers averaged $1,300 in 1964, compared with $3,259 for nonfarm laborers, $4,065 for service workers, and $5,130 for operators of industrial and other equipment.

Moreover, the relative position of farmworkers has deteriorated since World War II. When adjustments are made for cost-of-living increases, and fringe benefits, farmworkers fall behind

TABLE 1. *Farm Employment: Average Number of Persons Employed and Indexes, U.S., 1949–64* [1]

Year	Total employment		Family workers [2]		Hired workers [3]	
	Average number persons (thousands)	Index, 1910–14 = 100	Average number persons (thousands)	Index, 1910–11 = 100	Average number persons (thousands)	Index, 1910–13 = 100
1949	9,964	73	7,712	76	2,252	66
1950	9,926	73	7,597	75	2,329	69
1951	9,546	70	7,310	72	2,236	66
1952	9,149	67	7,005	69	2,144	63
1953	8,864	65	6,775	67	2,089	61
1954	8,651	64	6,570	65	2,081	61
1955	8,379	62	6,345	62	2,034	60
1956	7,853	58	5,899	58	1,954	57
1957	7,600	56	5,660	56	1,940	57
1958	7,503	55	5,521	54	1,982	58
1959	7,342	54	5,390	53	1,952	57
1960	7,057	52	5,172	51	1,885	55
1961	6,919	51	5,029	49	1,890	56
1962	6,700	49	4,873	48	1,827	54
1963	6,518	48	4,738	47	1,780	52
1964	6,110	45	4,506	44	1,604	47

1. Average number of persons employed during 1 survey week each month. Survey weeks selected are the latest week that excludes the last day of the month.

2. Includes farm operators doing 1 or more hours of farmwork and members of their families working 15 hours or more during the survey week without cash wages.

3. Includes all persons doing farmwork during the survey week for pay.

SOURCE: USDA data. Data for 1910–48 in "Agricultural Statistics," 1962, table 648.

wageworkers in other industries in all major regions of the country. Even in California, where the highest average farm wages are paid, the gap between farm and nonfarm wages has widened in the last 10 years. . . .

COMPOSITION AND LOCATION OF HIRED FARM LABOR FORCE

About 27 percent of the people in hired farm households are nonwhite, compared with only 12 percent of the general population. While Japanese, Filipinos, American-Indians and Mexican-

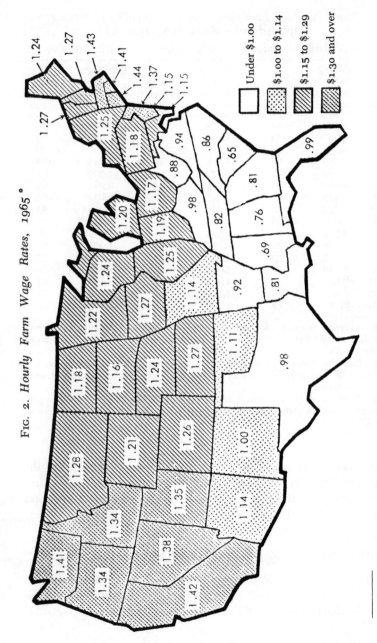

Fig. 2. Hourly Farm Wage Rates, 1965 *

Under $1.00

$1.00 to $1.14

$1.15 to $1.29

$1.30 and over

* For workers paid per hour without board or room. USDA data.

Americans are included, most of the nonwhites are Negroes.

Hired farmworkers are concentrated on a small proportion of the farms in the United States, and in certain types of farming—though the hiring farms are located throughout the country (Table 2). In 1964, more than half of the hired workers lived and worked in the South. About one-tenth lived in the northeastern States; the remainder were about equally located in the North Central and Western States. Three states—California, Texas, and Florida—accounted for about one-third of the total hired farm labor bill in 1964.

Only about 300,000 farms in the United States use one or more regular hired workers. These workers (around 700,000 in 1959) were hired most extensively in the Atlantic and Gulf Coast States, parts of the North Central Region, and California. Seasonal workers are somewhat more concentrated.

Livestock and dairy farms usually have a high proportion of regular workers. Tobacco and cotton farms, on the other hand, rely heavily on seasonal workers. Specialty-product farms were about the only users of the 36,000 foreign workers authorized by the Department of Labor in 1965. These farms will probably need to depend more on domestic seasonal workers in the forth-

TABLE 2. *Farm Employment: Type of Worker and Region in 1965, and Percentage Change, 1950–1965*

Region	1965			Percentage change, 1950–1965		
	Total	Family [1]	Hired	Total	Family [1]	Hired
	Thousands	Thousands	Thousands	Percent	Percent	Percent
Northeast	457	328	129	−51	−49	−56
Lake States	630	545	85	−36	−35	−41
Corn Belt	1,025	884	141	−40	−38	−46
Northern Plains	411	351	60	−39	−38	−43
Appalachian States	941	710	231	−44	−48	−26
Southeast	504	320	184	−49	−58	−19
Delta States	453	281	172	−56	−63	−34
Southern Plains	433	299	134	−48	−50	−44
Mountain	273	175	98	−35	−34	−35
Pacific	483	235	248	−28	−32	−25
U.S.	5,610	4,128	1,482	−43	−46	−36

[1] Family workers include operators and unpaid family workers.

coming years.

In 1964, nearly two-thirds of the hired farmworking force lived off farms at the end of the year (although some of them lived on farms at some time during the year). This contrasts with the situation in 1948 when approximately two-thirds lived on farms most of the year. Increasingly, farmworkers may commute from nonfarm homes; they may work on farms during the week and return home on weekends; or, they may work on farms during peak periods and turn to nonfarm work or drop out of the labor force for the rest of the year.

Thus, as hired farmworkers are increasingly drawn from nonfarm sources, their welfare is no longer solely a problem of farm areas.

FOREIGN LABOR FOR U.S. FARMS

Foreign labor has been used for many years to meet temporary labor shortages on U.S. farms. These workers were recruited primarily from Mexico, Canada, and the West Indies. The number of foreign nationals admitted to the U.S. for foreign jobs reached a peak of more than 400,000 per year during the late 1950's.

After that time the use of foreign labor declined, as a result of U.S. farm mechanization and particularly the mechanization of the cotton harvest. By 1964, the number of foreign workers was down to 200,000. These workers were employed on only 1 percent of U.S. farms, but were heavily relied on in such states as California, Texas, Florida, and Michigan.

In recent years, employment of foreign workers on U.S. farms has come under increasing criticism. Charges have been made that their employment restricts the job opportunities of domestic farmworkers, and eliminates the normal competitive pressures to improve wages and working conditions in agriculture.

As a result, Public Law 78—the "bracero program"—was allowed to expire at the end of 1964.

The bracero program was first enacted by Congress in 1951 as a temporary program to provide farmworkers during the Korean war labor shortage. Under this program, Mexican agricultural workers were allowed to work on U.S. farms during the seasons of peak labor needs, then returned to their homes. The program was renewed on an annual basis until 1964.

Foreign workers can still be admitted under the Immigration and Nationality Act, but only under stringent regulations issued by the Secretary of Labor. Prospective employers of foreign workers must offer domestic workers specific minimum wage rates (depending on the wage level prevailing in the given State), offer transportation costs, and provide family housing where feasible and necessary. Only after such incentives have failed can foreign workers be imported.

As a result of the termination of the bracero program and of Department of Labor regulations, the number of foreign workers admitted to the U.S. dropped from 200,000 in 1964 to less than 36,000 in 1965.

Foreign workers in 1965 harvested citrus fruit and sugarcane in Florida; tomatoes, strawberries and asparagus in California; and apples, shade tobacco, and potatoes in several Northeastern States. Foreign workers were eliminated from the cotton and sugarbeet fields and from the melon harvest.

The result seems to have been 1) a somewhat smaller available labor force for cultivating and harvesting specialty crops; 2) somewhat higher wages for domestic farm workers; 3) higher production costs for the affected crops; and 4) increased pressure to mechanize the operations formerly done by human labor.

Not all of the braceros were replaced, man-for-man, in the fields. In California, for instance, the domestic farm labor force in 1966 was up only 11,000 over 1964—when more than 60,000 braceros were also at work.

Termination of the bracero program did clearly increase farm wage rates. For instance, the California hourly farm wage rate climbed 22 cents, going from $1.36 in October 1964, to $1.58 in October, 1966.

The higher labor costs and somewhat smaller plantings in anticipation of labor difficulties were both reflected in higher prices for specialty crops.

The already rapid trend toward mechanization also received another push. The most dramatic instance involved processing tomatoes. Only about 3 percent of U.S. processing tomatoes were picked by machine in 1964, but by 1966 the figure has soared to over 50 percent. Mechanical harvesters are now well along in development for most crops, with the notable exception of strawberries.

THE FUTURE

The supply of migratory labor for agriculture will decline in the future and more of the part-time agricultural labor will have to come from local sources. Difficulties in recruiting workers, however, are not due mainly to a shortage of people to do the nation's farmwork, in fact, population increases and technological advances actually provide a manpower surplus in many rural areas.

The old relationship between farm employers and employees is changing rapidly. Traditionally, the less desirable farm jobs have been filled by workers with few job alternatives. But, today, a growing number of farmworkers can choose between the wages and working conditions of both farm and nonfarm jobs. This trend will continue and farmers must compete more and more directly with nonfarm employers. And, since the heavy seasonal need for farmworkers often exceeds the local labor supply, farmers must recruit workers who are not normally in the farm labor force.

Farmers are at a disadvantage in competing for these workers. Farmwork is seasonal, usually with little or no security. Wages are generally low—and the annual earnings relatively even lower because of the seasonality (Figure 3). Working conditions are often poor and the workers' status tends to be low. Most farmers have not developed the employer skills to be effective recruiters and managers.

Improved mechanisms for recruiting farm labor and moving it where it is needed, providing adequate housing and facilities, improving wages, and developing labor management relationships will be more important to tomorrow's farmer, even though the total need for farm labor continues to decline.

EQUAL PROTECTION FOR RURAL WORKERS

There seems to be no justification for treating farm labor differently than other workers in the labor force. Therefore, the

FIG. 3. *Median Money Income in 1964*
for Males, by Occupation

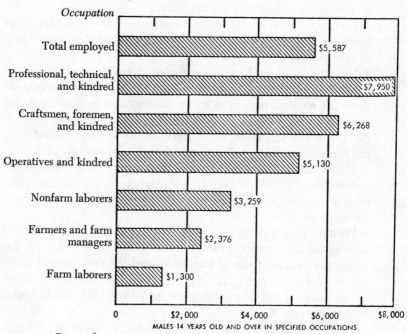

Occupation

Total employed — $5,587

Professional, technical, and kindred — $7,950

Craftsmen, foremen, and kindred — $6,268

Operatives and kindred — $5,130

Nonfarm laborers — $3,259

Farmers and farm managers — $2,376

Farm laborers — $1,300

0   $2,000 $4,000 $6,000 $8,000

MALES 14 YEARS OLD AND OVER IN SPECIFIED OCCUPATIONS

SOURCE: Census data

Commission recommends that farmworkers should not, by Federal or State exemptions, be denied the benefits of policies and standards that are deemed to be in the interest of other wage earners.

Rural workers should have protection equal to that of urban workers in such important areas as workmen's and unemployment compensation, social security, collective bargaining, and minimum wages.

Where the detail of existing law and regulation cannot sensibly be applied to rural or farm workers by simple extension or amendment, new enactments should be written to achieve the intent of commensurate regional and rural opportunity.

The Commission supports the extension of workmen's compensation coverage for persons employed in agriculture and agriculture-related industries. Special Federal legislation should be provided to meet the special interstate needs of migratory farmworkers, should it prove necessary.

Farming is one of the most hazardous of our industries, yet farm workers have not had the protection afforded other workers in case of injury.

No farm workers have been included under minimum wage legislation until very recently—and only about 30 percent of them are covered now by a lower minimum wage than exists for urban workers. Indeed, there is a real danger that simply extending the minimum wage to all agricultural workers would only price many of them out of agriculture—and out of jobs.

The Commission recommends that agricultural workers be covered under minimum wage legislation, while at the same time a positive program is pursued to offset the adverse effects on employment.

Without such a program, the wide variation in farm wage rates throughout the country, the fact that these wage rates are far below the existing Federal minimum, and the ever-present alternative of sharecropping all stand as important barriers to effectively working out a minimum wage policy that would really help farmworkers.

The Commission recommends that hired farmworkers be permitted to report as self-employment income, income from hired labor activities in situations in which the employer is not required to make a Social Security contribution.

However, we support extended coverage of hired farmworkers under the Social Security System in a manner similar to the coverage of industrial employees.

The Commission recommends that lower income limits to Social Security coverage for self-employed farmers be removed and that the income definition be expanded to include the commercial value of farm production, whether sold or not, for such farmers.

Rural workers must also have the same rights to bargain collectively for wages as urban workers. The Commission recommends that farmworkers be included under the provisions of the

National Labor Relations Act, to the extent feasible and wherever necessary to achieve equivalence of personal and social protection for the rural work force.

The Commission recommends more detailed statistical and related information on agricultural labor should be made available so that responsible decisions can be reached by growers, workers and policy makers.

These data can be had without setting up new agencies and new methods of collection. Increases in the proper budgets specifically for this detailed information and for the proper series of data should be undertaken immediately.

Part Five   Overcoming Rural Poverty

Rural Poverty

W. KEITH BRYANT

W. Keith Bryant is an Associate Professor in the Department of Agricultural Economics at the University of Minnesota. In 1966–67 he served as a staff economist with the President's National Advisory Commission on Rural Poverty. This article is from the February 1968 issue of Minnesota Farm Business Notes.

The People Left Behind, the report of the National Advisory Commission on Rural Poverty, was released by President Johnson in December 1967. It contains the findings and recommendations of a year's hearings, study, and debate by the Commission.

President Johnson's charge to the Commission was:

• to study the current economic and social situation and trends in American rural life.

• to evaluate the programs and policies affecting the welfare of rural people and communities, and

• to recommend action by governments and private enterprise to increase opportunities for rural people and communities to share in America's abundance.

The Commission's charge involved more than farms and farm people. Farm people made up only 24.5 percent of the total rural population in March 1965. Hence, the Commission had to concern itself with the conditions of the 55.3 million Americans who in 1965 lived in open country, villages, and small towns.

HOW MANY ARE POOR?

The number and characteristics of the poor depend on the definition of poverty. And, of course, poverty is a relative concept. The Commission was charged with studying the poverty of rural Americans in the 1960's. So the definition had to be appropriate to the United States in the 1960's and relative to its present abundance.

The poverty definitions used by the Commission were adapted from those of the Social Security Administration and were based on the income needed by individuals and families of various sizes to afford a low cost diet (developed by USDA) and other necessities of life. According to these definitions, the average nonfarm family of four required approximately $3,100 per year in 1965 to be "out of poverty"; smaller families required less and larger families more. The average *farm* family of four required about $2,200 per year. Individuals and families with incomes below the "poverty line" for their particular size and type of family were considered to be poverty stricken.

Table 1 shows a breakdown of the population and the poor by residence as of March 1965. Of the 55.3 million rural Americans in 1965, 13.8 million or 25 percent were poor. Relatively speaking, poverty was more widespread in rural than urban America. While one rural person in four was poor, one person in eight who lived in metropolitan areas was poor, and only one suburbanite in 15 was poor. Furthermore, while nearly 30 percent of our total population was rural in 1965, more than 40 percent of all poor people were rural.

TABLE 1. *Persons in Poverty, by Rural and Urban Residence, March 1965*

Residence	All persons		Poor persons		
	Number (millions)	Percent distribution	Number (millions)	Percent distribution	Percent poor
U.S.	189.9	100.0	33.7	100.0	17.7
Total rural	55.3	29.1	13.8	40.9	25.0
Farm	13.3	7.0	3.9	11.6	29.3
Nonfarm	42.0	22.1	9.9	29.4	23.6
Total urban	134.6	70.9	19.9	59.1	14.8
Small cities	27.1	14.3	6.4	19.0	23.6
Metropolitan areas	107.5	56.6	13.5	40.1	12.6
Central cities	58.6	30.8	10.2	30.3	17.4
Suburbs	48.9	25.8	3.3	9.8	6.7

source: *The People Left Behind,* Report of the National Advisory Commission on Rural Poverty, Sept. 1967, Washington, D.C.

Popular views to the contrary, most of the rural poor do not live on farms. Indeed, only about 28 percent of them live on farms: the majority live in villages, small towns, and the open country.

WHO ARE THE POOR?

Given the current emphasis on civil rights and their relationship to poverty, one might think that most of the poor are Negro Americans, Indian Americans, or Mexican Americans. Such is not the case. Of the approximately 34 million Americans who were poor in 1965, about 31 percent were nonwhite. Furthermore, about 3 million of the approximately 14 million rural poor were nonwhite. However, three out of five rural nonwhite families were poor. Some 90 percent of these families live in the poorest counties in America—in the South. The poor rural white population is scattered across the country.

Table 2 shows the incidence of poverty by selected characteristics. Though the information is relative to all families, it also is representative of rural families. The poverty picture that emerges from Table 2 is multi-faceted. A family is more likely to be poor if:

1. its head is very young or elderly,
2. its head is a female,
3. its head is not in the labor force or is unemployed,
4. it is a large family,
5. it is nonwhite,
6. the head is employed as a farmer or laborer.

Clearly, if a family has all or more than one of these characteristics, it is even more likely to be poor.

SOCIAL CONDITIONS IN RURAL AMERICA

As part of its study of conditions in rural America, the Commission considered the education, health, and housing of rural people. In general, rural people are less well educated and housed and are not as healthy in certain important respects as urban people. Also, the manpower and facilities for providing health and education services are more inadequate in rural than in urban America.

TABLE 2. *Selected Characteristics of Families and Families in Poverty, 1964 (in thousands)*

Characteristics	White Total number	White In poverty Number	White In poverty Percent	Nonwhite Total number	Nonwhite In poverty Number	Nonwhite In poverty Percent
All families:	43,081	4,956	11.5	4,754	1,876	39.1
Farm	2,815	676	23.2	283	208	73.5
Nonfarm	40,266	4,280	10.6	4,471	1,668	37.0
Age of head:						
14–24 years	2,609	416	16.0	322	152	48.1
25–64 years	34,284	3,313	9.3	3,892	1,458	37.5
65 years and over	6,188	1,227	19.9	540	266	47.5
Type of family:						
Male head	39,200	3,831	9.8	3,629	1,169	32.0
Female head	3,881	1,125	29.0	1,125	707	62.7
Size of family:						
2 persons	14,316	1,840	12.9	1,397	374	26.6
3–5 persons	23,217	2,071	8.9	2,189	745	34.0
6 or more persons	5,548	1,045	18.8	1,168	747	63.9
Employment status of head in 1965:						
Not in labor force	7,721	2,238	28.9	1,029	648	64.4
Employed	34,371	2,530	7.3	3,503	1,103	31.1
Unemployed	989	188	19.2	222	125	53.4
Occupation of employed head:						
Professional and technical	4,588	95	2.1	235	12	4.9
Managers, officials, and proprietors	5,799	315	5.5	138	31	21.1
Clerical and sales	4,878	188	3.8	240	27	10.8
Craftsmen and foremen	6,865	298	4.3	368	75	19.8
Operatives	6,523	535	8.1	920	231	26.1
Service workers	2,088	217	10.4	765	244	37.6
Laborers (except mine)	1,840	396	21.4	734	350	46.0
Farmers and farm managers	1,790	486	26.3	103	83	78.5
Region:						
Northeast	11,067	923	8.2	846	182	21.3
North-Central	12,531	1,317	10.5	932	261	28.7
South	12,151	1,990	16.3	2,350	1,299	53.8
West	7,332	726	10.0	626	134	21.9

SOURCE: Mollie Orshansky, "More About the Poor in 1964," *Social Security Bulletin,* Vol. 29, No. 5, May 1966, Table 2, pp. 6–7.

Health Conditions and Facilities. Rural people "have higher rates of injuries, more days per year of restricted activity, and lose more days from work per year due to illness and injury than their urban counterparts." Chronic health conditions restricted the major activity—working, keeping house, going to school, or playing—of 12.3 percent of all rural farm people, 9.9 percent of all rural nonfarm people, and 7.9 percent of all urban people during the period July 1963-June 1964. These percentages were higher for elderly than for young people and higher for the poor than for the rich. In 1963 rural people accounted for three out of every five deaths due to accidents.

Partly because of their lower income and partly because of fewer health facilities and manpower, rural people do not use doctors, dentists, and hospitals as much as urban people. "Rural residents, especially children, are less likely to have used the services of a physician during the year than urban people. And relatively more rural residents than urban residents have never seen a physician." Similar statements applied to use of dental services.

That health manpower is inadequate in rural America is widely known. Some facts highlight the urban-rural differences. While "about 30 percent of our population lives in rural areas, only 12 percent of our physicians, 18 percent of our nurses, 14 percent of our pharmacists, 8 percent of our pediatricians, and less than 4 percent of our psychiatrists are located in rural areas." There were 69 dentists per 100,000 people in large metropolitan areas in 1962 but only 27 per 100,000 people in isolated rural areas.

Education Conditions. What constitutes a good education is a hotly debated issue today. But almost everyone would agree that increased schooling leads to higher incomes, that school dropouts are more likely to be unemployed and more likely to have lower incomes than those who graduate, and that certified teachers probably are better teachers than the uncertified. The Commission found large urban-rural differences in these and other rough indicators of education and educational quality. For instance, in 1960:

The median urban adult had completed 11.1 years of school while medians for rural nonfarm and rural farm adults were 9.5

and 8.8 years, respectively;

Twenty-one percent of urban youths age 14–24 years dropped out of school compared to 28 percent of rural nonfarm and 23 percent of rural farm youths of the same age;

Nearly 50 percent of urban youths who had graduated from high school in 1959 attended college, while only about 33 percent of similar rural youths attended college;

Of the 8- to 17-year-old white urban males who were enrolled in school, 7 percent were retarded one grade and 2.3 percent were retarded two or more grades; the percentages for white rural nonfarm males of the same age were 10.2 and 6.3. For white rural farm males of the same age the percentages were 8.3 and 4.9;

The percentage of all rural teachers not properly certified was about twice as high as for urban teachers.

Housing Conditions. As with health and education, housing conditions in rural areas are not as good as in urban areas. According to the 1960 Census of Housing, 27 percent of occupied rural housing is substandard—deteriorating or dilapidated—compared with 14 percent of urban housing. Of the 9.2 million substandard occupied housing units in the nation, 42.4 percent were located in rural areas.

The housing of migratory farmworkers continued to be deplorable despite the fact that 28 states now have legislation specifying minimum housing and sanitary standards for the housing of these people. And "of the 76,000 houses on Indian reservations and trust lands, at least three-quarters are below the minimum standards of decency."

ECONOMIC CONDITIONS IN RURAL AMERICA

The Commission found that our nation's economic growth and technical change have affected many of our communities—rural and urban—in perverse ways.

Economic growth and technical change have increased labor productivity faster than output in industries typically found in rural areas—agriculture, forestry, fisheries, and mining, for instance. Labor productivity has increased less rapidly than output in industries typically found in urban areas—services and some manufacturing, for instance. And too few of the industries attracted to rural areas—textiles, apparel, food and kindred products, wood products, furniture, and miscellaneous manufacturing—have rapidly growing manpower needs.

Furthermore, "developments in transportation and communications systems along with the expanded network of roads and highways have confronted many villages with competition from large towns and cities. The result has been extension of the trade areas of the larger towns and cities into areas once served by villages. The same developments have made it possible for rural people to commute farther distances to jobs in cities and towns."

The results have been multi-faceted and severe. Many rural areas have been and still are suffering from declining employment opportunities, out-migration, lowered tax bases, meager local government revenues and hence inadequate or absent school, health, police, fire, road, library, water and sewer, and legal facilities and services. The results of these inadequacies are reflected in the social conditions described above. They also make rural areas less attractive to expanding and relocating industries, so the likelihood of reversing the downward trends in employment and population is lessened. The most severely affected areas are poverty-stricken. These are concentrated in the Southeast, the Ozarks, and Appalachia, but many are located in upper New England, the upper Great Lakes, and in the Southwest.

THE RECOMMENDATIONS

The Commission concluded that events have outrun the capabilities of many individuals and communities: that the rural poor—people and communities alike—do not have "the bootstraps" by which they might pull themselves out of poverty. Through its recommendations, the Commission would provide the aid—the bootstraps—for people and communities who are able to help themselves *and* would alleviate the poverty of those who by reason of age, disability, etc., cannot help themselves. A summary of some of the Commission's recommendations follows.

1. *Guaranteed Employment.* The spirit of the Employment Act

of 1946 should be fulfilled; i.e., government should provide employment for all those willing and able to work who are not provided employment by private enterprise.

2. *Manpower.* The Employment Service and Unemployment Compensation systems should be separated so that the Employment Service can concentrate on serving the employer and the person looking for work. A computerized nationwide service for matching workers and jobs should be established as an integral part of the U.S. Employment Service. Existing manpower development, training, and retraining programs should be organized as a single comprehensive job training program. A relocation program with training and relocation assistance should be established for disadvantaged workers who cannot find work where they live but for whom employment opportunities exist elsewhere.

3. *Education.* Every child age 3 should be afforded the opportunity to participate in a good preschool program. Every elementary school system should have continuing access to specialists in the early education of socially and economically disadvantaged children. An educational extension service should be created linking national and regional education laboratories and the universities with every school system. Federal funds should be appropriated to make rural teachers' salaries competitive with the salaries in good urban schools.

4. *Health and Family Planning.* Professional and subprofessional rural health manpower should be expanded and community health centers should be established to focus on the needs of rural people. Family planning programs should be expanded so that the rural poor may have equal access to the facilities, services, and information they need to plan the number and spacing of the children they desire.

5. *Public Assistance Programs.* City and state residence requirements as eligibility criteria for public assistance payments should be abolished. The federal government should provide funds to the states sufficient to cover payments required to meet nationally set minimum needs standards. Public assistance recipients should be permitted to earn a specified amount without a reduction in benefits and thereafter benefits should be reduced by less than a dollar for every additional dollar earned. This

setup would provide work incentives that present programs do not.

6. *Housing.* Funds for rent supplements should be greatly increased to provide rental housing for the rural poor. County-wide housing authorities should be established to administer programs of public housing in rural areas.

7. *Area Development.* Multicounty districts that cut across urban-rural lines should be created to plan and coordinate programs of area development cooperatively. Federal grants, loans, and industry subsidies should be made to finance public facilities and services and to induce industrial development.

8. *Agriculture.* Public programs to enlarge small farm operations and to retire submarginal land from commercial production should be undertaken.

9. *Government.* Involvement and participation of the poor in the planning and operation of poverty programs should be encouraged.

Six Reasons for Action on Rural Poverty Now

NATIONAL ADVISORY COMMISSION
ON RURAL POVERTY

The National Advisory Commission on Rural Poverty was a group of twenty-five prominent citizens appointed by President Johnson to study and recommend actions to eliminate rural poverty. In this selection from its 1967 report, The People Left Behind, *the Commission argues for swift action to meet the needs of the rural poor and the communities in which they live.*

THAT 14 MILLION rural Americans have been left behind, consigned to poverty and destitution, should be reason enough for action. Still, there are those who will say, "Any American who is poor has only himself to blame." The findings of this Commission are impressive proof to the contrary. On the basis of these findings, the Commission offers the following six reasons which justify prompt and effective action against rural poverty.

First, simple justice demands that we take action now. It is imperative that the United States provide rural poor people with the same opportunities to share in the fruits of our social and economic progress that all other citizens enjoy. Today's rural poor have been left behind in the wake of basic changes in the fabric of rural life. Many are refugees from an agricultural revolution. Others are refugees from similar revolutions in mining and other natural-resource-based industries. Cut off from opportunities to develop and prosper in rural areas, they are ill-equipped to help themselves. They, and the communities in which they live, are doomed to permanent and increasingly severe poverty unless they get help. Justice demands that they not be isolated from the rest of society.

Moreover, rural people have suffered severely because of discrimination. The incidence of poverty is especially heavy among Negroes, Mexican Americans, and Indian Americans living in rural areas. A much higher percentage of these minorities than of the rural white is poor. Unless the barriers of economic, social, and racial discrimination are removed, many of them will never have a chance to work their way out of poverty.

Second, we must act now because the rural poor, in their desire for the same goods and services enjoyed by most urban people, continue to pile up in the central cities of America. Yet, for many migrants who lack the training and skills for employment in the cities, the move is like jumping from the frying pan into the fire. The result is frustration, despondency, and despair.

The blight in our central cities, as well as the continued blight in rural America, is a national disgrace. The problems of rural America and central city America are closely linked through migration. A high proportion of the residents of our cities formerly lived in rural areas. Many more are one or two generations removed from a rural parentage.

The senseless piling up of refugees from rural America in our central cities provides no solution to the problems of rural areas or of the cities.

Third, we must act because our antipoverty programs have bypassed the rural poor. Rural poverty is not as apparent as urban poverty. The rural poor, especially the white rural poor, are not well organized, and have few spokesmen for bringing the nation's attention to their problems. The urban poor are more concentrated, organized, and vocal in their call for help, and they receive more help than the rural poor. Rural poor people have been shortchanged in public programs designed to improve transportation, housing, education, health services, area development, and income maintenance.

Even though living conditions in central city America are intolerable, the continuing stream of rural migrants to our central cities strongly suggests that conditions there are better than in our blighted rural areas.

This Commission questions the wisdom of massive public efforts to improve the lot of the poor in our central cities without comparable efforts to meet the needs of the poor in rural America. There is danger that programs limited to the needs of our central cities will be self-defeating. If economic and social conditions are greatly improved in our central cities without comparable improvement in rural areas, additional incentives will be created for migration to the cities. In the end, therefore, the special housing, education, employment, and other special programs for the central cities may lead to increased migration, thereby complicating the very problems we are trying to solve.

Even more important is the fact that there is a growing restlessness in rural America. Many people whose families have been deprived for generations are deeply resentful that little is being done to meet their needs. National action which in effect rewards the violence in the central cities is not unnoticed in rural America. Through such action, the nation is telling rural poor people that if they want effective programs, they must find more violent ways of making their demands known. This is a tragic message and it could have tragic consequences. The problems of poverty in both rural and urban America are so serious and so interrelated that we cannot ignore one group while helping the other.

Fourth, we must act now because our rural communities do not share the benefits of much of our nation's economic growth and technical change, and conditions in these communities are destined to become much worse unless basic changes are made.

The early rural community was largely self-sufficient. It performed the services needed by farmers and other rural people. But now most of these services are performed in small to medium-sized cities to which rural areas are linked by an increasing number of channels. Today the areas of an effective community is approximately 100 times that of the effective community of the early 1900's.

Many small communities have been unable to adjust and keep pace with the changing economic and social fabric of the more prosperous ones. Accordingly, many rural communities formerly providing service functions for rural families now find their economic base eroded away. They, and the people within them, are trapped in poverty.

Numerous rural centers have lost so much population they have become ghost towns and resemble abandoned gold-mining villages. Their economic and social facilities are not meeting the needs of the people in the communities they serve. Nor can they without help. Poverty in these communities promises to be self-perpetuating unless there are effective programs to reach and assist the people who live there.

The changes in the social and economic fabric of rural America are irreversible. Indeed, it is unthinkable that we should try to reverse them. The capacity of this nation to eradicate poverty stems from its rapid technological progress and its greatly expanded capacity to produce. But the same changes giving us greatly increased production and improved levels of living have created very difficult adjustment problems for many rural families and rural communities. And they will continue to do so. Fewer people will be employed in agriculture, forestry, fisheries, and mining in the future than today.

The job to be done is to restructure rural facilities and services on a broader geographical base and to connect them with their urban counterparts. There will be little or no abatement of rural poverty until this is done. We have to change our traditional view of rural America—its function, its relation with the rest of the nation, and the social and economic processes required to assure a better life for rural people.

Fifth, we must act because our rural communities are unable to prepare people to participate in the modern economy, and they will become increasingly less able to do so unless there are concerted and extensive changes.

There is in rural America today a serious and widespread failure to prepare the people for participation in a modern and advancing economy. In entirely too many instances the schools, libraries, health facilities, churches, and governments in rural America have failed to develop programs to meet the needs of the people. The extensive unemployment and underemployment in rural areas attest to the fact that our record is not good in preparing people for jobs and in helping them to locate productive employment.

State and local governments are not able to meet the needs of the people in most rural communities. At the same time that the citizens of rural communities have begun to demand the kind of services that cities offer, local governments are finding it harder and harder to provide even the basic services.

The winds of change have struck rural government, though

local leaders often seem unaware of it. Recent changes in rural America have rendered obsolete many political boundaries of villages and counties. Too many local governments in rural areas operate on too small a scale to be practicable. They are able to provide no more than the most elementary public needs. Their tax base is eroding as their more able-bodied wage earners leave for jobs elsewhere.

In a very practical sense, rural government has been left behind politically as well as economically. Though these governments continue to operate as they have for 100 years, the center of political power has shifted drastically. It has moved toward the more professional governments of urban areas and toward state and national governing bodies. The important decisions on education, health, welfare, and other matters of vital public concern are made, more and more often, at higher levels. Because local rural government has failed to change, it has isolated itself and its constituents from the political mainstream.

The problems of overcoming rural poverty are complicated by the fact that many rural poor have lost almost all hope of improving their situation. Many have attempted to keep up with the technological tide in farming and have failed. Many have been disillusioned in their efforts to obtain employment outside agriculture, forestry, fisheries, or mining. Their lack of the requisite skills to earn a decent living is discovered too late. It will not be easy to motivate these people to try again. But we must.

Part of our problem stems from our unwillingness to face realistically the limited employment potential of today's modern farming, and tomorrow's farming. Likewise, we have failed to comprehend the limited job opportunities in forestry, fisheries, and mining. We have not developed good employment opportunities for the people in rural areas. Worse yet, we lack the kind and quality of educational and manpower training services to provide rural people with skills necessary for other employment. Without forthright action, jobs will get scarcer in rural areas, and the skill gap between urban and rural people will widen.

Sixth, we must act now because our public programs in rural America are woefully out of date. Many of them, especially our farm programs and vocational agriculture programs, are relics from an earlier era. They were developed during a period when there was a strong belief that people born in rural America should stay there and work on farms, or in farm-related occupations. The programs emerged from legislation which equated the welfare of farm families with conditions on farms and the welfare of rural communities with the incomes of farmers. These conditions no longer prevail.

Although many farm programs were originally developed with the express purpose of increasing the incomes of low income rural families, they did not take into account the vast changes in technology of the last 30 years. As a result, instead of combating low incomes among rural people, these programs have helped to increase the wealth of landowners while largely bypassing the rural poor.

It cannot be emphasized too strongly that the poverty in rural areas is self-perpetuating. There will be little or no abatement and no real solution unless specific steps are taken to cope with it. Moreover, since the basic structure of rural America has been altered, the old programs are not sufficient for coping with problems of today. A new approach clearly is required.

The Commission has endeavored to chart a course to wipe out rural poverty. Emphasis is placed upon the many problems of the rural poor people. The problems of the people differ because of differences among them in age, race, education, geographic location and other attributes. The diversity of their needs is recognized, and recommendations are made to meet the diverse needs.

In developing these recommendations, the Commission gave consideration to problems of the rural poor and to problems of impoverished rural communities. Changes in existing programs and the development of new programs are proposed. The immediate needs of the rural poor are emphasized, but the necessity for changing the conditions that have made them poor is also stressed. Better programs for human resource development and the physical resources needed for their development are urged. Emphasis is placed upon improving the operation of the private economy so as to provide rural people with better opportunities for jobs and a decent living. Government is called upon to complement the private sector where necessary to erase rural poverty.

In the Commission's view, the complexity of the problems of rural poverty preclude the success of a single program or approach. Programs emphasizing immediate needs will not change the conditions creating and perpetuating rural poverty, and programs designed to change these deeply rooted conditions will take time. The recommendations complement and reinforce one another. Taken together, the recommendations will eliminate rural poverty, and thereby remove the basis for much of our urban poverty.

The costs to society for implementation of the Commission's recommendations will be high, but the costs will be immeasurably higher if we do not implement them. Over the long pull, the gains to society from wiping out poverty will far exceed the costs. The time for action is indeed now.

The Need for Improved Mobility Policy

C. E. BISHOP

C. E. Bishop holds a William Neal Reynolds Professorship in Economics on the faculty of North Carolina State University. Since 1966 he has been Vice President of the University of North Carolina. He served as the Executive Director of the National Advisory Commission on Rural Poverty in 1966/67.

THE MIGRATION OF PEOPLE was one of the paramount factors contributing to the development of the United States. The flow of people across the oceans to this continent and the great western migration of the people across the continent made possible the development of its agriculture, the establishment of its industries, and the building of its cities.

The vast movement of people that has taken place in the development of this country, however, has gone on largely in an unguided and an unplanned manner. For the most part, it has been assumed that individuals and families possess sufficient knowledge to pursue the search for employment of their resources in an optimal manner.

Only recently has migration come to be recognized as a form of investment in human capital. Sjaastad emphasized that spatial differences in earnings for similar work would lead people to invest in transfer of resources over space and that this movement would tend to equalize the differences in earnings.[1] Migration is a means of augmenting the value of the human resource in the same manner that education, training, and changes in occupations increase the productivity and thereby the value of the human resource. Both geographic and occupational mobility, therefore, should be treated as investments in increasing the productivity of human resources. Since both involve costs and yield returns associated with changes in the productivity of

1. L. A. Sjaastad, "The Costs and Returns of Human Migration," *Journal of Political Economy*, Vol. LXX, Supplement, pp. 80–93.

human resources, the optimal pattern of investments in human resource development should consider increases in the productivity of the human resource through changes in occupation and location as well as through education and training. Resources are optimally allocated when the last expenditures for the different forms of investment in the human agent bring equal returns.

Rapid technological and economic progress in industry have important implications concerning the need for mobility of manpower. The response of manpower in adjusting to these technological and economic conditions may affect importantly the economic growth of the nation, the structure of industry, and the distribution of income among the people.

This paper will summarize some of the findings of recent research pertaining to the occupational and geographic mobility of labor and offer suggestions concerning programs needed to improve mobility.[2]

THE LABOR MARKET IN RURAL AMERICA

Numerous studies have demonstrated that the United States population is relatively mobile. A recent study indicates that 15 percent of the family heads in the United States moved between labor markets during the period 1958 to 1963.[3] More than two-thirds of the family heads in the United States are living in labor market areas other than the one in which they were born.

Migration from rural areas has been very heavy in the United States. The manpower needs of farming are determined by the market conditions for farm commodities and the productivity of labor and other resources in producing farm commodities. Given the nature of the demand for farm commodities, the most important determinant of farm manpower needs in the immediate future likely will continue to be expansion in the use of capital and the accompanying increase in the productivity of labor. The development of technology which increased the productivity of

2. This paper draws heavily upon papers prepared for the President's National Advisory Commission on Rural Poverty.

3. Robert E. Marsh, "Geographic Labor Mobility in the United States, Recent Findings," *Social Security Bulletin*, No. 30, March, 1967, pp. 14–20.

capital relative to labor in the production of farm commodities has been the basic factor contributing to structural changes in farming. Technological innovations of a biological, chemical, and mechanical nature, and innovations in the organizational structure of agriculture all predominantly increase the productivity of capital relative to labor and provide incentives to substitute capital for labor and to increase the size of the farm firm.[4] While the elasticity of demand for labor in farming is relatively low and the substitution may not be very important in the short run, the elasticity increases rapidly over time as farmers are able to make the adjustments necessary to efficiently use the improved technology.[5]

Since the demand for farm products has been increasing rather slowly relative to the increase in the capacity to produce these products, and since the predominant impact of improved technology in agriculture has been to increase the employment of capital and decrease employment of labor in the production of farm commodities, the major burden of the adjustment to the changes in technological and economic conditions has fallen on the labor market. The major form of adjustment has been a sharp reduction in the amount of labor employed in farming and a concomitant shift of labor from farm to nonfarm employment. In many instances, these adjustments have involved geographic mobility in addition to occupational mobility.

Magnitude of the Shift · The transfer of the human resource from farming has been massive. Net outmigration has been so large that the base farm population declined rapidly from 31 million in 1920 to less than 12 million in 1967. The average annual net outmigration for the decade of the 1940's was 1.3 million persons per year compared with 1.0 million in the decade of the 1950's. During the current decade the average annual net outmigration is approximately 750,000. However, the annual migration rate as a percentage of the farm population currently

4. C. E. Bishop, *Geographic and Occupational Mobility of Rural Manpower*, Documentation in Agriculture and Food, No. 75, Organization for Economic Cooperation and Development, Paris, 1965.

5. G. Edward Schuh, "Interrelations Between the Farm Labor Force and Changes in the Total Economy," *Rural Poverty in the United States*, Chapter 12, National Advisory Commission on Rural Poverty, 1967.

is as large or larger than it was in the 1940's and 1950's.[6]

In a study of transfers from farm to nonfarm employment, Dale Hathaway and Brian Perkins concluded that most of the people who make the transfer do not change residence. Although their study does not include farm residents who elected nonfarm employment at the time of entry into the labor force, the behavior of those who change occupations at the time of transfer from farm to nonfarm residences likely is similar to the behavior of other migrants. Those farm residents who are most inclined to change residence when transferring from farm to nonfarm employment are young, Negro, farm wage workers and those who reside in relatively prosperous rural areas in close proximity to employment centers.[7]

Persons working in the farm labor force as unpaid family laborers or as hired laborers are more inclined to migrate than owner operators. Farm operators tend to be older, have larger investments in farms and in farm skills, have fewer alternative opportunities, and are less responsive to economic incentives to transfer to nonfarm employment than others in the farm labor force. Farm-owner operators are among the least mobile of the occupation groups in the United States. Approximately twice as high a percentage of hired farm workers migrate upon transferring from farm to nonfarm employment as farm operators. Schuh found that the short-run elasticity of supply of farm operator labor with respect to nonfarm income is considerably less than the short-run elasticity of supply of unpaid family labor hired farm labor.

Labor is not a homogeneous commodity. The characteristics of the people affect the productivity of their labor and also affect the demand for it. Although there is a heavy migration from the farm labor force, the size of the flow varies considerably from year to year and not all groups in the population participate in the transfer to the same extent.[8]

6. *Rural People in the American Economy*, Agricultural Economic Report No. 101, ERS, USDA, 1966, p. 9.

7. Hathaway and Perkins, "Occupational Mobility and Migration from Agriculture," *Rural Poverty in the United States, op. cit.*, Chapter 13.

8. C. E. Bishop, "Economic Aspects of Changes in the Farm Labor Force," *Labor Mobility and Population in Agriculture* (Iowa State University Press, 1961), Chap. 4, pp. 36–50.

Characteristics of the population which are related to the mobility potential of that population include sex, age, race, education, and training. The age distribution of the population in particular may exert an important influence upon its mobility potential. Migration involves costs as well as returns. Those in the younger groups have a longer working life after migration and, therefore, have a longer time in which to recover the costs of migration.[9] Furthermore, other things being equal, young people are given preference by employers. The young also have less investment in farming and may view the income foregone by transferring from farming as less than those with larger investments in farming.

The transfer from farm to nonfarm employment decreases rapidly with age. Hathaway and Perkins concluded that about one-third of the persons under 25 years old moved out of agriculture each year, and in each successive age class there was a lower rate of transfer than in the preceding age class. Since the rate of occupational transfer declines sharply with age, the major burden of reducing the number of farm operators and the labor input in farming has fallen heavily upon decreasing the number of young men entering farm occupations. Stated differently, the major means of decreasing the supply of labor in farming is to find nonfarm employment for farm youth entering the labor force.[10]

While the rate of outmigration from the farm population is higher for Negroes than for others, Hathaway and Perkins found that other things being equal, mobility from the farm labor force to nonfarm employment was significantly lower for Negro farm wage workers than for others, especially during periods of recession. It should be noted, however, that a relatively high percentage of the migration of Negroes was for long distances.

Major Determinants of Mobility · Many studies have been made of the factors determining transfers of labor among occupations and locations. From an economic standpoint, the choice among jobs and among locations is made on the basis of net advantage

9. C. E. Bishop, *op. cit.*, p. 38.
10. Marion Clawson, "Aging Farmers and Agriculture Policy," *Journal of Farm Economics*, February 1963, pp. 13–30.

to the persons making the decisions. Basically, therefore, the determinants of occupational and locational transfers are those conditions affecting the supply and demand for human resources in various occupations and locations. The costs of migration on private account include the costs of job search, the direct costs of relocation, the opportunity costs of moving and changing occupations, the nonpecuniary costs of changing locations and leaving friends and relatives, the diseconomies associated with living in the new location and any costs involved in acquiring the skills necessary to perform effectively in the new job or new location.[11] Marsh found that "most people in the labor force who had crossed county lines gave job-related reasons for moving and . . . it appeared that people with the strongest economic positions in terms of skill level and education were most likely to respond to economic incentives such as the opportunity for a better paying job."[12]

Several studies have emphasized the importance of employment opportunities and low unemployment rates in the areas to which migrants are attracted. Schuh found that increases in expected nonfarm income lead to reductions in the quantity of labor supplied to agriculture, other things being equal. Marsh found that most of the workers who did move between areas for economic reasons were attracted by lower unemployment rates rather than by higher pay scales. Bishop found that, during periods when the rate of unemployment is above 5 percent, the earnings of labor in nonfarm occupations relative to farm occupations have little effect upon the rate of migration. On the other hand, in a relatively full employment economy increases in the returns for labor in nonfarm employment relative to farm employment provided incentives for increased migration from agriculture. In another study of migration, Sjaastad concluded that "there can be no doubt that employment conditions in the nonfarm labor market are a crucial variable for off-farm migration."[13]

11. P. R. Johnson, "Labor Mobility: Some Costs and Returns," *Rural Poverty in the United States, op. cit.,* Chap. 14.

12. Robert E. Marsh, *op. cit.,* p. 16.

13. L. A. Sjaastad, "Occupational Structure and Migration Pattern," in *Labor Mobility and Population in Agriculture* (Iowa State University Press, 1961), Chap. 2.

All of the above studies suggest that the supply of farm labor to nonfarm firms is highly elastic at prevailing relative rates of return for labor in farm and nonfarm industries. Under these conditions, the actual migration is determined largely by the demand for labor in nonfarm employment. Furthermore, much of the nonfarm employment in the United States is governed by an institutionally established minimum wage. Employment, therefore, is limited to the number that employers can profitably employ at this wage. The behavior which one observes in the labor market in rural areas suggests that there is job rationing among migrants from rural areas.[14] In a sense, the farm labor force serves as a large pool from which nonfarm employers draw labor as needed. Nonfarm employers endeavor to obtain those workers whose productivity is highest from this pool. Since the institutionalized wage has not applied to agriculture, there has been free entry into the farm labor force. Consequently, the farm labor force has become increasingly a residual labor force.

The Migration Process · Few would contend that decisions concerning migration are made in a well-considered rational manner. On the contrary, there is increasing evidence that most decisions to migrate are based on very incomplete information. Furthermore, there has been no national program to provide information or other relocation assistance to potential migrants.

Marsh found that the planning period was "one month or less for about one-third of the moves reported; alternatives were not even considered in two-thirds of them; and, in over half of the cases, family heads who relocated consulted only one or even no other sources of job information."[15] He also noted that the more highly educated workers deliberated at greater length concerning migration and that they had greater access to specific information prior to migration.

Smith concluded that most farm migrants have little or no information concerning living conditions in the areas to which

14. C. E. Bishop, *op. cit.*, p. 40. Also see W. E. Hendricks, "Income Improvement Prospects in Low-Income Areas," *Journal of Farm Economics,* December 1959, p. 1070.

15. Robert E. Marsh, *op. cit.*

they migrate.[16] The vast majority of them do not have a definite job offer at the time of migration. However, a very high proportion of those who migrate have friends and relatives in the areas to which they go. These friends and relatives serve as a primary source of information concerning job opportunities.

The out-of-pocket costs for moving from farm to nonfarm residences are small for most migrants in the United States. Nevertheless, many migrants have little capital to invest in the job search. Johnson suggests that under these conditions a farm worker is apt to apply a high internal discount rate to nonfarm earnings, and that when faced with a sharp decline in demand for his services in farm employment, he tends to move where friends and relatives have preceded him, dismissing differences among cities in costs and returns.

There is no doubt that off-farm migration operates largely through an informal process dependent largely upon friends and relatives. The results are evident in the patterns established by migrants. The significance of established streams of migrants is demonstrated clearly in a study by Kain and Persky as follows:

The typical rural Negro lifetime migrant tends to move to large urban areas (greater than a million in population) outside of the South. The white movement is more diffused and has a marked orientation toward medium-sized Northern cities and the metropolitan areas of the South itself. While the Southern-born whites and Negroes each sent about 2-½ million (2.61 and 2.47 respectively) individuals to cities larger than a million outside of the South (1950–60), only .42 million Negroes went to non-Southern cities of between 250 thousand and a million as compared to 1.42 million whites. Moreover, all Standard Metropolitan Statistical Areas greater than 250,000 account for only 60 percent of the whites leaving the South as against 89 percent of the Negroes. With respect to movements within the South, only .86 million Negroes left their state of birth to move to Southern SMSA's greater than 250,000 as compared to 2.86 million Southern whites.

The five-year migration series (1955–1960) suggests no recent alteration of the basic pattern. Thus, 25 percent of the white outmigrants from the South moved to rural areas in the North and West, as

16. E. D. Smith, "Nonfarm Employment Information for Rural People," *Journal of Farm Economics*, August 1956, p. 815.

compared to 8 percent of the Negro outmigrants. Within the South, Southern cities account for 72 percent of all Southern whites moving to urban areas, but only 55 percent of all Southern Negroes. Moreover, there is evidence that Negroes moving North move in stages: first to a Southern city, then a Northern one. If this is so, the differences are even larger than indicated here. It is also important to note that these figures include considerable interurban migration. If the rural-urban stream could be isolated, it is likely that the pattern would become even sharper, with rural Negroes much less reluctant to move North than their white neighbors. . . .

Fifty-eight percent of Negroes born in the South Atlantic Division and now living elsewhere, live in the four North Eastern SMSA's greater than a million (Buffalo, New York, Philadelphia, and Pittsburgh). Similarly, about 40 percent of the Negro lifetime migrants from the East South Central Division have moved to the five East North Central SMSA's greater than a million (Chicago, Detroit, Cincinnati, Cleveland, and Milwaukee). Finally, about 36 percent of the same group from the West South Central Division live in the four Pacific SMSA's greater than a million (Los Angeles, San Diego, San Francisco, and Seattle). Thus, not only have Negroes from the South moved to large metropolitan areas, they have moved along clearcut lines to their destinations, forming at least three major streams, one up the Eastern seaboard, another up the Mississippi River to Ohio and Michigan, and one westward to California.

The pattern is more diffused for whites. While whites from the three divisions also tend to move along these streams, there is a much greater willingness to cross longitudinal lines and to go to smaller places.[17]

Movement of Population to Rural Areas · Migration involves a two-way flow of people. Studies of net migration are helpful in analyses of incentives for adjustment in employment of manpower. However, studies of gross migration provide better information on responsiveness of people to changes in economic and social conditions. Even if mobility were perfect, a substantial movement of people to rural areas could occur at the same time that a large exodus from rural areas was taking place. While a large movement of labor to rural areas in a country which is experiencing a mass exodus from these areas may be evidence of excessive mobility, mistaken expectations and social waste,

17. John F. Kain and J. J. Persky, "The North's Stake in Southern Rural Poverty," *Rural Poverty in the United States,* Chap. 17.

such migrations also may reflect differences in tastes or personal characteristics of inmigrants and outmigrants instead of a back-flow to rural areas.[18] Unfortunately, data are not available to separate those who move to rural areas because of their prefer-ences for employment or living in those areas and those who return to rural areas because of disillusionment and disappoint-ment in nonfarm employment. However, research demonstrates that there is a large gross movement of labor into as well as out of farm employment. For the period 1957 to 1963, the number of persons moving into farm employment averaged close to 90 percent of the number of persons moving from farm to nonfarm employment.[19] Earlier research established that most persons transferring from nonfarm to farm employment had formerly been employed in farming, but had failed to establish themselves in nonfarm jobs and moved back to farming. Hathaway and Perkins concluded that "the proportion of off-farm movers who returned to farm work decreased with city size. Employment stability increased with city size for all persons transferring from farm to nonfarm employment regardless of whether they changed residence." The authors concluded that those farm-employed persons who rely on small local labor markets for a nonfarm job have the lowest probability of successfully moving out of farm employment. However, a high percentage of those who return from nonfarm to farm employment try again to obtain nonfarm employment. For the period 1957 to 1963, 37 percent of those who moved from nonfarm to farm employment were employed in nonfarm employment again one year later.[20]

In an earlier study, Hathaway concluded that workers who leave agricultural employment are more likely to find employ-ment in industries that are subject to cyclical and secular down-turns in employment and thus subject to layoff when labor force reductions occur.[21] Because a relatively large share of the mi-

18. Hathaway and Perkins, *op. cit.*

19. B. B. Perkins and D. E. Hathaway, "The Movement of Labor Between Farm and Nonfarm Jobs," *Agricultural Experiment Station Re-search Bulletin 13* (Michigan State University, 1966).

20. Hathaway and Perkins, *op. cit.*, p. 74.

21. Dale E. Hathaway, "Occupational Mobility from the Farm Labor Force," *Farm Labor in the United States* (Columbia University Press, 1967), Chap. 5, p. 94.

grants from farms in the South are long distance migrants who are employed in the industries subject to heavy layoff, recessions have a relatively high impact upon the South.

The Gains From Mobility · Few studies have attempted to gage the private costs and returns associated with occupational and geographic mobility. The large number of persons who move back to farming suggests that many migrants become disillusioned with living conditions or earnings after migration.

Hathaway and Perkins found that more than 40 percent of those leaving farming had lower incomes in their nonfarm occupations the following year and that persons leaving farming after the age of 44 seldom are able to improve their earnings. They also found that the earnings of a person in agriculture are a reasonably good indicator of his subsequent nonfarm earnings. Higher earnings were obtained by moving to the cities of more than one million in size.

In order to assess the returns from mobility, one should give consideration to all of the costs and returns associated with mobility. Osborne presents a fairly complete accounting of costs and returns for a sample of migrants in North Carolina. Although his analysis is concerned only with costs and returns on private account, his results indicate a return on investments made in mobility greater than 100 percent.[22] Thus, the migrants covered in this study could have recouped the costs of occupational and residential shifts during the first year after migration.

After studying the experiences of the North Carolina Fund in relocation projects in North Carolina, P. R. Johnson also concluded that the return from the investments made in this project on private and social account were large enough to recoup the costs during the first year after migration.

On the basis of their study, Hathaway and Perkins conclude that the normal operation of labor markets in transferring labor among occupations and locations does not serve to reduce income disparities within agriculture or between persons employed in farm and nonfarm occupations. They conclude that in general

22. D. D. Osborne, "Returns to Investment in Human Migration," Unpublished PhD. Thesis, Department of Economics, North Carolina State University at Raleigh, 1966.

the mobility process works less well for those who need it most and that it may well result in a widening of income differences among people and among areas.

PROGRAM DEFICIENCIES

The studies of mobility leave no question concerning the fact that the rural population in the United States is highly mobile. In fact, there is an increasing body of evidence that suggests that migration is excessive as it now operates. The large number of people returning to farm employment and the fact that many had lower earnings in nonfarm employment than in farming suggests social waste in migration. The problem appears to be one not of increased migration, but of rationalizing the migration process so that a higher percentage of those who migrate actually benefit from migration. Several policy directions emerge.

The significance of cyclical and secular shifts in employment to successful migration is obvious. The attainment and maintenance of full employment is a necessary condition for a reduction in the backflow and for rationalization of mobility.

Since such a high proportion of those who migrate are in the younger age groups, it is imperative that a better job be done in occupational preparation. General education must be improved; training programs in rural areas must place greater emphasis upon nonfarm vocational training; testing and counseling programs must be expanded in schools in rural areas; and there should be effective coordination of counseling with consideration of employment opportunities through the services of the Employment Security Commission.

A nationwide comprehensive manpower program should be initiated to provide improved job information to potential employees. The well-established streams of migration in the nation at the present time suggest that, in the informal system now guiding migrants, the pattern of dissemination of information has a more important effect upon who migrates and where they go than the potential increase in earnings. The high rate of movement back to rural areas suggests the need for reception centers, guidance counselors, and improved housing in the cities receiving large numbers of migrants.

The meager evidence that is available suggests that the return received from investments in mobility assistance programs far exceeds the return from investments in education and training. Public assistance in defraying certain mobility costs may contribute greatly to the success of mobility efforts. In particular, a system of relocation payments provided through, and based upon, the advice and counsel of the Employment Security Commission, could yield very high returns for society.

Political Pressures and Income Distribution in Agriculture

VARDEN FULLER

Varden Fuller is Professor of Agricultural Economics at the University of California at Berkeley. This paper was presented at a session of the American Farm Economic Association meetings in August 1965.

WE ARE NOW well into the fourth decade of experience with a series of obligations assumed by the American society to involve its national government intensively in the alteration of income flows on behalf of farmers. Throughout these years, the rationalizations of the actions taken have been fully as diverse and evanescent as the composition of political support which gave them sanction. The composite of net political support has embraced not only varying perceptions of "the farm problem" but also varying and changing perceptions of the proper role of government, the latter being particularly true of the perceptions arising from within agriculture. Depression, war, and technological impact have been the principal elements of environmental change, but the political support essential to the actions taken has apparently depended heavily upon a pre-existing and long-surviving endowment of sympathy for "the farmer," who, according to prevailing ideology, was unfairly treated by the economic system and therefore entitled to protection and redress.

That conceptions of disadvantage should emerge, survive, and attain great political significance is perhaps not truly remarkable. Despite a heritage of land and opportunity almost without parallel in the modern world, American farmers—some more than others—have suffered economic adversity ranging from poverty to disillusionment. What is remarkable is that so much political sympathy for the farmer as an undifferentiated eclectic abstraction has not been matched by an equal concern for the

255

really poor as against the not-so-poor within agriculture. It may be close to self-evident why those who articulate the interests of organized farmers might wish to maintain an undifferentiated image of disadvantage, but why the nonfarm sources of political support have not required that aid to farmers be more nearly calibrated to individual needs is far from evident.

The failure of political sympathy for "the farmer" to be specific as to need and to carry through to the needy has meant that the bulk of the program benefits for more than thirty years have been distributed in disproportion to need and that they have been rewarding to the owners of land and unrewarding to the owners of labor.

Proposals have been made to graduate the benefits of various programs or to place ceilings upon them, thereby making the distribution more egalitarian. With some few exceptions, these proposals have been the casualties of sharp opposition centering in the leadership of farm organizations. The Brannan proposal with its 1800-unit ceiling is possibly the most renowned failure, while the Jones-Costigan graduated-sugar-payment system, including its labor provisions, is perhaps the outstanding success.

Over the years, there have been many opportunities to make egalitarian choices, either in the distribution of general-benefit programs or in programs selectively directed towards remedying or alleviating poverty. Because of their generality and the immense magnitudes of money involved, the price-support programs ranked first. The victory of the nonrecourse-loan system over the compensatory-payment system is one of the major triumphs of American farm politics. The nonrecourse-loan method not only provides its own blanket of obscurity as to who gets how much and who pays for it; it also is not vulnerable to ceilings or graduation. Although there have been shades of difference in enthusiasm among organizations as to the choice of system, the real differences have been on the level of support.

In addition to price supports, other choice situations involving selectivity or differentiation have been principally the following: action programs, such as the Farm Security and Farm Home Administrations, designed to improve asset ownership and managerial ability among low-income farmers; clientele priorities

directed toward identified needs, such as Land Use Planning in
1938–1942 and Rural Development since 1956; and finally, any
and all of the proposals and efforts such as minimum wages,
unemployment insurance, and social security, none of which have
enjoyed much popularity in farm politics and all of which were
centered on human beings rather than land or commodity.

That eligibility for programs of any monetary consequence
has tended to center upon land and upon commodity, that benefits have tended to be in proportion to the amount of land owned
and the production therefrom, and that the rationalizations for
these arrangements are firmly embedded in political consideration are, I believe, matters of considerable familiarity. Assuming this, I shall not now undertake a detailed documentation of
who supported or opposed what and when. Rather, I wish to
examine some of the aspects of organizational behavior and institutional influence that have affected the choices that have been
made.

First to be considered is the farmers' association as an organizational entity. As these organizations customarily give the
impression of speaking for "the farmer" and for "agriculture" and
since they seem to be voluntary, self-initiating, mutual-benefit
associations, it is not completely illogical that many people expect
them to represent the full spectrum of farmer interest. These
are the people who are dismayed that the organizations seldom
show much sympathy for the poor and unsuccessful—and that
their philosophies are so divergent. Among those dismayed on
the latter score is Secretary Orville Freeman, who on occasion
admonishes farm leaders to bind up their schisms and present
a unified picture of what the farmers really want.[1] For two principal reasons these views of the farm organization are naive and
imperceptive: they deny the importance of diversity and hetero-
geneity, including class, in the broad spectrum of farm interests;
they are not realistic of organizations in the environment of
American agriculture, or of their means of acquiring power and
of survival.

I suggest that organizations representing segments of economic

1. As in his speech to a conference of 200 farm leaders in Kansas City,
Mo., Apr. 13, 1964, mimeo., U.S. Department of Agriculture. *The New
York Times,* Apr. 14, 1964, reports on the reception.

interest can most usefully be looked upon as agencies engaged in the business of marketing organizational ethos, political posture, and bargaining power. These are products that must be fashioned to a market or they do not sell. Within the heterogeneous range of American farm enterprises and occupations, the agencies whose products are organization and representation can, do—and perhaps must—differentiate their product: hence, the American Farm Bureau Federation, the National Grange, the National Farmers Union, and, as well, numerous additional commodity, area, and special-purpose organizations. Obstinate, divergent philosophical commitments of farm leaders do not any more explain organization fragmentation in the United States than does the uniqueness of Lord Netherthorpe[2] explain unity in Great Britain.

The market for organizations seems to be best among those who already have interests to be protected as well as promoted; it is poorest among those who have little to protect and whose "needs," exteriorly defined, might be judged to be the greatest. It is not just coincidence that the organizational strength of the American Medical Association, the National Association of Manufacturers, and the skilled crafts is so sharply in contrast with that of sharecroppers, migratory farm workers, and janitors.

In this affluent, pluralistic stage of American society, effective political pressure comes much more from organizations associated with success than from those based on protest—a generalization I believe to be valid even with the exception of the civil rights movement. In any event, the poor of agriculture have not been a good market for organization in this century. Consequently, it has followed that all of the farm organizations—even as each has seemed to be speaking for farming generally—have actually been constrained, for the sake of their own organizational prosperity and survival, to serve the interests of those who were conscious of their interests, however differentiated.

The entrepreneurs of organization have done a fair job of assessing the diversity of their markets. Even more to be admired

2. [Farmers in Great Britain have demonstrated far more cohesiveness as a political pressure group than have U.S. farmers. Lord Netherthorpe was president of the National Farmers' Union of Great Britain from 1945 to 1960.—*Editor*.]

is their agility in designing ideological doctrines that would serve as vehicles to carry the particular interests of their segment without clearly revealing the nature of these interests to nonfarm supporters. Thus the nonrecourse loan has the alleged merit of permitting farmers to earn their incomes in the market place; it avoids government handouts; it does not reward failure and punish efficiency. Getting rid of Farm Security meant a great achievement in avoiding duplication of services and governmental inefficiency. Terminating Land Use Planning was essential to the preservation of local government against federal encroachment.

The Grange, the Union, and the Federation in their policy resolutions give consideration to the low-income farmers and to rural underemployment. The three statements reflect varying combinations of piety and punch. For the Federation, the mix is mainly piety, for it said in 1959: "We insist that control of the Rural Development Program remain at state and local levels. All agencies participating in the program should support it, but the agricultural extension service should have the primary leadership responsibility. We are opposed to the creation of a new agency to administer this program."[3]

This instruction was for the benefit of the Ezra Benson regime, but judging its merits was soon to be up to Orville Freeman. Apparently the instruction has been found meritorious, for despite two changes in name for rural development and a great step-up in rural-renaissance rhetoric, contemporary rural development consists of a minute staff with no action program of its own, on the ready to supply coordination, expedition, and liaison—all to an assortment of federal, state, and local agencies, each firmly hinged by comfortable political symbiosis to its own respective clientele.

When one extends his examination of organizational ethos into ideology and its manipulative possibilities, he soon discovers a more obscure and elusive source of political pressure from within agriculture. It is one which interrelates with the size attributes of farm enterprise and with the concept (or slogan) of the family farm. In varying proportions, all farmers except the very largest are self-employed workers as well as self-capitalists and entre-

3. *Farm Bureau Policies for 1960*, Chicago, Dec. 17, 1959, p. 50.

preneurs; many also are at least incidental employers. But for most American farmers, the main occupational component is self-employment. Even the fairly large full-time farmer whose farm is worth $40,000 and who hires 100 man-days of supplemental labor should be more interested in the level of labor returns than in high capital earnings or in low wages for hired workers. Only for those few whose investment approaches or exceeds $100,000 and who hire most or all of their work done should the logical interest alignment be that of capital owner and employer. Yet it can scarcely be denied that the pro-investor, anti-labor psychology generally prevails among American farmers. The varying degrees of intensity in which it prevails are one of the main bases for organizational differentiation.

The American farmer has a long history of property and capital-gains consciousness. Alexis de Tocqueville noted in the 1830's: "It seldom happens that an American farmer settles for good upon the land which he occupies: especially in the districts of the far West he brings land into tillage in order to sell it again and not to farm it: he builds a farmhouse on the speculation that, as the state of the country will soon be changed by the increase of population, a good price will be gotten for it. . . ."[4]

Richard Hofstadter, 120 years later, concluded that the agricultural society, emerging from the conflict between the agrarian myth and an environment of commercial realities, was one which cherished not the land but land values.[5]

For the farm-organization leader (i.e., entrepreneur), the concept of property ownership as transcendent over occupation is something not to be ignored. On the contrary, it is an attitude to be exploited, not the least of reasons being that the active minority which normally constitutes the leadership group of an organization is likely to have considerable property interest. Consequently, farm-organization ideology is saturated with the psychological postures of the property owner and employer. And accordingly, the great mass of American farmers do their thinking in these terms even when their roles of property owner and employer are at most quite incidental to their self-employment.

4. Alexis de Tocqueville, *Democracy in America* (1899 ed.), Vol. II, p. 644.
5. Richard Hofstadter, *The Age of Reform*, 1955 (Vintage ed.), p. 41.

Under the circumstances, it is not remarkable that production allotments and marketing quotas mostly have their eligibility in land rather than in people; nor is it remarkable that program benefits tend to flow into the hands of land owners through capitalization rather than into labor returns, either of the self-employed or of hired workers. This outcome results from the behavior pattern of American farmers in the land markets. They do not appear to regard a large investment in land as an obstruction to an occupational career but rather as a prospect for further capital gains. They seem to be quite prepared to sacrifice current labor income in the competition to acquire land.

This is not the entire explanation of the doubling of land values since 1950, during which time aggregate farm income has not risen. Yet, during the period 1950–1962, as a fairly stable aggregate of net income was realized by a declining number of recipients, there was the opportunity for a significant rise in labor incomes. And if land, rather than labor, were the residual claimant—as classical theory says—there was something like 45 cents per hour more for labor in 1962 than in 1950.

But the markets for land and labor have operated in such a way as to award this increment of income mainly to land owners. On the ever-rising valuation, "comparable returns" (i.e., the going interest rate on comparable investments) use up almost all of the per-capita income increment. It scarcely needs to be added that realizing income as capital gains and in proportion to land ownership is a far less egalitarian form of distribution than is labor income.

If the initial endowment of sympathy for the farmer which sanctioned the epoch of price and income support has been badly used, as I believe it has, and if one seeks an explanation, I would find it in off-farm politics rather than in political pressure originating within agriculture. Farm political pressures have been somewhat on the side of the inevitable; their internal conflicts have had some cancellation effect, and farm pressures alone would have been an insufficient force. For concurring support, the banks, the machinery and fertilizer industries, and others similarly situated have had their motives, mostly ulterior. But the final and critical support has come from legislators and party leaders who by opportunity or obligation have become committed to supporting, not directly the farmer or his welfare, but the welfare of even more obscure abstractions—cotton, wheat, corn, rice, or particular geographic regions. Since commodities are specialized to regions and therefore to congressional districts and constituencies, the opportunities for vote-trading[6] and political reciprocity are abundant. In this environment, it has not been easy for those who cared to be vigilant that the income benefits created so unspecifically should do something to alleviate poverty within agriculture; and, regrettably, the motives of many politicians and officeholders have been such that they did not care.

That program benefits have mostly been distributed regressively and have done little to alleviate or remedy rural poverty are not, I am sorry to say, my gloomiest conclusions. It is bad enough that income diversions have been converted mainly into a spiral of capital gains and mortgage obligations but it is worse that a political commitment thereby comes into effect to protect and guarantee these capital gains and the banks which facilitate their realization.

In November 1964, the National Agricultural Advisory Commission in its report, *Farm Policy in the Years Ahead*, proposed six goals, of which this was the second: *A level of farm income enabling efficient producers to earn returns on their labor and investment comparable with returns realized on similar resources outside of agriculture.* This sounds reasonable, and, except to those aware of what has been happening to the distribution of farm income, it is quite innocent. However, the Commission itself apparently felt a bit doubtful, for its discussion included the observation that "computing returns on investment in land presents a difficulty, for in the long run land values themselves are considerably affected by the level of farm income."[7] This sort of observation may get the attention of economists but it is not likely to have much constraining influence upon politicians.

When the Secretary of Agriculture and others of the administrative and party establishments say, as they do frequently, that "the country cannot afford the terrible cost of ending commodity

6. A recent important example is the swapping of support in the House on the repeal of section 14(b) of the Taft–Hartley Act for support of the Administration's farm bill.

7. National Agricultural Advisory Commission, *Farm Policy in the Years Ahead*, Washington, D.C., Government Printing Office, Nov. 1964, p. 10.

programs," what do they mean? Are they worried about losing another half-million small farmers? Are they worried about invoking a "farm-led, farm-fed" depression? Are they thinking about a fearful political windfall to the rival party if commodity price programs were to be terminated, thereby putting such a squeeze on land inflation as to invite some well-publicized mortgage foreclosures? If these questions were to be put, I am quite certain that the first two, with no harm done, could and would be answered in the affirmative; the third, not likely to be answered at all, might provoke a shudder.

In any event, I am only using this as a way of trying to say that I believe that land and mortgage owners, in becoming the principal beneficiaries of programs supposedly designed for disadvantaged working farmers, have established a most cloying political commitment. So long as it stands, this commitment is likely to be served at the expense of the rural poor and of working farmers whose primary interest in agriculture is only occupational. A further, and more specific, conclusion to be drawn is that the administrative agency most directly afflicted by such a commitment is not in good position to lead a campaign on rural poverty or to be the champion of rural renaissance.

PART SIX   Agricultural Trade, Aid, and Development Policy

Agriculture and Foreign Economic Policy

D. GALE JOHNSON

This article is the text of the author's presidential address to the American Farm Economic Association in 1964, published in the Journal of Farm Economics, December 1964. In it, Dr. Johnson, Professor of Economics at the University of Chicago, traces long-run developments in the agricultural trade policies of the United States and other developed nations.

ALTHOUGH THE ORIGINS of the English Corn Laws are obscure, it is clear that in a rudimentary form this peculiar group of economic regulations existed at the beginning of the fifteenth century. Over the next four centuries the regulations became increasingly complex, until the combined effects of Cobden and his Manchester liberals and the potato famine led to their abolition in 1846. Contrary to general belief, the Corn Laws were not simply a set of import duties but also consisted of export bounties, variable import levies, and export and import prohibitions, with special preferences for using British ships.

During this period of British history, and also after the repeal of the Corn Laws until World War II, agricultural and trade policy were closely linked though there was more to agricultural policy than the regulation of trade. The objectives of the Corn Laws have a modern ring. Their aims were to stabilize the price of corn for the "benefit" of both producer and consumer; reduce the dependence upon foreign supplies of a critical food; achieve adequate land rent, since rent was viewed as a good measure of national prosperity; and maintain a large and prosperous rural population.

CORN LAWS ALL OVER AGAIN

The Common Agricultural Policy of the European Economic Community could well be called the European Corn Laws. The variable import levy was introduced into the Corn Laws in 1670. But the parallel with the Corn Laws is even closer. When direct payments and subsidies to farmers are withdrawn, the Common Agricultural Policy will be basically a trade and agricultural policy. The agricultural price and income goals will be sought through manipulation of international trade by variable import duties and export bounties.

To an increasing extent, especially during the last decade, the United States has come to rely upon international trade as an adjunct of agricultural policy. Import limitations and export subsidies were a necessary adjunct of farm price programs beginning in 1933, but with the inception of P.L. 480 export subsidies have become a major and positive aspect of our agricultural policies. Limitations on imports have begun to play an even more important role in recent years, especially with the "voluntary" limitations on certain dairy products and beef and veal that were negotiated with New Zealand, Australia and Ireland in 1963 and 1964. The Sugar Act of 1962 introduced the variable import levy into our agricultural policy. We have long used variable export subsidies—the size of the subsidy representing the difference between domestic prices and whatever was needed to export the desired volume.

On July 1, 1964 the British imposed minimum import prices on grains. An offer of grain at a lower price results in the imposition of a duty to bring the landed cost of the grain to the specified minimum level. Both the EEC and British minimum import prices are an open invitation for sellers to collude to raise the cost of grain.

The industrial countries seem to have come almost full circle for the English Corn Laws are now the pattern for agricultural and trade policy. Thus, there are important lessons for students of current agricultural policy to be drawn from English history prior to abolition of these laws in 1846. This is particularly true when we consider the outcome of the recent trade negotiations in Geneva. The U.S. position was especially similar to that of the British following the War of 1812 up to the abolition of the Corn Laws in 1846.

The repeal of the Corn Laws was a part of a general movement toward free trade, just as the negotiations at Geneva were part of an effort to achieve freer trade. Prior to the repeal of the Corn Laws, as now, the difficulties of modifying barriers to trade in agricultural products were an important consideration in general trade relations among nations. This was made clear by J. S. Nicholson in his lectures on the Corn Laws when he discussed efforts to reduce barriers to trade.[1]

At the same time, both at home and abroad, the Corn Laws were the most prominent and noticeable part of the protective system. When foreign nations were invited to reduce their tariffs, they always pointed to our Corn Laws. A remarkable instance occurs in connection with the framing of the tariff of the United States in 1824. Our Minister at Washington, in that year, wrote to Mr. Canning: "Had no restriction existed on the importation of foreign—i.e., American—grain into Europe, and especially into *Great Britain*, there is little doubt that the tariff (that is, of the U.S.A.) would never have passed through either house of Congress, since the great agricultural states, and Pennsylvania especially, the main mover of the question, would have been indifferent, if not opposed, to its enactment."

In the same despatch, it is said that the retention of the Corn Laws by Britain led the Americans to suspect the real intention of any removal of other restrictions as in the modifying of the Navigation Acts. . . . They suspected this country of insidious designs, with the view of afterwards taking advantage of the concessions obtained from other countries.

How similar these views and concerns are to those of today! The view exists in some quarters that the current U.S. interest in reducing the barriers to our agricultural exports is largely a self-serving one and that any concessions we might make on agricultural products will be negated subsequently if the increase in our imports becomes embarrassing. Actions that have been

1. J. S. Nicholson, *The History of the English Corn Laws* (London, 1904), pp. 129–130.

taken under Section 22 to limit imports, our recent responses to increases in imports of certain dairy products and of beef through negotiations of so-called voluntary agreements, or recent congressional consideration of beef import quotas that would violate our GATT[2] obligations serve as a basis for the view. Thus just as we suspected the British almost a century and a half ago of "insidious designs," our behavior in negating reductions that we have made in tariff duties leads others to suspect us.

There is also a growing concern in the United States of the long-run effects of the Common Agricultural Policy of the EEC. This concern is due to the adverse effects of that policy upon our agricultural exports, for example, the effects of the variable levy upon poultry meat; our government cried foul and exercised its right to retaliate under GATT regulations. But exercising the rights did not prevent a sharp decline in our poultry exports to the EEC.

It is feared that high grain prices and consequent high prices for livestock products will both increase EEC production of grain and reduce EEC consumption of livestock products, which in turn implies a reduction of imports and perhaps even some export surpluses in the EEC.

The EEC has rejected the use of deficiency payments to meet price support commitments. Thus the difference between a support or intervention price and world prices must be maintained by an import restriction—the variable levy—or, if there is an export surplus, by an export subsidy. Thus, in effect, the EEC price support effectively determines the EEC trade policy for those agricultural commodities produced in the EEC. The United States finds that it must negotiate with the EEC about the Community's price support levels. In turn, the U.S. must be willing to negotiate with respect to our domestic farm programs.

Secretary Freeman, in presenting the negotiating plan of the United States for agricultural trade for the then forthcoming GATT meeting in Geneva, summed up the objectives and hopes of that plan:

2. [GATT stands for General Agreement on Tariffs and Trade. This is a 72-nation agreement which provides general guidelines for the conduct of international trade and a framework for multilateral negotiation of trade barriers.—*Editor*.]

Finally, it is a plan for trade liberalization, and that is what the trade negotiations are all about.

It would require tariff cuts. . . .

It would assure markets to efficient producers and would require some limit to the measures encouraging inefficient production.

It would expose the trading practices and the domestic farm policies of the Free World to the test of the high principles under which the trade negotiations were launched.

It would inject new strength and vigor into the world's established commercial trading system, a system which has served man well through the ages and which continues to offer best promise for effective and rewarding distribution of his production.[3]

I consider the above to be an extremely important statement. It represents a new direction; it is the clearest official statement that I have seen which says that it is wrong for us as a nation to continue to develop our agricultural programs without concern for their effects upon others. As the Secretary said on an earlier occasion, "No matter how much it complicates our problems, agricultural policy must be considered in terms of the needs of all our people, of every segment of our economy, and of the position and responsibility of this Nation as a leader of the free world."[4]

If the present trade negotiations are to have a successful conclusion, the close interconnections between agricultural and trade policies require that the negotiations concern themselves with price support levels, subsidies, and other methods that tend to encourage output increases. The export subsidies, the quantitative import restrictions and the variable levies are only the obvious requirements of the domestic farm policies. These interferences with trade are not desired for themselves, but only as means for achieving the objectives of domestic agricultural policies.

If present policies are maintained, the EEC will expand its high cost agriculture and will burden its population with high food prices; the United Kingdom will be saddled with a huge drain upon its treasury to finance the deficiency payments and

3. From a speech given by Secretary of Agriculture Orville L. Freeman to the annual meeting of the Rice Millers Association, Houston, Texas, January 31, 1964.

4. From a speech given to the Agricultural Policy Forum, Chicago Board of Trade, Chicago, December 12, 1963.

production grants unless it, too, transfers these costs to consumers; and the U.S. will continue to incur farm program costs of upwards of 6 billion dollars. And the farm problems of these countries will be no nearer solution in 1970 than today.

But my main concern here is not the problems that the rich industrial nations of the West have made for themselves. They have what they well deserve! I am concerned about *the consequences of the agricultural policies of the industrial nations for the less developed areas of the world.* The industrial countries no doubt can easily afford their present farm programs from a purely domestic viewpoint. But is this true when all of the international implications are taken into account? I do not promise to answer this question, but I know that it is a critically relevant question which requires analysis and which, in terms of policy choices, calls for an open mind.

THE WEB OF TRADE

It should not be necessary here to show the importance of the expansion of agricultural production and the growth of agricultural exports as significant contributors to the growth of per capita incomes in the underdeveloped areas. In most of the less developed countries agriculture provides employment for half or more of the labor force and for three-fourths or more of total foreign exchange earnings. More farm output is required to feed a growing population and to feed it better; more farm exports are required to provide some of the capital and other requisites for modernization.

The primary link between the agricultural policies of the industrial nations and the development of agriculture in low income countries is the value, origin and composition of international trade in agricultural products. The major industrial nations influence the value of agricultural exports from the less developed countries by restricting imports and expanding exports. Western Europe reduces the value of exports of the less developed areas by expanding indigenous agricultural output. If present policies are maintained in Western Europe, that area may become an important exporter of some farm products for which it has been a traditional importer. The United States also reduces the value of such exports by the use of export subsidies and by expanding domestic production in the face of less costly imports.

The less developed countries suffer from two important disabilities because of the composition of their export trade. The first is that the major components of that trade—food, fibers and beverages—have relatively low income elasticities which means that the growth in demand in the industrial countries for products of the type they produce is primarily a function of population growth and only secondarily a function of increases in per capita income. The second difficulty is that the industrial countries are engaged in protecting or subsidizing their own producers of similar products. The first disability should not be confused with the second. At best, the growth in demand for the exports of the less developed areas will be much slower than the growth in real national income of the major industrial countries, unless there is a substitution of imports for domestic production in the industrial countries.[5] When this difficulty is added to the second—the practice of most industrial nations of subsidizing a number of competing products—the outlook for future growth of exports is indeed bleak.

It is argued by some that since most of the lesser developed countries are semitropical or tropical and most industrial nations are in the temperate zone, there is relatively little competition between the agricultures of the two areas. While it is true that a wide variety of tropical products are admitted into industrial countries under favorable terms and that tariff rates on many of these products are zero or nearly so, there are some tropical products that face relatively high internal excises—coffee in West Germany and France, for example. And while this point is not directly within the province of this paper, it should be noted that generally only the raw tropical products are found on the free list. Most industrial nations, including the U.S. and the EEC, have what appear to be moderate duties on the first processed product or products (oil and oil meal from an oilseed) but have what in fact are duties that are a very high fraction of the value added during such first processing. A 10 percent tariff on the first processed product, with a zero duty on the raw

5. Most of the exports of the less-developed regions are to industrial countries—in 1962 approximately 75 percent.

material, can result in protection of the first processing of 50 to 150 percent. It is virtually impossible for the underdeveloped countries to develop certain processing industries that could compete for international markets.

But let me return to the competition between the tropics and the temperate zone. Some of it is very direct—sugar, tobacco, cotton, rice, fats (butter and lard versus vegetable oils), many fruits and nuts. In recent years, for example, approximately 40 percent of the world's output of sugar has been grown in temperate areas subject to all manner of protection and subsidization. But the less direct forms of competition—one food grain for another (e.g., wheat for rice) and one food relative to all others—must in the aggregate be of substantial importance. If the output of temperate zone food products increases as a result of the policies of the industrial countries, the demand for tropical zone products in the industrial countries will almost surely decline.

DEVELOPMENT AND TRADE

As already noted, the economic growth of the developing countries is dependent upon agricultural exports. This statement is an oversimplification; what the developing countries require is a substantial increase in imports. An expansion of imports can be financed in only two ways—by an increase in exports, or by loans, grants and aid from the industrial nations. The expansion of agricultural exports is emphasized because the present composition of the exports of the less developed countries is so largely agricultural, and especially so when areas that have large petroleum exports are excluded.

While loans and grants to the less developed areas are likely to increase in value over time, it is difficult to imagine that loans and grants can ever provide for most of the total import requirements of the poor countries. Only about 16 percent of total imports of the developing countries were provided by all forms of private and governmental loans and grants in 1960–1961.[6] If the capital flow from rich to poor countries in 1960–61 had conformed to the standard that is now being put forward as an objective—

6. UN, *World Economic Survey 1962, I. The Developing Countries in World Trade*, p. 115.

namely, 1 percent of the gross domestic product of the advanced countries—it would have financed about 21 percent of the total imports of the poor countries.[7] Thus the magnitude of the capital flow actually achieved in 1960–61 was rather close to what some consider to be a reasonable upper limit to the amount of transfers. While it is not possible to predict exactly how much the imports of the less developed countries would need to increase over the next decade or two if they were to achieve rapid economic growth, projections made by the Economic Commission for Europe indicate the probable order of magnitude of the required increase. If the less developed areas achieve an annual growth rate of per capita income of 3 percent between 1957–59 and 1980, the commission's projection is that their imports would increase from $22.5 to $60.0 billion.[8] If net capital inflow stays at a constant fraction (approximately 16 percent) of imports, exports would have to increase by more than $30 billion. Put another way, this projection implies a required increase in the exports of the developing countries in two decades that is greater than their exports as of 1957–59.

The share of agricultural exports in the total exports of the less developed countries will decline if per capita national output increases. However, a large increase in the absolute value of agricultural exports must be achieved. But if the industrial countries maintain their present domestic agricultural policy course, is this in the realm of what is possible?

Agricultural protection of a significant magnitude is almost universal among the industrial countries. This protection takes numerous forms—higher prices, deficiency payments, production grants and input subsidies. Because of the many forms that protection takes, it is difficult to measure.

Gavin McCrone has made an estimate of the amount of one type of protection for Western Europe for 1955–56.[9] His estimate is the difference in the value of output measured at the prices

7. Based on *ibid.*, p. 119.
8. Economic Commission for Europe, UN, *Economic Survey of Europe in 1960*, Geneva, 1961, Chap. 5, p. 6. The estimates and projections exclude the major petroleum exporters.
9. Gavin McCrone, *The Economics of Subsidizing Agriculture*, London, 1962. Rather similar estimates for the major agricultural products may be found in ECE, *Economic Survey of Europe in 1960*, Chap 3.

received by farmers and the value of output at import prices of the same year. He did not consider any of the many other forms of subsidization. I have slightly modified his estimates and have made similar estimates, on a consistent basis, for 1961–62.[10] The degree of protection, indicated by the percentage excess of output valued at national prices over output valued at import prices, was the following:[11]

	1955–56	1961–62
France	24	17
West Germany	22	39
United Kingdom	33	29
Italy	19	25
Sweden	26	41
Norway	20	43
Netherlands	5	14
Belgium	6	13
Denmark	3	0

By the limited measure used, the degree of protection decreased significantly only in France during the six-year period, though there was also a small decrease in the United Kingdom. Major increase occurred in West Germany, Sweden and Norway. Tiny Denmark had virtually no protection in either year.

How does the United States compare with Western Europe? I have made estimates similar to those made by McCrone and they show that the difference in value to output valued at national prices and import or commercial export prices amounted to 16 percent of the latter in 1961–62. This estimate does not include the direct payments to farmers which were about 6 percent of the value of farm production for sale and home use. However, similar payments (except the deficiency payments in

10. The modifications included a change in the basis for measuring the degree of protection—from output valued at national prices to output valued at import prices—and the inclusion of poultry meat in the calculations.

11. The estimates of agricultural protection are not subject to a simple interpretation; in all of the countries, other sectors of the economy are protected in varying degrees and in ways that are not reflected by calculations of average tariff rates. Furthermore, the specific percentages should be considered as general approximations of the degree of protection since many difficult problems of comparison are involved. These include differences in quality of products imported or exported and local production, exchange rate complications and location and stage of processing effects upon prices.

the United Kingdom) were not included in the estimates of protection for Western Europe.

The amount of protection afforded agriculture in the industrial countries has increased significantly in the last three decades, and the ratio of farm output to domestic use of farm products has risen both in the United States and Western Europe. Food and Agriculture Organization of the United Nations (FAO) estimates indicate that Western Europe imported 31 percent of its food supply before World War II; by the late 50's the area imported only 25 percent of its food; projections made before the implementation of the Common Agricultural Policy of the EEC and other recent protectionist measures in Western Europe indicated that by the mid-60's, 22 percent or less of the total food supply would be imported.[12] During the past decade, U.S. imports of agricultural products have remained approximately stable in value terms, while exports of farm products have increased by more than 60 percent and total agricultural exports which at the beginning of the decade were no larger than imports now exceed total agricultural imports by roughly 60 percent.

An admittedly extreme example of agricultural protectionism in the industrial countries is that of sugar. U.S. sugar production has long been highly protected, first by tariffs and since 1934 by import quotas and direct subsidy payments to farmers. Since the first sugar act, the quotas allocated to continental U.S. have more than doubled. In the late 20's, U.S. producing areas (excluding the Philippines) supplied only 37 percent of U.S. sugar consumption; during 1956–60, 51 percent. Under the Sugar Act of 1962, the share of the sugar quota reserved to U.S. producers was increased from 53 to 60 percent. Sixty-five percent of any increase in total quotas due to increased U.S. consumption is now allocated to U.S. producers.

The record of the EEC with respect to sugar is about the same as ours. Before World War II, the present EEC imported about a quarter of their sugar even though all domestic sugar was heavily protected.[13] Between the late 30's and 1957–58 sugar imports declined 68 percent while internal use increased about 60 percent

12. "Trends in European Agriculture and Their Implications for Other Regions," *Monthly Bul. of Agr. Econ. and Stat.*, November 1960, pp. 1–8.
13. The Netherlands was an exception until recently.

and local production doubled.

While sugar appears to be an extreme case, it is extreme only because the degree of protection has been so great and not because protection is atypical. Moreover, it is exceedingly relevant to this analysis because sugar is a commodity that can be grown throughout much of the underdeveloped world—and sugar would be produced to a much greater extent in that part of the world than it now is if the major markets were not so protected and so precarious.

Of course, not all the agricultural policies of the industrial countries work to the disadvantage of the underdeveloped countries. For more than a quarter century, the U.S. has set a floor under the world price of cotton and tobacco. There was a marked response on the part of producers in other regions to the relatively profitable prices achieved by the efforts at output restriction and stock accumulations in the United States. In the case of cotton, some of "the bloom has been taken off the rose" in recent years by export subsidies equal to roughly a quarter of the U.S. domestic price. However, there is evidence that U.S. output of cotton would not be much if any below the present level if there were no farm program for cotton. In both tobacco and cotton the U.S. has lost its position of dominance in international trade. In the late 20's the U.S. exported about two-thirds of the cotton moving in international trade; now its share is little more than two-fifths. The loss in the case of tobacco is not so dramatic—from in excess of 40 percent in the late 20's to about 30 percent recently.

The United States, alone among the industrial countries, has some programs designed to limit the output of certain agricultural products and to some degree, total agricultural output. Although the official view of the Department of Agriculture is that the United States is effectively limiting the output of farm products, I believe, as I have argued elsewhere, that the net effect of all federal farm programs—irrigation, reclamation, soil conservation, conservation payments, high support prices, imported labor, soil banks and acreage allotments—has been to increase farm production.[14]

14. "Efficiency and Welfare Implications of United States Agricultural Policy," *J. Farm. Econ.*, Vol. 45, May 1963, pp. 331–342.

It is important to emphasize that we have not been able to convince our major trading partners that our farm programs, including both output restrictions and inducements, have had any effect other than to increase output and depress world prices. One of the important rationalizations of the EEC variable levy system is that it is required to protect EEC farmers from subsidized farm product exports from the U.S. This argument was used during the poultry dispute, with little justification in my opinion, but this does not mean that their position is without general validity. The following two quotations are from material that came to my desk in the same week—in one case the authorship is French and in the other it is American:

The variable levy applied by the EEC to agricultural imports from nonmember countries is aimed at making up the difference between the abnormally low world prices at which products are usually sold and prices within the Community. It is therefore nothing more than the counterpart of the export subsidies used by these nonmember countries; these subsidies also vary in relation to world prices so that products may be marketed below domestic prices. While this variable levy presents an effective counter to the disturbing effects of dumping foreign surpluses, it is not intended to prevent the entry of products that meet a need on the Community market, either because of their quality or the services provided.

. . . if market prices plus the certificate result in wheat being priced higher than world prices, appropriate adjustments will be made by way of export subsidies so we will continue to be competitive.[15]

So long as these two positions on the output effects of U.S. farm programs prevail, there is little possibility of reaching mutually acceptable solutions to the major agricultural trade problems. It would appear to be in the interest of the United States to ask for an independent evaluation of the output effects of our farm programs, just as we asked for an evaluation of the trade impacts of the EEC variable levy on poultry.

15. *France and Agriculture,* no author, distributed by French Information Service, New York, December 1963, p. 48, and speech by Secretary Orville L. Freeman in Wenatchee, Washington, June 11, 1964.

TRADE REALLY MATTERS

In 1960–62, world exports of major agricultural products totaled approximately 22 billion, of which $12 billion was exported by the less developed regions.[16] According to USDA estimates, the total value of agricultural output in the developing countries was approximately $53 billion in 1958; by coincidence, the value of agricultural output in Western Europe and the United States was also estimated to be $53 billion.[17] Thus if the industrial countries displace a billion dollars of the agricultural exports of the less developed countries by decreasing imports or by subsidizing exports, the amount is large relative to either the value of LDC's agricultural exports or the value of their total farm output.

During the 50's the annual rate of growth of the quantity of exports from the less developed countries was 3.6 percent compared to 6.9 percent for the industrial countries.[18] But what is even more important is that much of the growth in exports occurred by 1956. In value terms the exports from the nonindustrial countries to the industrial countries increased by 33 percent between 1950 and 1956; from 1956 through 1962 the increase was only 14 percent.[19]

Some of the reduction in import growth of the industrial countries of the products of the underdeveloped countries may have been due to a decline in the rate of national income growth during the 50's and to overcoming the effects of World War II on agricultural production in Western Europe. But some role must surely be assigned to the rising tide of agricultural protectionism in Western Europe after the end of the Korean War and the

16. FAO, *The State of Food and Agriculture 1963*, Rome, 1963, p. 50. The data exclude the trade of eastern Europe, USSR and Mainland China. The data also exclude intraregional trade.

17. USDA, *The World Food Budget, 1962 and 1966*, Foreign Agr. Econ. Rpt. No. 4, Rev., January 1962, p. 9. Values based on 1958 wholesale or export prices of major exporting countries.

18. UN, *World Economic Survey 1962, I. The Developing Countries in World Trade*, Chap. 1, p. 1.

19. GATT, *International Trade, 1962*. The country classifications differ slightly in the GATT and UN studies.

large increase in surplus disposal by the United States, especially under P.L. 480 beginning in 1954 and increasing in later years.

The significance of the increase in surplus disposal resulting from P.L. 480 can be seen by comparing it with the change in the value of world exports of the main agricultural products among the major regions between 1952–53 and 1960–62.[20] The increase in the interregional trade in agricultural products was $3,283 million during the period. This increase may be partitioned as follows: 1) the increase in the exports of the less developed countries was only $815 million; 2) the increase in commercial exports of the industrial countries was $1,097 million, and 3) the increase in the value of products made available as economic aid or surplus disposal by the United States was $1,371 million. Thus the increase in the value of shipments by the U.S. under programs such as P.L. 480 was much greater than the increase in exports of agricultural products from the less developed regions and somewhat greater than the increase in commercial sales by industrial countries, even though a substantial fraction of the latter increase was due to the use of export subsidies. How much substitution there has been between P.L. 480 shipments and commercial exports of all countries, including the U.S., is subject to dispute, but it is highly probable that there has been a significant degree of substitution.

The protection given agriculture in the industrial countries restricts exports from the less developed countries in one or both of two ways—increasing output and reducing consumption. Only in the United Kingdom have the consumption effects been largely eliminated through the use of deficiency payments. If the increase in prices received by producers averages 20 to 25 percent and if the increase in prices paid by consumers averages 15 to 20 percent, even very low elasticities of supply and demand will result in substantial contraction in the demand for exports of the less developed regions. If supply elasticities are as low as 0.15 and demand elasticities 0.2, the effect on the value of agricultural imports of the industrial countries would be as much as $3.5–4.5 billion. Some of the increased import demand would be met by

20. FAO, *State of Food and Agriculture 1963*, p. 51. Data exclude the communist areas and the changes in value of exports are for broad regional groups, not the change in the value of trade of each country.

developed countries such as Canada and Australia. But if the increase in LDC exports were to be only half that indicated or about $2 billion, the importance is very great when compared with total LDC exports of agricultural products of approximately $12 billion.

TRADE AND AID AND AGRICULTURAL POLICY

For a number of years, the slogan, "Trade, not aid," had a certain attractiveness in some circles in the United States. If current trends in agricultural policy in the industrial countries persist, the situation in the years ahead, as viewed by the less developed countries, may be best described as "Aid, not trade." Western Europe will import less and less and the United States will export more and more.

One of the most alarming prospects facing the less developed areas is that the United States soon may lose its near monopoly on the provision of food aid. This is a dim prospect, not because the new participants will be less concerned about the export implications of their activities than the U.S. has been, but because it will mean that the total flow of such aid will increase, more and more markets will disappear and relative farm prices will be further depressed in the world markets and in the recipient countries. If farm output in the EEC continues to expand relative to EEC consumption, the EEC will have no acceptable alternative but to inaugurate its own version of P.L. 480.[21]

An expansion in the volume of food aid will not offset the adverse effects of a decline in export earnings. While it is comforting to the rich to believe that their bounty is being used to prevent malnutrition among the poor and, perhaps on occasion, to prevent actual starvation, it is a delusion to assume that such aid will be a major factor contributing to a rise in real per capita incomes in the recipient countries.

If, as a result of the agricultural policies of the industrial nations, the less developed countries are not able to finance the imports that will contribute to rapid economic growth, the alter-

21. See *France and Agriculture,* pp. 50–55; and Pierre Uri, *Partnership for Progress, a Program for Transatlantic Action* (New York, 1963), pp. 27–40, esp. pp. 33–40.

natives are to follow policies of autarchy or for the industrial countries to substantially increase the flow of aid, grants or loans. If export earnings are demonstrably decreased by the farm policies of the industrial countries, the claim of the less developed countries for increased aid or other capital flows will be a strong one. Thus it is not at all unlikely that a reduction of export earnings will be offset, at least in part, by an increase in aid and loans.

If present agricultural policies in the industrial countries are continued, the costs to consumers and taxpayers will surely increase as they have for the past decade. When the cost of additional foreign assistance necessitated by the consequences of these policies is added to the direct costs, the case for searching for alternative methods of meeting the income objectives of the agricultural policies of the industrial countries becomes even stronger.

The very high cost of the current farm programs—to consumers and to taxpayers—is due to a substantial degree to the measures that result in increased output. A very high fraction of the total costs of the farm programs is required to pay for additional inputs attracted to or retained in agriculture as a result of production subsidies or high product prices. I refer not so much to labor or land, though these are involved, but more to capital inputs, fertilizer and other current purchased inputs. The U.S. farm programs, with an emphasis upon acreage limitations, appear to be no more effective in creating additional income for farm labor and management than the programs used in Western Europe.

Almost exactly two decades ago I argued that while price policy could be used to improve the efficiency with which resources were used within agriculture, price policy was not an effective tool for meeting important income goals.[22] Price policy can make little or no contribution to the elimination of poverty in agriculture, to the reduction of the dispersion of income within agriculture or to the achievement of returns for farm labor equal to the returns to comparable labor in the rest of the economy. The most that price policy can do is to contribute to greater

22. "Contribution of Price Policy to the Income and Resource Problems in Agriculture," *J. Farm Econ.*, November 1944, pp. 654–664.

stability of farm income. But most industrial countries have placed major or sole reliance upon price policy as the means for increasing farm incomes.

The adverse consequences for the less developed countries of the agricultural policies of the industrial countries are primarily due to the efforts by the latter to achieve income objectives by the use of commodity price policy. Only as the industrial countries turn to direct approaches for meeting their farm income objectives—education, training, aids to mobility, health, employment services, and income grants not associated with production or productivity—will it be possible to eliminate the existing inconsistencies between their agricultural and foreign economic policies.

If we are guided by consideration for the interests of others and if we are imaginative in devising ways for meeting the legitimate income objectives of the farm populations of the industrial countries, we can improve upon the present highly unsatisfactory state of international trade and create a basis for international trade in which the less developed countries will have a real opportunity to compete effectively for markets. If, for lack of imagination and consideration for the interests of others, we continue along our present paths, we must accept responsibility for the adverse consequences of our actions upon others who are immeasurably less fortunate than we are.

Malthus, Marx, and the North American Breadbasket

ORVILLE L. FREEMAN

As Secretary of Agriculture under Presidents Kennedy and Johnson, Mr. Freeman helped move our food aid programs away from surplus disposal toward more positive efforts to encourage economic development abroad. In this article, published in For- eign Affairs, July 1967, he documents the crucial role played by U.S. food aid in recent years.

NORTH AMERICA's dramatic emergence over the past generation as the world's principal supplier of food can be illustrated with a half dozen numbers. During the late 1930s, three of the world's seven major geographic regions supplied virtually all of the grain moving into the world market. Latin America, with exports of nine million metric tons yearly, was the leading food exporter, and grain exports were an important source of foreign exchange earnings. North America and Eastern Europe (including the Soviet Union) were each exporting five million tons yearly. Most of the grain exported from these three regions, principally wheat and corn, went to Western Europe.

Thirty years later the pattern of world grain trade has been altered beyond recognition. As of 1966, Latin America, with net grain exports of two million tons, was scarcely self-sufficient. Exports from Argentina were largely offset by imports into Brazil and other smaller importing countries. Eastern Europe, including the Soviet Union, no longer exported grain but on the contrary was an importer; in 1966 the area imported some fourteen million tons, largely from Canada.

Of all the changes in the pattern of world grain trade between the late 1930s and 1966, the change in the position of North America was most pronounced. As shown by Table 1, net grain exports increased from five million tons to sixty million tons, providing in 1966 some 85 percent of the combined grain exports of the net exporting regions. Australia has substantially increased its exports, but its share of the total has remained at about 12 percent. North America has clearly emerged as the breadbasket of the world.

About three-fourths of North America's grain exports originate in the United States; the remaining one-fourth, coming from Canada, consists largely of wheat. U.S. grain exports are presently rather evenly divided between wheat and feedgrains. Significantly, the United States alone could export easily the entire sixty million tons yearly if it were to remove all remaining production constraints.

Several factors have contributed to North America's growing importance as a source of food for the rest of the world. Three of these stand out. On the demand side, both the forces identified by Malthus and the adverse influence of Marxian thought on agriculture in the communist countries have contributed to the steadily growing excess of food consumption over production outside North America. On the supply side, the massive application of science to agriculture in the United States has resulted in an impressive increase in its capacity for producing food, making it possible to respond to growing needs abroad.

Malthus first described the threat of uncontrolled population growth in 1797, nearly 170 years ago. His theory that population would tend to grow geometrically while food production would increase arithmetically has proved valid throughout much of the

TABLE 1. *World Grain Trade by Major Geographic Regions (in million metric tons)*

	1934–38	1960	Est. 1966
North America	+5	+39	+60
Latin America	+9	0	+2
Western Europe	−24	−25	−23
Eastern Europe (incl. U.S.S.R.)	+5	0	−14
Africa	+1	−2	−3
Asia	+2	−16	−30
Oceania (Australia & N.Z.)	+3	+6	+8

NOTE: plus = net exports; minus = net imports. Minor imbalances between world imports and exports in a given year may be due to rounding or variations in reporting methods used by various countries.

world. Half a century after his gloomy prognosis Ireland's population was sharply reduced by a famine.

It is commonly supposed that food shortages exist in the less developed countries because agriculture is performing poorly there. This is not exactly the case. Food production is increasing almost as rapidly in the less developed countries as in the developed ones. Between 1957–59 and 1966, total food production in the less developed countries increased 19 percent as compared to 22 percent in the developed countries. But population growth rates in less developed countries were double those in the more advanced countries, largely offsetting the overall gains in food production. Latin America and Western Europe illustrate this. Both have expanded food production at about 2.5 to 3.0 percent annually over the past decade. In Europe, where population is increasing at about 1 percent per year, this has meant progress and a steady upgrading of diets. But in Latin America, where population has been multiplying at nearly 3 percent per year, food output per person has not been gaining.

Rates of population increase in the less developed countries today are without precedent. In several they are well above 3 percent yearly, in some instances approaching the biological maximum. Populations growing at 3 percent yearly double within a generation and multiply eighteenfold within a century. To the agriculturalist, this Malthusian arithmetic is frightening. A less developed country today is, almost by definition, one with a rapid rate of population growth. There are not many exceptions. The impact of modern health measures has reduced death rates, but comparable reductions in birth rates have not been achieved. Even a population growth rate of 3 percent could be tolerable if there were vast areas of fertile, well-watered land to be brought under the plow. But unfortunately, most of the frontiers have long since disappeared and the supply of new land which can be brought into production quickly and cheaply is fast diminishing.

The world food problem is, however, more than a race between food and people. In reality it is a race between the production of food and the demand for food. There are two reasons for the sharp increase in the world demand for food: population growth is one; the other is rising per capita incomes.

In some countries, rising incomes are generating more growth in the demand for food than is population increase. This is certainly the case in Japan, where incomes have risen 7 percent annually over the past decade, but where population has grown less than 1 percent annually. The same is also true for many countries in Europe, particularly West Germany, France, Sweden and Italy. To construe the problem merely as a race between food and people fails to grasp the whole issue.

In no country prior to World War II had population growth rates or per capita incomes risen rapidly over an extended period. High, sustained rates of growth in both population and income per person are largely postwar phenomena, and to make things more difficult, they have occurred simultaneously. The result, in recent years, has been a rate of increase in demand which the world's farmers have not matched (see Chart 1).

The difference in diets between a low-income, less developed country and a more advanced country such as the United States or Canada is much more than merely the difference between 2,000 calories per person per day and 3,000 calories. Caloric intake measures only the quantitative aspects of diet. It gives no indication of quality; it does not show whether malnutrition exists—from, say, the lack of protein.

To provide the high-protein diet enjoyed by North Americans requires close to one ton of grain per person per year. Of this total only about 150 pounds are consumed directly as grain. Most of the remainder is consumed indirectly in the form of meat, milk and eggs. The amount of grain available per capita in the less developed nations averages about 400 pounds per year. Deducting some 10 percent of this for seed leaves 360 pounds for consumption, or less than one pound per person per day. Nearly all of this must be consumed directly to meet minimum energy requirements. Little is left for conversion into meat, milk and eggs—the traditional sources of protein in the more developed nations.

For every $2 rise in annual per capita income there is a corresponding rise in grain requirements of at least one pound. (See Chart 1). The significant point is that virtually every country, regardless of its level of development is striving to improve per capita income over the next few years. If these plans succeed, much more food must be obtained somewhere.

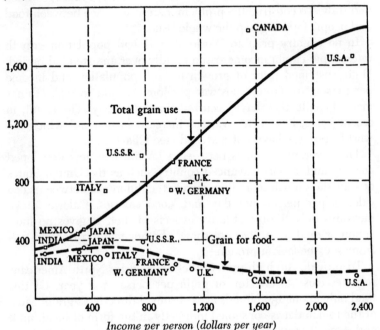

CHART 1. *Income and Per Capita Grain Consumption,*
Total and for Food

Pounds of grain
per person per year

Income per person (dollars per year)

Just as the developing countries are, almost by definition, countries with rapid rates of population growth, so communist countries are countries with a poorly performing farm sector. There are few, if any, significant exceptions. To name a communist country—Poland, Czechoslovakia, East Germany, the Soviet Union, Albania, Mainland China, Cuba—is to name a country having problems with agriculture.

All of these nations have claimed allegiance to Marxian thought —in agriculture as well as in the rest of the economy. Actually, Marx himself had little to say about agriculture. He was a city boy, primarily interested in diagnosing the social ills of early industrial societies. It was largely his followers who assumed that agriculture, like industry, could be readily organized on a large scale under state control. And it was they who went on to exploit agriculture in order to provide the basis for industrialization. Agriculture was given neither sufficient inputs nor incentives.

The communist countries are beginning to pay dearly for this policy. Food shortages have become a drain on their foreign exchange and a drag on their economic growth. The decision to organize agriculture on a large-scale, authoritarian basis has cost the communist countries literally billions of dollars in inefficiently used resources and lost economic growth.

Khrushchev's rise to power was closely followed by several efforts to cure Russia's farm ills. The Machine Tractor Stations were abolished; large areas were planted to corn in an effort to emulate successes in the American Midwest; and vast areas of virgin land were plowed and planted to wheat in areas of marginal rainfall. Output did increase from 1954 to 1957, and in 1958 Khrushchev promised the Soviet people that they would soon surpass the Americans in per capita production of meat, milk and eggs. At the same time, however, investment in agriculture was reduced. In the following years, output stagnated at 1958 levels. Yet in 1963 when I visited the Kremlin, Khrushchev was still bragging loudly. That year drought struck, accentuating an already weak position, and in 1964 the Soviet Union imported more wheat than any country in history. Khrushchev was out of office before drought occurred again in 1965.

The dramatic reversals in Chinese agriculture, following the Great Leap of 1958 and during the early 1960s, were equally abrupt. Many, principally those who had failed to gauge the weaknesses of the Great Leap, particularly in agriculture, were much surprised in 1961 when China turned to Western countries for several million tons of imported grain. This continuing dependence on food from abroad probably reveals more accurately than any other available information the true state of affairs in Chinese agriculture. Another indicator is the reported effort to move twenty million urban immigrants back to the rural areas from whence they came "to provide more labor to produce food." What it may disclose is not so much a shortage of labor in the countryside as the inability of the Peking régime to procure food in the countryside for movement to the cities. To avoid hunger and possibly famine in the cities, Peking has imported food from abroad and exported people back to the countryside where their village kin are more willing to share their food with them.

A generation ago Mainland China was the leading producer of soybeans, supplying some 90 percent of all the soybeans entering the world market. In recent years, however, a steadily expanding population has reduced the outflow of soybeans to a trickle. Today, the United States produces three-fourths of the world soybean crop, enabling it to provide some 90 percent of the soybeans entering a vastly enlarged international market.

Mainland China is, perhaps ominously, suffering from both the influence of Marx and the forces identified by Malthus.

Offsetting the effects of the forces described by Malthus and the adverse influence of Marxian thought on food production has been the impressive development of North America's capacity for producing food. Several factors have contributed to this. To begin with, the United States has an excellent piece of agricultural real estate. Its Midwest, or Corn Belt, is one of the largest areas of fertile, well-watered farmland in the world. The only other areas even remotely approaching it in both size and inherent fertility are Northwestern Europe, the pampas of Argentina and the Gangetic plain of India.

Not only did we start with good farmland but we have done an excellent job of developing it. Through scientific soil and water management we have made inherently fertile soils even more fertile. Perhaps the most important single factor contributing to our unparalleled productivity has been the family farm. As a production unit it is the most efficient yet devised. Other forms of production organization are in use or have been experimented with, but most have not worked well. This is particularly true for most of the systems embodying very large production units such as collectives, communes or haciendas. The family farm, where the social unit and the production unit are identical, provides a stronger link between effort and reward than any other system. As a result, they are continuing to grow in both size and efficiency. Although many of these production units run up to several hundred acres in size and have assets frequently exceeding $100,000, they are not corporate farms. They are still family units, owned and operated by the family, using mostly family labor. The number of large corporate farms is exceedingly small, and actually declining.

Another factor contributing to the success of American agriculture has been the careful delineation of the government's role. There seems to be a great deal of confusion as to the proper role for the public and private sectors in many of the hungry countries today. The record of U.S. agriculture provides some clues. The government has never been directly engaged in agricultural production. Actions such as the Homestead Act of 1862 were specifically designed to encourage private settlement and production. Neither has the government engaged in producing and distributing any of the multitude of inputs that modern agriculture requires. This has been left entirely to private industry.

Conversely, we did decide that government should conduct agricultural research and education. The idea that problems in agriculture should be subject to systematic research took root over a century ago. The first publicly supported agricultural research in the United States took place before the Civil War in the Patent Office, the predecessor of the Department of Agriculture. Since the passage of the Hatch Act in 1887, the Land Grant Colleges have been an important partner in agricultural research. This government-sponsored work was the precursor of the concept of research and development in modern industry. We also decided at an early date that the government should be involved in extending new ideas and techniques from the laboratory and experimental plot to the farm. The result has been our widely respected Extension Service. The discoveries made through research sponsored by the Department of Agriculture are public property. As soon as new varieties are developed they are released, to be multiplied and distributed by private industry, hopefully at a profit. Similarly, when the process for developing frozen citrus concentrates had been perfected in Department laboratories, it was turned over to private industry.

Public policy recognized, after much struggle, that three million production units—producing literally dozens of different commodities and scattered throughout the United States—are not likely to be able to bargain effectively with the non-farm economy. As a result, government has influenced the terms of trade between farmers and the rest of the economy, generally by means of price supports. This policy, dating from the late 1930s, was instrumental in triggering what we now term the modern agricultural revolution. The effect of an assured price level backed by government is to encourage farmers to invest both short-term production capital in fertilizer and in superior but expensive seed of new and improved varieties; and longer term capital in productive capacity—in irrigation, drainage and other improvements in land and other capital assets.

Governments in nearly all of the countries with modern, productive agriculture now operate price-support programs for principal crops. Thus we see government serving as a guarantor of minimum price, a referee in the marketplace and a catalyst to technological progress. This is not to say that the pattern we have chosen to follow in the United States is the precise policy that should be adopted by the developing countries, but it may be a useful guide. Involving government too directly in agriculture—often for political reasons—has resulted in a great waste of resources in developing countries.

Inevitably, the agricultural successes of the North American breadbasket and stagnation in communist agriculture have affected the balance of power between East and West. Indeed, North American food and our capacity for producing it have been instrumental in tilting the scales in favor of the West.

About the same time as Khrushchev's 1958 promise of a better diet and, implicitly, a better performance in agriculture, the Soviet leaders were also challenging the United States to a general economic competition. This was to replace the more overt military and political competition characterizing the earlier stages of the cold war. In some areas of economic competition the Soviets are performing exceedingly well. The overwhelming advantage we once enjoyed in the production of steel has been narrowed; the generation of hydroelectric power has increased rapidly in the Soviet Union, narrowing the gap between the two economies; in the space race we do not know whether the language first spoken on the moon will be English or Russian.

But in agriculture there is no contest. The United States, with scarcely 6 percent of its people still on the farm, is feeding 200 million Americans, 60 million Indians and the equivalent of at least another 100 million people in other parts of the world. The Soviets, by contrast, with close to half of their labor force still tied to agriculture, are importing grain to provide bread for their people. If we were as far ahead of the Russians in the space race as we are in agriculture, we would by now be running a shuttle service to the moon.

The impressive food-producing capability of North America and our growing lead over the countries of the East are beginning to have an impact on the countries of the Third World. During the early post-colonial years, many of the newly independent peoples could be satisfied with slogans and flag waving. Now they are hungry; they want food, not slogans. Rising rice prices in Djakarta helped to undermine Sukarno. Empty shelves in the food shops of Accra contributed to the overthrow of Nkrumah. More and more, the less developed countries are turning for assistance to those with food and food-producing know-how.

Our unmatched food-producing capability has strengthened our foreign policy immeasurably. For instance, during the period since World War II, and particularly since the Communist take-over of the Chinese Mainland in 1949, the Japanese and U.S. economies have become increasingly integrated. Traditionally, China and Japan were natural trading partners, with China supplying basic raw materials and foodstuffs in exchange for Japanese manufactures; Japan looked to China for much of its imports of soybeans, rice and other farm products. But China can no longer supply Japan's needs. Today, Japan looks to the United States for the bulk of its imports of farm products—wheat, rice, feed-grains, soybeans and cotton. The flow of farm commodities crossing the Pacific from the United States to Japan may exceed $1 billion in 1967. Without our ability to generate huge farm exports, these strong economic ties could not have developed. In geographic terms Japan is off the cost of China, but in economic terms it is just off the coast of California. This is but one of the more dramatic illustrations of the value of a productive farm sector in supporting our foreign policy.

The growing food deficits common to nearly all the communist economies are causing them to become politically and militarily vulnerable. During the early 1950s the Communist Chinese did not hesitate to intervene massively in the Korean conflict, but today, though they have threatened to intervene in Viet Nam, in fact they have not done so. Nor do I think they will. During the early 1950s China was self-sufficient in food production. During the 1960s, however, it has imported five to six million tons of grain annually. In addition, its dependence on imported fertilizer has increased to the point where it is now the world's leading importer. Significantly, nearly all the imports of both food and fertilizer come from the West—Australia and Canada in the case of grain, Western Europe and Japan in the case of fertilizer.

Combined imports of food grains and fertilizer into China now require nearly 40 percent of her total export earnings. Data on food production trends within China are unreliable but the fact that the Chinese leadership, intent on industrializing, is willing to use such a large share of available foreign exchange for food and fertilizer—essentially consumer goods—indicates just how hard pressed the Chinese are on the food front. In the event of a showdown with the Chinese in Viet Nam, or anywhere else in Asia, it is quite likely that exports of food from Australia and Canada would cease. Imports of fertilizer might also be halted, and China would then face a near famine or possibly worse.

Food deficits in Eastern Europe are also affecting the relationships between countries. The fact that nearly all the COMECON[1] countries have grain deficits has loosened the economic and, therefore, the political ties binding them together. As recently as the early 1960s, the Soviet Union was supplying large quantities of grain to the East European countries in exchange for industrial products, such as chemicals from East Germany and machine tools from Czechoslovakia. As of the mid-1960s, however, the East European countries are turning increasingly to Canada for wheat and to the United States for feedgrains. East Germany, once the breadbasket of all Germany, must today import large and growing quantities of food and feed. The East European countries are finding that their natural trading partners

1. [COMECON is the Council for Mutual Economic Assistance. Its purpose is to encourage economic cooperation among Eastern European nations and the USSR. There are eight permanent members: Bulgaria, Czechoslovakia, East Germany, Hungary, Poland, Mongolia, Rumania, and the USSR. Yugoslavia is partially affiliated.—*Editor.*]

lie to the West as well as to the East.

The embarrassing food shortages plaguing almost every communist economy are causing governments to invest more resources in agriculture, with the result that production is likely to increase. The Soviet Union enjoyed a bumper crop in 1966. This is not to say, however, that it, or any of the other communist countries, will become a leading grain exporter. The pressure for internal improvement in diets, as the standard of living improves, is too great. Some very substantial gains in grain production will be required before the Soviet Union can satisfy the growing desire of its people for more meat, milk and eggs.

As agriculture failed in one communist country after another, and they turned to the West for food imports, the communist strategists in Moscow must have faced a dilemma as they plotted their takeover of the world. What if they were successful? Who would be left to feed them?

As the East-West ideological conflict begins to fade, it is clear that a new North-South polarization is beginning to take shape between the have and have-not countries. This new polarization —which is essentially economic rather than political—threatens to be a pervasive and divisive force. In spite of all the rhetoric describing the need to narrow the gap, the gulf is widening, both absolutely and relatively. Nowhere is this growing gap so painfully evident as in the case of food.

For the past seven years, increases in world food production have almost exactly equalled those in population growth. But the expansion in production plus the continuing reduction in stocks in recent years have not been sufficient to cover the additional demand created by rising incomes. The result has been rising prices for basic food commodities such as wheat and rice, both within individual countries and in world markets.

Those countries which are more advanced and which have stronger purchasing power have been increasing their per capita consumption. In several countries where purchasing power is weak, either because of a lack of income or lack of foreign exchange, per capita consumption has declined. Two drought years are only a partial explanation of why per capita food supplies in India in 1966–67 were 5 percent below those of the early 1960s.

This decline, of course, has been concentrated in the low-income groups. Those of middle and upper income have increased their expenditures for food to offset at least partially the rise in prices. Those at the bottom of the economic scale, already using most of their income to buy their meager daily rations of food, have not been able to do so. When they have tightened their belts to the last notch, they take to the streets. Food demonstrations or riots erupt periodically, and with increasing frequency, in the major cities of Asia, North Africa and Latin America.

Perhaps the best illustration of just how acute this problem is becoming is the trend in rice prices in recent years. Nearly all of the world's rice-consuming peoples, except the Japanese, are continuing to multiply at an unabated rate. The area of land which can be used to produce rice, however, is rather rigidly defined by temperature, the availability of water and type of soil. The result has been a growing worldwide shortage of rice and rising prices over the past few years, and particularly the last several months. The price of rice, traditionally somewhat higher than wheat, has now climbed to the point where a ton of rice can be exchanged for two tons of wheat in the world grain market. Although this has not seriously affected the more advanced countries such as Japan or the smaller rice-importing countries of Europe, it has sharply reduced the ability of low-income, rice-consuming countries to import the rice they need.

An analysis of the trends in world stocks of grain—held almost entirely by the major exporters of wheat, feedgrains and rice—shows the emergence of some new and disturbing trends. During the eight years from 1953 to 1961, world grain stocks increased by an average margin of nine million tons each year. During this period world production was running ahead of consumption. During the six years from 1961 until 1967, world stocks of grain declined each year. Most of this decline, averaging fourteen million tons per year, took place in the United States. This means that since 1961 grain consumption has been exceeding production by 1.4 percent a year. (See Figure 1) Stated otherwise, production is going up only 2 percent a year, while consumption has been increasing at about 3.4 percent annually.

This excess of consumption over production has been met by using the surplus stocks held by the major exporting countries, particularly the United States. But if food deficits continue to grow in the less developed countries, the exporting nations will not be able to fill the growing food gap. Five years ago, we in the United States had the world's two major reserves in the race between food needs and food production: some fifty million tons of excess grain in storage, and a large area of fertile cropland made idle under our farm programs. During the early 1960s, idle cropland increased and in 1966 exceeded fifty million acres. Decisions within the past year to increase acreages of wheat, feedgrains, rice and soybeans will bring nearly one-half of this cropland back into production. Once this ready reserve is exhausted, it will become much more difficult for the world to achieve any abrupt increases in production to meet additional demand.

Since World War II, and more particularly since passage of Public Law 480, the 1954 enabling legislation for our food aid program, the United States has been attempting to alleviate world hunger by shipping food abroad. By the end of 1966, about 176 million metric tons of food worth $15.7 billion had been

Fig. 1. *World Grain Production Now Lagging Behind Consumption*

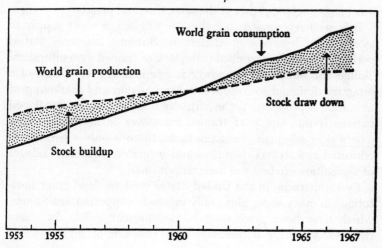

shipped abroad under concessional terms. Despite this massive program we are still as far from solving the problem as when we began—perhaps further than ever.

The growing economic distance between the have countries of the North and the have-not countries of the South is, moreover, now a source of social unrest and political instability. Secretary Robert McNamara gave a speech in Montreal in May 1967 in which he pointed out the relationship between the living standards in various countries and the incidence of social unrest and violent political upheaval. In that speech he made a short but very significant statement: "Security is development." For our purposes I would like to narrow that a bit and say "Security is food." Without an adequate supply of food in the developing countries, the prospects for economic and political stability are not good.

If we are ever to solve the world food problem, we must now begin concentrating in earnest on increasing food production in the less developed nations. We have a pretty good idea of what is needed. In varying proportion according to particular situations, the hungry countries need: increased quantities of fertilizer and other farm chemicals, improved varieties of seeds, increased availability of water, added credit, productive price policies, improved marketing facilities and expanded research and education. What makes progress so difficult is that most of these must be brought together at the same time and place.

It is well recognized that these inputs are in short supply in most of the less developed nations. But one key item that is perhaps less well recognized is the lack of trained agriculturalists. Skilled and educated manpower is essential in every phase of a program designed to improve the production and marketing of agricultural products. Yet in virtually none of the less developed nations is the supply of trained manpoyer in agriculture anywhere near adequate. In many cases, there is only a handful of educated researchers, planners and extension workers. Colleges of agriculture are few and their output small.

By comparison, in the United States we have land-grant institutions in every state, plus many privately supported institutions, which have been graduating trained agriculturalists for many decades. We have a relatively vast reservoir of highly skilled professional manpower (although still more is needed). In the Department of Agriculture alone we have 40,000 professional agriculturalists, only a few of whom are in Washington; most are working in the field throughout the 3,100 counties in the United States. These professionals include agronomists, entomologists, plant geneticists, agricultural economists and a host of others needed to develop and maintain high levels of productivity.

Until the less developed nations can build up cadres of trained personnel of their own, the logical approach is to make use of agriculturalists from the advanced nations. The United States has, for many years, been loaning know-how through the Agency for International Development (AID) and its predecessor agencies, and through programs operated by State universities and private consulting organizations. More recently these programs have been broadened to include the Department of Agriculture through the establishment of an International Agricultural Development Service which is financed by, and works closely with, AID.

In addition to providing biological and social scientists, the Department is increasingly called upon to assist in formulating the policies so essential for rapid progress in agriculture. Food price policies must become producer oriented, providing the farmer with a price for his products which makes the use of modern agricultural technology profitable. Policies governing foreign private investment must encourage the influx of capital, management and marketing know-how needed to product and distribute the sorely needed inputs.

This is not a job government can or should do alone. The participation and coöperation of industry—with its special skills and resources—is also urgently needed. As a nation we must cease asking how much it will cost to solve the food/population problem and begin asking how much it will cost if we fail to solve the problem in the allotted time. Time is the critical dimension. Today's hungry countries must compress the progress of centuries into decades and decades into years if they are to feed their rapidly multiplying peoples. Our aid is essential. As a nation we must now exercise the same imagination and resourcefulness which brought us to our current position of world agricultural leadership. We must devise more effective ways of linking our skills in producing food with the needs of the less fortunate multitudes abroad. The challenge has never been greater, or the stakes higher.

What Ails World Agriculture?

THEODORE W. SCHULTZ

*Professor Schultz is among the world's foremost agricultural econ-
omists. This article, published in the* Bulletin *of the Atomic
Scientists, January 1968, is a capsule summary of his views on
agricultural investment, technical assistance, research and economic development policy for agriculture. He is Hutchison Distinguished Service Professor in the Department of Economics at
the University of Chicago.*

THE PATTERNS OF U.S. investments pertaining to the production
of food are beset with four classes of malinvestment. In a nut-
shell, these malinvestments are as follows:

1. We are still committed to publicly-induced over-investment
in material forms of capital contributing to agricultural production. The current food grain shortages in parts of the world
could start us off on another binge of federal irrigation programs
and the like to increase the capacity of U.S. agriculture. It might
also postpone once again bringing U.S. farm product prices in
line with their economic values here and abroad.

2. We persist throughout the agricultural establishment to
underinvest in the human forms of capital. Fortunately, other
parts of the federal government are beginning to correct this
long-standing underinvestment in farm people. But meanwhile,
the six and more billions of dollars appropriated annually for
agriculture become ever more simply subsidies to U.S. commercial agriculture.

3. We still have not developed a set of successful public programs for investing in agricultural research and technology in
poor countries. The Rockefeller Foundation has done well on
this score, and in recent years the Ford Foundation has joined in
this successful approach. A few of the agricultural colleges, despite the uncertainties of AID financial assistance, have begun to
forge a successful pattern. But in terms of U.S. public expendi-

tures to this end, the investment in general is woefully inadequate both in the manner in which it is being accomplished and in the amounts spent for this purpose.

4. While we have succeeded in putting family planning and birth control on the U.S. foreign aid agenda, we are still a long way from having developed meaningful public programs in this area. U.S. private groups, notably the Population Council and the Ford Foundation, are far ahead of the U.S. public sector.

Before turning to the harder and more important underlying issues, there are two preliminary matters which call for comment. One pertains to the poor performance of agriculture in so many of the disadvantaged countries and the other to the changes under way for the better.

AGRICULTURE'S POOR PERFORMANCE

It has been convenient to conceal the mistakes in economic policy that account for the failures in modernizing agriculture by blaming the poor performance of the agricultural sector in disadvantaged countries on the adversity of nature, or the perversity of farmers, or the fecundity of man.

A sequence of bad monsoons or droughts, a spell of bad weather—thus nature is to blame. As one who was reared in the Dakotas with its volatile weather, I look upon this aspect of nature as perfectly natural. It should be an integral part of any normal expectations with respect to agricultural production. The bad monsoon of South Asia will return from time to time, but there will be good crop years, too. The droughts that have burdened the Soviet Union will pass, and in good years there will be wheat enough, even some for export once again. These adversities of nature do not account for the poor performance of agriculture.

In the minds of many who shape economic policy, farmers are ever so perverse. When a national economic plan calls for more agricultural production, farmers fail to respond; when instructions are issued to shift from wheat to corn, they fail to produce enough of either crop; when given the command to make a big leap forward, they step backward; and when they are heavily subsidized to reduce the acreage of particular crops, they proceed to increase the yield to more than offset the reduction in acreage. It has been convenient to believe that farmers, especially in poor countries, are loafers who prefer leisure to doing the extra work that will increase production; are squanderers who will not save for investment with which to increase agricultural production, and are inefficient in using the resources at their disposal. Thus these poor, lowly farmers are to blame. But farmers are not perverse in their economic behavior. If there is perversity, it will be found in the minds of those already mentioned, in what they behold in agriculture, and in national economic plans that fail to provide economic incentives for farmers.

It is now fashionable to attack the fecundity of man as the culprit, as if it were to blame for the poor performance of agriculture. The excessive growth in population is indeed a serious matter, for surely it has major adverse social and welfare effects in what can be done to improve health facilities, to enlarge cultural opportunities, and to provide schooling; and it can be a heavy drag on economic development. This excessive growth in population, of course, also increases the demand for food; nevertheless, the rapid growth of the population is not responsible per se for the poor performance of agriculture.

In my judgment the real culprit causing the poor performance of agriculture in the less developed countries is the lack of economic opportunities in agriculture—opportunities that are rewarding to farmers.

SOME CHANGES FOR THE BETTER

Despite past economic policy mistakes and the many unresolved problems in transforming traditional agriculture, the world food supply prospects are not as bleak as the exponential population growth curves would have us believe. The height of absurdity is revealed in a full two-page advertisement in *The Atlantic*, July 1966 issue, by Olin, with its half-page heading. *"Of the billion people who may starve in 1976,"* followed by a paragraph saying, "The statisticians say that in ten years over a billion—not a million, but a billion—people may be dying of hunger." These naive projections treat human beings as if they were mechanical robots without preference and choice when it comes to reproduction. There is under way throughout the world a fundamental change with respect to human reproduction, because parents clearly prefer smaller families and because of wholly new possibilities of achieving effective family planning. To satisfy these preferences for smaller families much can, should, and will be done.

But to return to agriculture: the long, wasteful swing toward imbalance on the part of economic policy in the less developed countries *underemphasizing agriculture* has fortunately reached its trough. In general terms, the corrective process consists of the following parts:

1. The less developed countries are beginning to correct their underpricing of farm products; also, their overpricing of agricultural inputs and of the consumer goods and services that farm people buy.

2. It has been fashionable since the mid-forties for less developed countries to embark on import substitution (substituting home-produced for imported foreign-produced goods) virtually without regard to cost. But on this policy too there are now many second thoughts. I would expect some freeing of international trade, which will reduce the monolithic push for import substitution. As this occurs, agricultural input prices will decline and the prices of consumer goods farm people buy will also decline in some of these countries.

3. Foreign aid from the more well-to-do countries will be tied less than it has been to the export of surpluses of farm products of U.S. Public Law 480 vintage, and there will be more aid in the form of fertilizer, insecticides, farm tools, machinery, and personnel who have the skills required to modernize agriculture.

4. The valuable stock of scientific and technical knowledge—a critical and major resource for increasing agricultural production, now located predominantly in Western countries—will become increasingly available to farmers in the less developed countries.

5. The endowment of natural resources in most countries will not prove to be a limiting factor to large increases in agricultural production.

In more specific terms, I call your attention to the following developments:

1. There is a radical change in the economic plans of the Soviet Union, providing a much better deal for agriculture (better prices, more investment, more consumer goods). The recent large crops may already be in part a payoff.

2. East European countries are beginning to adopt the approach of West European countries in their efforts to modernize agriculture.

3. The new U.S. legislation replacing Public Law 480 is likely to help agricultural development in countries receiving U.S. foreign aid.

4. Mexico's success in maintaining a balanced increase on the part of industry and agriculture is an approach that some of the other Latin countries are likely to adopt.

5. In South Asia we have the improved performance of agriculture in Pakistan, induced by the availability of relatively cheap nitrogen, tube wells, better roads and, above all, a more efficient system of prices.

6. New productive varieties of wheat coming out of Mexico as a result of the work of the Rockefeller Foundation and the Mexican government are being adapted rapidly to the climatic requirements and soils of other less developed wheat-growing countries. Similar progress is under way with respect to corn, grain sorghums, and millets. India, for example, and importantly, is now benefiting from these.

7. The picture with respect to improved varieties of rice is not as clear as that for wheat, but it now appears that the research under way at the International Rice Institute in the Philippines is achieving for rice what has been accomplished for wheat.

8. The Tropical Food Research Institute, which is in the process of being established in Nigeria (pending the political stability of that country), should also be mentioned, although it will take a decade and longer before it can discover and develop new and better varieties of food crops for this part of the tropics.

9. The cost of producing fertilizer in the advanced countries has declined by about one-half, relative to the price of major farm products. Most of the less developed countries have so far failed to take advantage of this important decline in the real price of fertilizer. But I would expect a marked change for the

better on this score during the next ten years. India is now proceeding to take advantage of this cheapness of fertilizer.

10. A specific deterrent is the lack of organized agricultural research to develop new and better sources of plant proteins. Protein food and feed from plants are already in short supply relative to the supply of carbohydrates and fats. The price of soybeans is a sign.

UNSETTLED QUESTIONS

In economic analysis, in clarifying the world food and population problems, we should consider a number of unsettled questions that go far beyond the realm of agriculture, nutrition, and demography. There are five key questions.

1. *Why are so many poor countries placing a low economic value on their farm products?*

I assume that it reveals a *policy preference* and that it is an *economic possibility*. I assume, also, that when countries such as Nigeria, Chile, or India want to and can keep their farm product prices low, the investment incentive for increasing the capacity of agriculture is thereby reduced. The policy preference is for industrialization, and agriculture's contribution to the attainment of it is cheap food, a source of cheap labor, and public revenue. This policy preference implies a low regard for agriculture as a source of economic growth. It means that low farm product prices and cheap food are an integral part of this type of policy.

What makes this type of policy possible? Politically, it is clear enough: where the rank and file of farm people have little or no voice in shaping policy, other interest groups presumably would dominate. But from whence the economic possibilities? Where there is an export surplus of these products, it is possible —by reducing the export surplus by an amount that is sufficient to increase the domestic supply of food, and thereby depressing the internal price. There have been many countries making this shift during the postwar period, especially throughout Latin America. Mexico is a noticeable exception. Where the losses in foreign exchange earnings caused by such a reduction in exports are offset by foreign aid, it is easier still. It is also possible whenever there is enough foreign aid in the form of farm products. Then it becomes necessary to reduce farm product prices below what they would be without such aid, in order to utilize such concessional farm products—unless the country is prepared and able to administer a two-price system.

As I have argued repeatedly, U.S. concessional exports of the P.L. 480 vintage have made this policy of cheap food and low farm product prices possible. This is not true in Nigeria, where the heritage of the marketing boards is predominantly to blame. But surely our aid in the form of farm products to Chile and especially to India and to many other countries has had the effect of reducing farm product prices below what they would have been without such forms of aid. During the period when we had large CCC surpluses, it was convenient to be blind on this issue. Now that we are less blind, the remedy frequently advanced is a two-price system—cheap food for the poor in the cities and higher farm product prices for farmers—as if it were possible for these countries with their public personnel already burdened to the limit to administer such a two-price system. It is sheer folly, so it seems to me, to urge these countries to undertake such a difficult administrative task and to assume that they could do it successfully.

There is still another part of the question here under consideration. We who are from rich countries are inclined to the belief that policymakers and people in poor countries should rate good nutrition much higher than they appear to do. But better diets entail costs. For them, it is very much a matter of what they can afford. Closely related, as one takes the long view, is our belief that the people in poor countries will, in the near future, want diets in which the proteins will come mainly from animal sources. Our belief on this point will undoubtedly prove to be wrong. During the relevant future and except where there are forage crops which cannot be utilized otherwise, dairy cows for milk and other animals for food will not become the major source of food proteins for all populations, as people improve their economic lot and can afford better diets.

2. Why are most of the less developed countries foregoing many of the gains to be had from international specialization and trade?

National defense considerations aside, such foregone gains are commonly viewed as temporary "losses," the price of achieving rapid industrialization. Thus, here too, the policy objective is industrialization and the development of new industries. Such infant industries require all manner of protection. For this, there is a ready-made economic doctrine and established policies to imitate in what some of the developed industrial countries have done. Furthermore, under the stress of foreign exchange disequilibrium, import substitution has become popular with policymakers as a way of "saving" on foreign exchange while further protecting their own domestic industries from foreign competition.

But with few exceptions, this rash of import substitution (and the accompanying protection) has not favored the agricultural sector. On the contrary, in countries that have had viable markets abroad for some of their farm products, these markets have been thereby impaired. In addition, and not to be overlooked, is this fact: if agriculture is to be modernized, farmers must have access to modern inputs—machinery, insecticides, fertilizer, and other— at prices that will make it profitable for farmers to proceed to use them. Where such modern agricultural inputs are produced by highly protected infant industries, the prices of such inputs are far too high to bring about a rapid modernization of agriculture. The gains that could be realized by many of these new forms of agricultural inputs are large.

Still another development reducing the gains to be had from international specialization and trade is the use of an export tax on farm products as an easy source of public revenue, especially in a number of West African countries, where marketing boards were established before or during the war. These marketing boards take a certain amount of the price as revenue—by selling the products at the world price but paying farmers much less. For example, in Nigeria, farmers have been receiving about half of the world price for their palm fruits, and production has been declining. Moreover, palm oil is being "wasted," for it has become so cheap in Nigeria that it is used in place of kerosene as a fuel. Yet if there is a "gold mine" in Nigeria (in pure economic values) it is palm fruit! One reason for the comparative advantage of palm fruit is the genetic breakthrough on the part of biological research. But the potential economic gain from this advance is being wasted by the export tax on this product.

When it comes to increasing the capacity of agriculture in these countries the investment implications are patently clear. The World Bank turned down Nigeria's request for a large loan to expand the production of palm fruit because of her export tax and its adverse effects on the profitability of that industry. India has been beset with endless difficulties in developing an adequate supply of cheap fertilizer for her farmers. The investment required for this purpose has not been forthcoming. Although Chile is an exporter of nitrogenous materials which she sells at world prices, these materials are anything but cheap to farmers in Chile. Strange as it may seem, it is a fact that the price is very high in Chile, and the obvious reason for this price distortion is that the price is rigged. Chile appears to be playing a monopoly game in producing and selling nitrogenous materials. The government is a partner of private producers in this game of exploiting Chilean farmers. The logic of this game is as follows: The material that is exported must be sold at the world price. This price is low; thus, it is presumed that it is sold at a loss. To offset this presumed loss, the price in Chile is set high, for it is sold in Chile at a price that is far above the world price. What a sad perversion of economic logic!

It would be remiss not to comment on the economic policies of the more developed countries that impair the gains to be had from international trade. No one can doubt that sugar cane produced in the semi-tropics has a marked, comparative advantage over sugar beets grown in Europe and the United States as a source of sugar. U.S. imports of fresh fruit from Chile are required to meet higher standards than domestically produced fruits. We too engage in all manner of substitution of home-produced goods for foreign-produced by the use of rules and regulations to protect particular farm products. But much more serious for agriculture are the explicit and implicit exporter subsidies that permeate our federal farm programs.

3. *Why are efficiency prices so low on the policy agenda of many less developed countries?*

It could be they have learned it from us! We were preaching not so long ago the Cochrane doctrine that farm prices could only be inefficient in guiding the allocation of resources. Cobweb models, backward-sloping supply curves, and perverse responses by farmers to price changes were the order of the day. While there have been second thoughts, in view of the contrary behavior of farmers, this doctrine of depreciating the function of prices has no doubt had some influence in shaping price policies in some of the less developed countries.

But policymakers in these countries have their own special reasons. They want to industrialize rapidly. This objective, as I have noted above, has among other things expressed itself in a policy preference for cheap food and relatively low farm product prices. For some of them this policy preference has been in the realm of economic possibility for reasons that I have set forth. One must add here, also, the widely held view that rent performs no allocative function. There is, of course, strong economic logic which shows that Ricardian rent is "unearned." Moreover, the income from rent is as a rule a relatively large income stream in most poor countries. Then, too, landowners are generally obstructionists (politically) with respect to planning for economic growth, and essentially functionless (economically). On top of all this is the cultural and intellectual orientation that looks upon the rank and file of farm people as belonging to an inferior occupation, and thus "deservedly" subject to all manner of social, political, and economic discrimination.

Economic theory also enters, performing two parts. Income and employment theory (macro-economics) extols the quantity of capital and labor using fix-price models. Price and allocative theory (micro-economics) defends efficiency prices. In this connection, it is noteworthy that modern economists have greatly clarified the relevance of price theory. The major advance has been in treating different forms of economic organization predominantly with respect to the relevance of price theory. Price theory—originally conceived to determine how resources are allocated and income distributed in a competitive, capitalist economy—has now been extended to a planned economy. As Robert Solow has noted in *Capital Theory and the Rate of Return,* modern work has rediscovered the same price theory "in the guise of shadow prices or efficiency prices." Accordingly, we now know "that the theory of perfectly-competitive capitalism is in many respects the theory of a planned or socialist economy."

In modernizing and increasing the capacity of agriculture in poor countries so that investments in agriculture will take forms that will produce the best rates of return, *one of the necessary economic requirements is a system of efficiency prices*. But it would take a book to show why this is true, and what is happening with respect to only three sets—namely, the prices of *farm products*, the prices of *agricultural inputs*, and also very importantly, the prices of the *consumer goods and services* that farm people buy for consumption. These prices are indispensable as an organizing device where there are many farmers. It makes no difference whether there are thousands or millions of them. No alternative system has as yet been devised that can integrate and organize efficiently the activities of many farmers. But it is a fact that these three sets of prices are, as a rule, badly distorted. Most of the less developed countries have inefficient systems of prices.

In my comments on question one, I have presented a picture of the low economic value being placed on farm products. I did not elaborate on the price distortions among farm products within such countries. There are many.

The picture of agricultural input prices is even more beset with price inefficiencies, and these are serious obstacles to the path of modernizing agriculture. If they are to modernize, farmers must buy fertilizer, insecticides, other chemicals, tools, equipment, machines, fuel, and repairs. In general, where they are available they are very expensive. These input prices are not only high, but they are also distorted one to another in most poor countries. Competition is weak because of all the barriers intended to protect the domestic producers of these inputs from foreign competition. Internal competition is also weakened *by domains of monopoly*. In some countries the production of some key agricultural inputs is restricted to the public sector. Where it is in the private sector, the suppliers of these inputs are, as a rule, not subject to effective competition.

Fertilizer deserves a special comment because it has become one of the principal inputs in increasing agricultural production. Although the discovery that nitrogen, phosphate, and potash can increase yields is not new, the profitability of using vast quantities of commercial fertilizer in farming throughout the world is largely a post-World War II development. The dominant factor underlying this development has been the decline in the supply price of commercially produced fertilizer materials, relative to farm product prices. Farmers, of course, must learn how to use fertilizer efficiently, which is not very difficult provided the variety of wheat or rice they grow is responsive to the application of fertilizer and provided there is sufficient rainfall and supplementary water.

Although relatively cheap fertilizer opens the door for large increases in agricultural production, this door still remains closed in most of the less developed countries. As a consequence, it has not been profitable for farmers in these countries to buy and use large additional quantities of fertilizer, because the advantage of lower world prices of materials that provide nitrogen, phosphate, and potash has not been extended to them.

In some countries there are already many types of complex machines and tractors. With respect to these, the lack of organization and the pricing of repair parts is appallingly inefficient. Tractors stand idle after a couple of years of use for lack of parts that have broken or have worn out. The cost and the time it takes to obtain repair parts is the explanation.

A brief reference to the prices of the consumer goods and services that farm people buy will suffice. There is all too little recognition of the economic importance of this set of prices. They really matter because they are the key to the purchasing power of the net income that farm people earn. In general, farm people in the less developed countries have fared badly in what they can buy with their earnings. While it is to be expected that the prices of consumer goods and services produced in urban areas will be somewhat higher when they reach the countryside, the rub is that these appear to have been rising, relative to the prices at which farmers sell their products; and, in many instances, the quality of the items farmers buy has been declining.

4. Why is the record of U.S. investment for increasing the agricultural capacity of poor countries so unsatisfactory?

For want of an investment policy in this area, no meaningful investment programs have been developed. Our policy preference has been very ambiguous. For years, the agricultural committees of Congress (with some change for the better recently) have been opposed to such programs because they might develop agricultural capacity abroad that would compete with U.S. farm products. The thrust of Congress has been toward surplus disposal and toward the subsidization and promotion of larger foreign sales.

The established dogma has been that the economic growth of poor countries is largely dependent upon industrialization and, for all practical purposes, is independent of the development of the agricultural sector. This dogma has long been compatible with the biases of agricultural committees of the Congress, with the instructions given to U.S. aid missions abroad, and with the general orientation of the State Department. All had been bitten by the industrialization bug.

While there is now under way a marked policy change in favor of increasing the agricultural capacity in poor countries, it is an exceedingly difficult policy to implement. How can public agencies of the United States make efficient investments in traditional agriculture? Loans to provide additional funds for millions of small farmers and thus augment the stock of the forms of capital used in traditional farming would be very hard to organize and administer. They would also be of little avail, because the payoff on such investment would be low indeed.

But the problem that confronts us in the modernization of agriculture in poor countries is compounded by three basic errors:

We must first rid ourselves of the false belief that traditional farmers are, in general, highly inefficient in allocating the agricultural resources at their disposal and that they will not respond to better economic opportunities.

Second, we must face up to the fact that efficient prices for farm products, agricultural inputs, and the consumer goods that farm people buy are necessary before it is possible to invest appropriately and efficiently in agriculture abroad. Nor do I exclude rent; for it is the price of the services of land and the price of resident entrepreneurs (farmers) in this connection which will require land reform in some countries.

The third error, especially in the minds of some economists, is the assumption that efficiency prices are sufficient. It is very much an error in modernizing agriculture because the investment opportunities, *the new high payoff inputs, must be discovered, developed, and supplied before farmers can turn to them in making their investment.*

In our failure to see the lack of new payoff opportunities we make the following mistakes:

a) We assume that in these countries usable and profitable new agricultural techniques; varieties of crops, vegetables, and fruits; and other agricultural inputs are available.

b) We start with extension programs before there is anything worthwhile to extend to farmers.

c) We link agricultural colleges to the ministries of agriculture abroad in order to concentrate on improving administration and information, instead of on a college-to-college arrangement with at least some emphasis on research.

d) We undertake countrywide community development programs without sufficient attention to the profitability of such programs for farmers.

Although a system of efficiency prices will usually reveal some rewarding opportunities, once these have been exhausted the further progress of agriculture is dependent upon a wide array of modern agricultural inputs—modern in the sense that they are the fruit of organized agricultural research.

AGRICULTURAL REVOLUTION

At this point it should be said that we live in a period in which there is indeed an agricultural revolution. In terms of what is theoretically possible, the scientific and technical knowledge in the West is so far ahead that what we see in more than half of the world is obsolete by a very wide margin. It is this stock of knowledge that warrants a large measure of optimism. This knowledge is exceedingly valuable, although much of it is still theoretical in the sense that the appropriate varieties of rice, wheat, and so on are not yet available for many countries. This situation, of course, calls for applied research, although much of it is more basic than many of us perhaps realize.

Clearly, the new inputs to increase world food supplies must come from outside agriculture. To develop these inputs, mainly through organized agricultural research, calls for both a transformation of the existing knowledge so that it will be economically useful in the less developed countries, and a further advance in knowledge that will be applicable in agricultural production.

But we have fallen far short in meeting these requirements. Look back two decades and see how little the Point Four Programs accomplished in Latin America. At that time, a third of the U.S. expenditures in Latin American countries were for agriculture. Nevertheless, not a single first-rate agricultural research center was developed by this program. I have already given the reasons why this research was grossly neglected. It was taken for granted that the supply of usable and profitable agricultural knowledge was large. Extension, yes—crash programs are always given top priority; the organization of viable agricultural research centers, no.

Fortunately, there have also been a few successful ventures and models to emulate. The success of the Rockefeller Foundation and the government of Mexico in agricultural research is such a model. So is the International Rice Institute and the new Corn and Wheat International Corporation that has just been put together in Mexico. The fairly recent and still modest agricultural research program taking place in India, in which the Rockefeller Foundation again is joined, also rates high.

But, let me underscore, a good research enterprise by itself, while essential, may not lead to increases in agricultural production. To go back to Chile, where the agricultural research program is quite advanced: in forage crops, food crops, vegetables, and fruit, Chile has generally good varieties. But, clearly, Chile has not been successful in its agricultural production during the last two decades.

In India, despite the breakthroughs that have been made in corn research, grain sorghum, and millet, there has been a long delay in getting the new varieties propagated, multiplied, and distributed to farmers.

In the Philippines, where Cornell has been for a long time and no doubt has done a fine job, there is as yet nothing to show for it in agricultural production.

Thus, price and related economic policy can indeed keep a country from realizing the gains in productivity to be had from successful agricultural research.

High on my investment agenda, as I look ahead, is additional capacity to produce and distribute fertilizer and land structures to increase and improve the supply of water as fertilizer and improved varieties become available.

Surely it is obvious in retrospect that our investment record for increasing agricultural capacity in poor countries is a sad affair. I am moderately optimistic that we will begin to do better during the decade ahead as we learn from our errors.

5. *Why are economists shy on population analysis?*

It is an odd bit of intellectual history. Economists were the first to stake a claim to population; they built the Ricardo-Malthus skyscraper, and then abandoned it. What has been built since then we owe to the demographers, a new specialization with sociologists in on the enterprise and economists out of it. Thus, it could be said that there is no demand now for this type of economist and accordingly no supply—no graduate instruction and PhD research in the economics of population. But the failure of economists in this connection is not so simple. It is true that specialization is the order of the day and that studies of population belong to demography, which is not the forte of economists. It is also true that economists have not developed a theoretical core to explain differences in the growth, composition, and quality of different populations over time and cross sectionally as an integral part of factor demands and supplies, and also to explain differences in family planning behavior in these terms.

Instead, economists long ago put population aside despite the pioneering work of the classical economists. Thus, our economic boxes are empty for the purposes at hand.

Before turning to aspects of the analytical problem, I want to mention some doubts with regard to the way population and food are linked here and elsewhere these days.

a) The growing demand for food in many poor countries is not simply a matter of population growth, but is also becoming (and increasingly so) a function of the rise in per capita income, because the income elasticity of the demand for food in these countries is relatively high. Surely this is true in the Soviet Union, throughout most of East Europe, in parts of Latin America, and in some part of South Asia.

b) The economic supply restraints in poor countries on the capacity to produce are, in general, less restrictive when it comes to increasing agricultural production than they are in providing the additional goods and services (health services and schooling, for example) required by the demand of a growing population with rising income. In my judgment, it is a narrow and misleading view to look upon the growth in population throughout the world as if it were predominantly a problem of running out of food. To concentrate only on the future supply of food misses the heart of the matter, which is the supply of factors to satisfy the demands—not only for food, but also for other goods and services. In principle, this issue encompasses both rich and poor countries.

c) It is altogether naive and very misleading to project for the next decade or two the recent and rising net-reproduction curves. The assumption that the family planning of parents will show little or no downward response in birth rates to the decline in death rates is, I am sure, invalid.

d) The notable advance in biological knowledge with regard to human reproduction and the rapid improvements in low cost and usable techniques of birth control will, in all probability, prove to be fully as important in this area during the next two decades as the advance in science and technology has been during the past in modernizing agriculture.

FAMILY PLANNING

In closing, I want to propose an economic approach in analyzing the behavior of parents in family planning. The key assumptions on which my proposal rests are as follows:

1. Parents the world over have preferences for a family of a particular size. Accordingly, they are not indifferent about the number of children they will have over their reproductive span of years. A strong assumption in this regard is that these basic underlying preferences are essentially similar—regardless of whether the sub-population is rural or urban, living in traditional or modern economic sectors, rich or poor.

2. Parents the world over engage in family planning.

3. In their family planning, parents make subjective appraisals of the benefits and costs, psychic and pecuniary, associated with enlarging their family size. They respond to declines in death

rates by reducing the number of births as such declines become reasonably certain and known to them. Their response influenced by uncertainty with regard to family births and deaths.

4. The possibilities of realizing these preferences of parents depends strongly on the availability, practicality, feasibility, and relative costs of birth control techniques.

If these assumptions prove to be valid, clearly the U.S. programs to assist poor countries in the extension and adoption of birth control knowledge and techniques should not concentrate on endeavors to alter the preferences of parents for children, but on the improvement of the possibilities for such parents to attain their family preferences.

The economic components that enter here are several. The price of the new birth control techniques is subject to patents, which can seriously delay the production and distribution of such techniques in poor countries. Whereas the improvement in the possibilities associated with the production and distribution of IUDs are substantial, their use places a considerable burden on the medical and nursing professions. We should therefore develop alternative and cheaper possibilities. Oral pills may become one such. If they can be supplied at a cost of not more than $1.70 for each year of a woman's requirements (as now offered by particular private firms) a new and cheap alternative would be at hand. More important still are wholly new techniques being developed by biomedical research. These techniques are likely to be still simpler to use, and less costly in terms of private and public expenditures.

The Old Agricultural Lag

KENNETH BOULDING

Professor Boulding of the Department of Economics, University of Colorado, penned this verse in deft appraisal of a recent conference on agricultural productivity and development.

I

O why does agriculture lag?
The answers all are in the bag
But the bag in which the answer lies
Turns out to have enormous size.

II

The ardent fertilizer buff
Thinks fertilizer is enough
(Such buffs, it's interesting to know
Are much produced in Buffalo).

III

Then some there are who argue that
The major culprit is the rat,
And so encourage, far and wide,
The massive use of pesticide.

IV

Economists, it's plain to see
All think that *Prices* are the key
For no economy will grow
With inputs high and outputs low.

V

Markets and competition now
Must be the hand that speeds the plow
Making, in one Rostovian leap
Corn dear, and fertilizer cheap.

VI

Some think the answer lies in Risk
Others, that land reform's the whisk
To brush away the blocks that bar
Development's immobile car.

VII

Some say, when growth occurs, what fed it
Is careful grants of shaky credit,
With Government to underwrite
The debts of those who fly by night.

VIII

For Anthropologists, Tradition
Remains the major inhibition.
And peasants, oftener than we think,
When led to water, do not drink.

IX

With facts too many now to list 'em
The answer is a General System.
So what has got to be advised,
Is, "get the stuff computerized."

X

When scientists use common sense
They fall into mistakes immense.
It's better far to place reliance
Even on the softest social science.

❋   ❋   ❋

Suggested Further Readings

Bird, Alan R., *Poverty in Rural Areas of the United States*, U.S. Department of Agriculture, Agricultural Economic Report No. 63, November 1964.

Bishop, C. E. (ed.), *Farm Labor in the United States* (Columbia University Press, 1967).

————, "The Urbanization of Rural America: Implication for Agricultural Economics," *Journal of Farm Economics*, vol. 45, no. 3 (1963).

Bonnen, James T., "Rural Poverty: Programs and Problems," *Journal of Farm Economics*, vol. 48, no. 2 (1966).

Breimyer, Harold F., *Individual Freedom and the Economic Organization of Agriculture* (University of Illinois Press, 1965).

Brewster, John W., "The Machine Process in Agriculture and Industry," *Journal of Farm Economics*, vol. 32, no. 1 (1950).

Clawson, Marion, "Rural Poverty in the United States," *Journal of Farm Economics*, vol. 49, no. 5 (1967).

Cochrane, Willard W., *Farm Prices: Myth and Reality* (University of Minnesota Press, 1958).

————, *The City Man's Guide to the Farm Problem* (University of Minnesota Press, 1965).

Fuller, Varden, *Labor Relations in Agriculture* (University of California Institute of Industrial Relations, 1955).

Hathaway, Dale E., *Problems of Progress in the Agricultural Economy* (Scott, Foresman and Company, 1964).

Heady, Earl A., *A Primer on Food, Agriculture, and Public Policy* (Random House, 1967).

Heimstra, Stephen J., "Concentration and Competition in the Food Industries," *Journal of Farm Economics*, vol. 48, no. 3 (1966).

Hildreth, R. J., *Readings in Agricultural Policy* (University of Nebraska Press, 1968).

Houthakker, Hendrik S., *Economic Policy for the Farm Sector*, American Enterprise Institute for Public Policy Research (1967).

————, "The Rationality of United States Agricultural Policy," *Journal of Farm Economics*, vol. 45, no. 2 (1963).

Knutson, Ronald D., "Cooperatives and the Competitive Ideal," *Journal of Farm Economics*, vol. 48, no. 3, part II (1966).

Kristansen, Thorkil, "The Approaches and Findings of Economists," *International Journal of Agrarian Affairs*, vol. V, no. 2 (1967).

McGovern, George (ed.), *Agricultural Thought in the Twentieth Century* (The Bobbs-Merrill Company, Inc., 1967).

Moore, John R., "The Causes and Consequences of Major Changes in the Organization of Agricultural Marketing Activities," *Journal of Farm Economics*, vol. 48, no. 3, part II (1966).

Mosher, Arthur T., *Getting Agriculture Moving: Essentials for Development and Modernization* (Frederick A. Praeger, 1966).

National Advisory Commission on Food and Fiber, *Food and Fiber for the Future* (Government Printing Office, 1967).

National Advisory Commission on Rural Poverty, *The People Left Behind* (Government Printing Office, 1967).

National Commission on Food Marketing, *Economic Regulation of the Food Industry* (Government Printing Office, 1966).

Paarlberg, Don, *American Farm Policy: A Case of Centralized Decision Making* (John Wiley and Sons, Inc., 1964).

Padberg, Daniel I., *Economics of Food Retailing* (Cornell University, 1968).

Panel on the World Food Supply, *The World Food Problem*, A Report of the President's Science Advisory Committee Panel on the World Food Supply, The White House, May 1967.

Perkins, Brian, and Dale Hathaway, *Movement of Labor between Farm and Nonfarm Jobs* (Michigan State University Agricultural Experiment Station, 1966).

Schnittker, J. A., "Farm Policy—Today's Direction," *Journal of Farm Economics*, vol. 48, no. 5 (1966).

Schultz, Theodore W., "Our Welfare State and the Welfare of Farm People," *The Social Science Review*, vol. 38, no. 2 (1964).

———, "Reflections on Poverty within Agriculture," *The Journal of Political Economy*, vol. 58, no. 1 (1950).

———, *Transforming Traditional Agriculture* (Yale University Press, 1964).

———, "Urban Developments and Policy Implications for Agriculture," *Economic Development and Cultural Change*, vol. 15, no. 1 (1966).

Soth, L. K., *What's Ahead for the Family Farm* (Iowa State University Press, 1966).

Swerling, B. L., "Income Protection for Farmers: A Possible Approach," *Journal of Political Economy*, vol. 67, no. 2 (1959).

Talbot, Ross B., "The USDA Embarks on Its Second Century of Service," *Journal of Farm Economics*, vol. 32, no. 1 (1950).

Tontz, Robert L., *Foreign Agricultural Trade: Selected Readings* (Iowa State University Press, 1966).

Tweeten, Luther G., *The Role of Education in Alleviating Rural Poverty*, U.S. Department of Agriculture, Agricultural Economic Report No. 114, June 1967.

U.S. Congress, Joint Economic Committee, *Policy for Commercial Agriculture: Its Relation to Economic Growth and Stability* (Government Printing Office, 1957).

U.S. Department of Agriculture, *Rural People in the American Economy*, Agricultural Economic Report No. 101, October 1966.

U.S. Department of Labor, *Manpower Report of the President* (Government Printing Office, April 1967).

Wilcox, W. W., "The Rationality of United States Agricultural Policy," *Journal of Farm Economics*, vol. 45, no. 2 (1963).

Wood, Arthur W., "The Marketing Board Approach to Collective Bargaining," *Journal of Farm Economics*, vol. 49, no. 5 (1967).

Yande, James G., and Peter G. Helmberger, "Marketing Cooperatives in the U.S.: Membership Policies, Market Power, and Antitrust Policy," *Journal of Farm Economics*, vol. 48, no. 3, part II (1966).

DATE DUE

JAN 11 1971			
DEC 5 1973			
APR 0 2 2004			
			PRINTED IN U.S.A.